# THE BURDEN
# OF VISION

# THE BURDEN
# OF VISION
## Dostoevsky's Spiritual Art

*by*
## GEORGE A. PANICHAS

William B. Eerdmans Publishing Company

Printed in the United States of America

**Library of Congress Cataloging in Publication Data**

Panichas, George Andrew.
  The burden of vision.

  Includes bibliographical references and index.
  1. Dostoevsky, Fyodor Mikhailovich, 1821-1881—Religion and ethics. 2. Spirituality in literature. I. Title.
PG3328.Z7R435      891.7'3'3      76-44503
ISBN 0-8028-1671-1 pbk.

To

ALFRED OWEN ALDRIDGE

"Of the things that wisdom prepares for lifelong happiness, by far the greatest is the possession of friends."

# CONTENTS

*My Lord, I stand continually upon the watchtower in the daytime, and I am set in my ward whole nights.*

Isaiah 21:8

*I have yet many things to say to you, but ye cannot bear them now.*

John 16:12

# INTRODUCTION

*Veni Creator Spiritus*
*Mentes tuorum visita,*
*Imple superna gratia,*
*Quae tu creasti pectora.*

Fyodor Dostoevsky's highest and most permanent achievement as a novelist lies in his exploration of man's religious
complex, his world and his fate. His probings have an intrinsically religious ambiance; his purposes are impellingly spiritual; his meanings are metaphysical. Dostoevsky's interi-
orizing concerns—moral, spiritual, and religious—deepen and,
what is more important, justify his aesthetic form. In his art
the world of experience, that totality of living, though it remains inescapable and though it has a germinal priority in the
creative process itself, becomes an experience of transcendence. It is true that Dostoevsky may be contradictory, but "he
is never confused," as Joyce Cary notes. The clarity, as well as
the scope and power, of his imagination—his religious imagination—is exemplified in his last five great novels, on which
the strength of his reputation must finally rest. In the confluence of their design and thought they have a pentateuchal
continuity of theme and relevance which provides rich poetic
truths about man's religious values. And in the end the novels
are revelations that give meaning to life. *Crime and Punishment, The Idiot, The Devils, A Raw Youth, The Brothers
Karamazov*: these novels must compel recognition of a special
sensibility that translates into the language and experience of
spiritual art.

Religion is the matrix of Dostoevsky's sensibility; it is, first
and last, the education and discipline of his imagination. His
basic ideas are religious, formed and informed as they are by
ultimate concerns and ultimate questions. Not "I know" but "I

9

believe" empowers the confession of his beliefs, of which his novels are dramatized analogues. As an existential historical experience, religion occupies a central place in Dostoevsky's imagination. It is an imagination with roots, and its frontier is everywhere. When speaking of Dostoevsky and religion, one must, at least initially, delineate an historical framework. Ancient traditions assert rigorous, discriminating principles of faith, of which the Judaeo-Christian heritage remains the most abiding substantive basis. Any consideration of the operative religious constituents in Dostoevsky's imagination must start from this affirmation. Inevitably, indeed even mysteriously, Dostoevsky's imagination returns to the framework of a religious experience. And inevitably its metaphysics is ordained by a vision of order whose sources are biblical and apostolic, sacramental and eschatological. Dostoevsky's imagination is chronologically modern, but in its beginning and ending it belongs to what Charles Péguy terms *"le système de chrétienté."*

By no means must these distinguishing Christian contexts of Dostoevsky's religious imagination restrict the meaning of his art. His imagination, to repeat, is religious; his art is spiritual. No undue subtlety is intended here, but some clarification is required. Imagination can be placed directly in its historical actuality. A vision of the world in which it exists and to which it responds, imagination is pregnant with all the tensions and pressures of existence. The creative essences of this vision are invariably, consciously and unconsciously, colored by historical governances, which crystallize into what can be called a metaphysics. "Men live and see according to some gradually developing and gradually withering vision," D. H. Lawrence reminds us. "This vision exists also as a dynamic idea or metaphysic—exists first as such. Then it is unfolded into life and art." This metaphysics, in short, becomes the alphabet of the imagination. In his vital, at times frantic responses to his age, to its ever-ascending and ever-threatening problems, Dostoevsky was impelled by a religious metaphysics, Christian in foundation and overview, Orthodox Christian in canon and outlook. To deny the religious fundamentals of his imagination is to diminish, and in the end to destroy, his rendered vision of man in the historical vortex. No critical estimation or appreciation of Dostoevsky's imaginative vision can be complete without a recognition of the specificity of this religious thrust in his metaphysics.

Yet Dostoevsky's Christianity must be seen in its radical and prophetic aspects. His is hardly a quietistic or irenic Christianity. It is very much an endangered Christianity, challenged by upheavals brought about by the positivist empiricism of contemporary society. In a final sense, Dostoevsky's Christianity is a modern, apocalyptic Christianity. His is a world in which people confront each other's broken souls. Proofs of faith are defied by proofs of negation. Distress and struggle are rampant in a dark, gray world in which the image of the city mirrors the schism of the soul. It is an undulant world in which terror is endemic to the human situation and in which the demonic breaks forth repeatedly with vicious fury and unparalleled power of disruption and dissociation. Here there is no rest from nagging doubt; inner torment is a constant reproduction of outer chaos. Extremes of life become Dostoevsky's extremes of fiction. Everyone stands at the very edge of something frightening. Madness, isolation, misery, pain, nightmare, chaos, smouldering sexual passions: these are the "fearful sights" in a world assaulted by godlessness. Of Dostoevsky's characters it can well be said that "this generation shall not pass away, till all [these] things be fulfilled" (Luke 21:32). Theirs is the agony of being caught "between those two abysses of the Infinite and Nothing," as Pascal phrases it. For Dostoevsky the true measure of suffering is found in this entrapment.

The religious situation is one of crisis. Necessarily, then, Dostoevsky's religious metaphysics, subject as it is to all the spiritual wars and turbulence of the age, bears the marks of incessant wandering and seeking. Disjunction and disharmony are the chief characteristics, and effects, of Dostoevsky's religious significance. His novels are not essentially about the religious life but are instead about religious problems. Dostoevsky affirms the permanence of religious values, but at the same time he is, as an artist, agitated by the collapse of values. The religious value of life is inspiring, but is it viable? It is to this recurring question that Dostoevsky addresses himself, and his discoveries are not the derivative results of the intellectual process but are the almost overwhelming results of what can best be described as a prophetic consciousness. This latter process is always the more perilous, for it involves creating a vision of faith in which the passional force is much greater than that of thought. (Passions, declares Lessing, "make us . . . more conscious of our existence, they make us feel more real.") Intelligence posits the exertive element of human control, and it is undergirded by some degree of the rational. It speaks in thoughts. Prophecy, on the other hand, lies at the frontier of endless searching; it is an ever-threatening communication of experience possessed in vision rather than in ratiocination.

Prophecy is Dostoevsky's vestibule of faith. It is also his burden of vision. He bears a heavy responsibility of utterance in a time of peril, when men live in "dark times." He must be ready to answer the voice that now calls to him: "Watchman, what of the night?" (Isaiah 21:11). Nowhere else in modern fiction has the prophet's burden of vision been more heavily borne than by Dostoevsky in his five great novels. And with the same kind of creative inspiration, instinctive concern, prophetic insight, and inward vision he announces with Isaiah: "For it is a day of trouble, and of treading down, and of perplexity by the Lord God of hosts in the valley of vision, breaking down the walls, and of crying in the mountains" (22:5). No less than Isaiah in ancient times, Dostoevsky in modern times sees and re-creates the terrible costs of man's estrangement from God. Spiritual death as a universal experience of judgment is Dostoevsky's most awesome prophetic preoccupation—and announcement. His novels revolve around this living form of death, as sign and portent, and in this respect their primary themes can be said to contain eschatological prophecies of judgment and salvation. If Dostoevsky reveals "the line of confusion, and the stones of emptiness" (Isaiah 34:11), he also speaks a message of hope and regeneration, when "the parched ground shall become a pool, and the thirsty land springs of water" (Isaiah 35:7). Throughout his novels the prophetic topography is as clear as the prophetic voice.

Moral questions constitute for Dostoevsky an organic part of his burden of vision and also weigh heavily on the creative act. Continuously he responds to the substance and consequences of moral actions. The problem of evil, the onus of sin and guilt, the depth of suffering are some of the moral questions that Dostoevsky examines. His excursions into the realm of the moral life are characterized by a prophetic subtlety. Since the human element is never for Dostoevsky a normative one, the range and focus of moral distinctions and valuations are affected. That moral vision does not contain or prescribe a systematic moral theology is one of the implicit aspects of his creative imagination. Dostoevsky recognizes the primal existence of moral law in the area of what he renders as the universal struggle between good and evil. But what counts most for him is not the assertion of moral law nor the imposition of moral criteria, but rather the manifestation of moral energy. The spiritual nuances of this moral energy incite his imagination. His major characters are identified by the strength and range of the moral energy that they actualize, whether as moral self-realization or as antimoral self-disintegration. The dramatization of this intrinsic moral process is Dostoevsky's most intense artistic impulsion, culminating, as Lawrence observes, in "a more vivid life circle, and giving the clue towards a higher circle still."

But if the moral process in Dostoevsky's novels is problematic, it is in the end unconditionally religious. His awareness of the consequences arising from moral conflict and action is decisive in its projected meaning and lessons. No matter how much Dostoevsky values freedom, he knows that its boundary stops at the moral point of connection. All human actions attain their validating sanction, their *telos,* in a moral perspective. The moral condition has a divine limit that defines man's situation. The acceptance of this truth marks the religious dimension of Dostoevsky's spiritual art in all its moral implications. It also marks the point of transcendence that distinguishes self from self and self from otherness. In Dostoevsky's novels the most revealing moments are those in which this experience of moral discrimination evolves. The moral process is one of transfiguration, or, in antimoral instances, of negation. The religious meaning of experience occurs precisely in this process and simultaneously reveals its moral essences. Human predicament and human paradox, which Dostoevsky captures and comprehends with a visionary power, are facets of the moral process. They are always there in the human encounter as a seminal part of the totality of existence: as the motivating constituents of moral energy. Their very presence implies teleological significance and reinforces man's essential possibility. They are the most real evidences of moral energy that, within the spectacle of the full materialization of human experience and possibility, give form to moral discrimination. Moral action attains its ultimate meaning as an encounter of natural and supernatural.

Dostoevsky's novels push the reader into the relentless complexity of moral war in which no human emotion is spared and no intricacy is reduced. Here Dostoevsky's prophetic subtlety appears in its most concentrated artistic form: moral energy, as impulse and act, emerging as moral revelation, compels moral judgment. This is a paramount example of spiritual art as a rejection of empirical-relativistic values. Such art always has fateful moral repercussions, since it makes one vulnerable to contact with the fight between good and evil, as well as the inexorable nexus of cause and effect in the moral order.

Dostoevsky's moral sense, always heightened and prophetic, underlines the ultimate decisions of *kairos,* that is to say, a strong consciousness of the historical moment when, as Paul Tillich notes, "something new, eternally important, manifests itself in temporal forms, in the potentialities and tasks of a special period." It is what gives to Dostoevsky's work a sense of eternity. In his novels, then, any expenditure of moral energy, in whatever form or structure, has continuous implications for both personal and transpersonal destiny. His art posits the conditions of moral experience requiring judgmental participation. These conditions are not only aesthetically ordered but also metaphysically centered, and from this confluence the moral perspective of Dostoevsky's fictional world emerges. The moral situation is inseparable from the human situation. This inseparability is unconditional; it is a bedrock of Dostoevsky's religious imagination. In their relational validity, moral and human values are interlocking; any debasement of the one inevitably leads to debasement of the other. Moral life gains its meaning and hence its standards in this dynamic process.

Sin-consciousness is a powerful undercurrent in Dostoevsky's fiction. In the main he conceives of sin as an anti-moral act of a defiant will that assaults and cheapens the values of spirit. Capitulation to sin is the denial of transcendence, the abrogation of reverence, the triumph of lack of conscience. Dostoevsky depicts sin as the outgrowth of confusion, which he sees as the mixture of good and evil and consequently as a problematic human condition. The historical situation, shaped by this tragic paradox, induces Dostoevsky's compassion. Yet his vision is spatially and temporally suprahistorical. Dostoevsky sees beyond history and beyond man; his prophetic vision singularizes the eschatological.

Sin and personal destiny are inextricably tied to the evil that is synonymous with the pain of spiritual loss or absence. Dostoevsky's novels often take on the form of "spiritual exercises" in the consciousness of sin as the one and only entrance into the life of faith. Sin that in any form leads to internal suffering and to the slightest reactivation of conscience is never without hope of redemption. The sinner who knows that he can never be the same again has been rent by the spirit of the absolute. "Evil has to be purified," writes Simone Weil, "or life is not purified." But there is, too, the sin beyond sin, when spiritual loss is a permanent condition and the sinner stands fast, immobilized in his non-being. Satan, "always, night and day," has his successors, and his name, as Dostoevsky realizes, is Legion. For Dostoevsky the burden of vision must include the vision of evil, for evil, as Claude Tresmontant says, "is the work of man, and not of matter," "is the work of created freedom."

Spiritual art is art that contains a fundamental religious category and that conveys implicit religious values of experience. It evolves from an immutable premise: God is Spirit, the world is Spirit. Its purposes are transcendent in their orientation, which always connotes an extra-dimensional aspect of human existence. Man is not seen in finite terms but in relation to values above and beyond himself. Human spirit in relation to Divine Spirit characterizes the principles of spiritual art. Urgent spiritual concerns inspire and shape the themes, and beliefs, of this art. The desecration of Spirit, particularly in such forms of breakdown as distrust, doubt, cynicism, despair, indifference, denial, is at the heart of the concerns. Desecration unleashes schismatic forces that dramatically alter the character of man and of the world itself. The entire value-system of human existence and its ultimate meaning undergoes radical change.

To the resultant actions, effects, influences, and significances of this change, spiritual art renders a constancy of response. Inner spiritual disintegration in all its ramifications demands attention in such art. If it is spiritual art, it is also tragic art: Divine Spirit is ever besieged by demonic energy. This interminable struggle is fraught with the meaning of human destiny, even as it personifies the apocalyptic note, or, better, the apocalyptic tension, that is central to the contexts of spiritual art. Spiritual art can be said to communicate the meaning of "last things"; in it human action and interaction are captured at their utmost point of temporal peril and must inevitably end in eternal revelation: "It is done." Spiritual art is spiritual experience insofar as it awakens consciousness of the "wholly other."

As spiritual art Dostoevsky's fiction attains a significance of the first rank and places him, as has been rightly claimed, with such religious visionaries as Dante, Cervantes, Milton, and Pascal. It is hardly enough to see Dostoevsky as "the Shakespeare of the novel," for his incessant concern with the needs of the soul and with the depth-experience of spiritual man takes him far beyond secular craft. He is, as Nicolas Berdyaev observes, the novelist as pneumatologist and symbolistic metaphysician. Yet Dostoevsky is not a theologian; he is not a builder of a religious system, although at the same time he accepts *le système de chrétienté* as one that possesses and discloses the true historical unity and order of man's existence and destiny. Here Dostoevsky's own words indicate the religious orientation of his art: "The Holy Spirit is a direct conception of beauty, a prophetic consciousness of harmony and hence a steadfast striving toward it."

His novels are not an elaboration of ideological issues but a penetration of spiritual life. Even the peculiarly Russian cultural and religious motifs of Dostoevsky's thought must be seen in their proper perspective, since his explorations of the human soul—of man's *mysterium*—are transcendent in meaning and application. "To become a genuine and all-around Russian," Dostoevsky declared, "means...to become a brother of all men, a universal man." Spiritual art is the re-creation of universal truths. From this point of view Dostoevsky is, in Lawrence's words, a "marvellous seer" whose "diagnosis of human nature is simple and unanswerable." In their universal human significance Dostoevsky's novels belong to Spirit, which overarches all boundaries. Spiritual art contains the triune of time, death, and eternity, of which Dostoevsky's novels are, with all the assurance of first principles, both a synoptic vision and a contemplation.

However reverential it is in its foundations, Dostoevsky's vision is modern in its cosmography. The world remains his map of action. The soul of man is his obsessing concern. Dostoevsky focuses on the drift of modernism: on people caught in a world in which change becomes the new moral imperative. The momentum of this change is often so swift, so immense and engulfing, that at every moment and turn old certitudes are threatened. The tremendous nervous energy pervading Dostoevsky's novels is synchronously commensurate with the depth of the changes occurring in man and his world. No feature of man's outer or inner life is left untouched by this energy; no human attitude remains for long the same.

Impermanence and incompleteness are the characteristics of a society in transit. Dostoevsky's characters show the shock of transformation, particularly as it affects their inner lives. They live in a world invaded by new values and half-finished ideas and simultaneously tempted by strange gods. This is a world filled with daring and excitement, communicating the power of defiant experimentation. Here, freedom becomes, like those long streets in Dostoevsky's novels, an endless adventure in self-assertion. Significantly, darkness overshadows the choices and actions of freedom, as if to emphasize its illimitable opportunities, as well as its paradoxical consequences. At what juncture do freedom and Spirit collide? How and where are limits ascertained? What happens to one who provokes Spirit and limits? What happens to society itself? With prophetic intensity Dostoevsky's novels delineate modern questions and underline the modern dilemma. It is no wonder that the whirlwind and the whirlpool are his images of change and that terror possesses his people.

With what Thomas Mann calls a "surging fullness of visions and passions," Dostoevsky probes the condition of the modern human consciousness. His comprehension is total and prophetic. The inner life, Dostoevsky insists, is filled with mysteries, and to discover these is to discover the world. More than anything else, perhaps, Dostoevsky illuminates power-concepts—power of mind, power of will, power of body, power of passion. The material, exploitative, non-spiritual manifestations of power lead to the fragmentation of consciousness.

Power can become a demonic entity, absolute unto itself, often assuming such forms as nihilism, blasphemy, cruelty, boredom, suicide, murder. Such power is a destructive agent in the consciousness and neither knows nor recognizes spiritual standards, without which fragmentation and disorder thrive. As a unilateral entity power constitutes the corruption of consciousness. For Dostoevsky a disoriented consciousness is a sign of spiritual disinheritance, the inevitable climax of rising indifference to the religious sense that he has in mind when he writes: " . . . the love of mankind is unthinkable, unintelligible and altogether impossible without the accompanying faith in the immortality of man's soul."

Dostoevsky depicts human consciousness in unrepentant isolation, without past or future; it is very much a self-parasitizing psychic process. It epitomizes man's abandonment in time, as well as the abandonment of the principle of order in the world. The fragmented consciousness is a denial of the concept of limits, and the concomitant denial of humility, a virtue that Dostoevsky sees as indispensable to a positive concept of life. In Dostoevsky's novels the psychology of consciousness makes great leaps. But Dostoevsky is not a materialist. The spiritual quality of consciousness remains for him an absolute category of life and art.

Inevitably the condition of man's consciousness gives an index to the external situations that Dostoevsky creates in his novels. The outer images of disharmony heighten and complement the chaos of soul. Yet man's dehumanization, which particularly occupies Dostoevsky, is not for him at the root of modern civilization's plight. The metaphysics of Dostoevsky's vision, it is important to remember, is inherently religious in origin. His view of dehumanized man is not prompted by what could be called a secular existentialism of chronolatry. For the causes of dehumanization Dostoevsky looks to interior conditions, personified, he feels, in a continuing process of despiritualization. He categorically rejects the solutions to dehumanization offered by modern liberalism and rationalism. Their solutions merely erect one "secular city" on another. The spiritual and not the human prospect is Dostoevsky's final concern. Man's spiritual condition is the only basis for formulating an absolute metaphysical standard, in the dissolution or absence of which there is no possibility of human renewal.

It is precisely this condition that Dostoevsky focuses on in his novels and that subdues all other, if co-existent, conditions. The outer physical properties, or architecture, of the novels serve to portend the spiritual situation. They make us aware of the pain of spiritual displacement. Dostoevsky's sense of place has a subterranean, a Dantesque—and metaphysical—emphasis that is pertinent to the struggle of the soul to find a way out of an oppressive darkness. Again and again, for example, we find Dostoevsky's protagonists breathlessly climbing up and down stairs. And we overhear the desperate cry repeated through the centuries: "O my dove, that art in the clefts of the rock, in the secret places of the stairs, let me see thy countenance, let me hear thy voice" (Song of Solomon 2:14).

Dostoevsky's characters are in a state of constant movement or agitation. They are in flight from one place to another, even from one house to another. Or they are engaged in long philosophical disputes with others—and with themselves. There is a ceaseless outpouring of emotions and words. Stillness and reflection cannot be afforded by these people. One hardly knows, or can predict, what will happen in the next minute or around the next corner, or who will be waiting in his cramped lodgings, in the next room, or at the top of the staircase. In mood, in atmosphere, in tone, in significance, the words and gestures and actions of Dostoevsky's men and women communicate a biblical, an apocalyptic sense of time, when "in the last days perilous times shall come" (II Timothy 3:1). For them this is "the last time," "the last state," "the last end." And now, in these "last days," "at the last trump," they shout, or whisper, "the last words." A feeling of urgency and expectancy prevails everywhere; one thought fills immensity.

Although Dostoevsky is not an epic novelist, he reveals an epic sense of things in that whatever action occurs and whatever decision is made is charged with meaning. The war of might that one finds in Homer becomes the war of the soul in Dostoevsky. The ethical design and the heroic ideal of the *Iliad* become the spiritual design and the tragic vision of Dostoevsky's "epic-tragedy," as it has been called. Spiritual war rages on a tremendous scale as God and Satan, to use Dostoevsky's own words, fight for the destiny of man. The war being fought here is no less fateful or heroic, and no less furious, than that fought on the plains of Troy. At stake is the soul's damnation or redemption. Homer and Christ, it can be said, come together in Dostoevsky. (Homer, he wrote, "was sent to us by God, as Christ was . . . [and] in the *Iliad*, gave to the ancient world the same organization in spiritual and earthly matters as the world owes to Christ.") Novelists, too, to paraphrase Clement of Alexandria, are children unless they have been made men by Christ.

To mention Christ in connection with Dostoevsky is to introduce an inexhaustible subject. One can only hesitate to make even an estimation of what Christ meant to Dostoevsky or how He affected his religious imagination. Dostoevsky's own often-quoted words underline this difficulty, even as they show that for him Christ occupies the Omega Point: "If anyone could prove to me that Christ is outside the truth, and if the truth really did exclude Christ, I should prefer to stay with Christ and not with the truth." Majesty, fear, reverence are the numinous qualities that characterize Dostoevsky's view of the Divine. A prophetic element of transcendence generally governs his response to man's attitude toward God. And repeatedly he shows that the man who rejects God rejects life, and himself: "Divinizable" man becomes "man-brute," perhaps the most frightening and awesome process that he recreates in his fiction.

The person and the image of Christ, however, signify a difference of supernatural power. Christ is an immediate and immanent figure in relation to Dostoevsky's belief and imagination. God represents infinite power, whereas Christ is passion. Dostoevsky sees God in the light of man's supernatural destiny; he sees Christ in the light of human experience. Christ represents the symbiosis of the divine and the natural, of reality and Revelation; He marks the quintessence of Dostoevsky's Christian anthropology. For him the figure of Christ makes meaningful, and redeeming, the tragedy of existence. Christ, as the cosmic Christ and the Incarnate Christ, achieves his completion in the world. "In him the whole fulness of deity dwells bodily" (Colossians 2:9), writes Saint Paul. In the deepest spiritual sense Christ, as "completion" and "fulfilment," is for Dostoevsky the divine *pleroma*. Above all He singularizes the biblical, and hence the metaphysical and spiritual, contexts of Dostoevsky's burden of vision.

Dostoevsky's metaphysical point of view, especially as it

affects the theses and currents of his fiction, cannot be fully grasped without a sympathetic understanding of and response to what is ultimately an aesthetic and critical process of meditation. Indeed it is more than a process *per se*. It is the experience of a spiritual vision of life. Action of every kind and of every degree of intensity fills the pages of Dostoevsky's novels. His people are both the creators and the victims of action, whether physical or mental or both; this action is centered in the struggle between the One and the Many. But for Dostoevsky the cosmogenic and theogenic processes are parallel and consubstantial, possessing a metaphysical structure. In this key respect the Christian perquisites of Dostoevsky's religious philosophy cannot be underestimated.

Human action in Dostoevsky's novels is ultimately to be judged on the basis of meditation, which is, too, his answer to the rational and positivist mind of the modern world. All human action will yield "ontosophic truths" (to use Jacques Maritain's phrase) only to religious attention. It is meditation and not action that finally measures progress. "Action is the pointer of the balance. One must not touch the pointer, but the weights," Simone Weil warns. Meditation is a spiritual experience; more specifically it is the faculty of divination that spiritual art helps to engender. In their integral continuity and totality, Dostoevsky's five great novels constitute a sequential meditation on man's human and superhuman destiny. It is as an artist that Dostoevsky first sets down, renders, his meditations. Inevitably, these return to and revolve around metaphysical principles anchored in a religious consciousness and a biblical theology.

It needs special stressing in any scrutiny of Dostoevsky's religious philosophy that his Christian metaphysics is biblical but not ecclesiological. Though his religious philosophy is colored by Orthodox Christian spirituality, it transcends Orthodox ecclesiology. This fact has always discomforted Russian and non-Russian Orthodox adherents. Dostoevsky speaks as a religious visionary and not as a religious doctrinist. His vision is both anthropological and sacramental: he never fails to see the divine in man and the eternal in the temporal. The revolutionary meaning of his fiction, particularly as it culminates in the Legend of the Grand Inquisitor (in which, according to one critic, Dostoevsky is at one with his Devil-Inquisitor in offering only extreme choices—"either a life of spiritual freedom in the 'wilderness' or a life of slavery in society"), is inescapable, and it can severely test the credibility of his Christian metaphysics. But Dostoevsky does not formulate Christian metaphysical principles; he sensualizes them, he subordinates them to the requirements of the symbolic imagination. His "experience in Christianity" is always dynamic. His art is theological in its perspective, but it does not state a theology. No critical judgment of Dostoevsky's novels can be complete without accepting two primary truths of his creative impulse and vision: he creates the concepts of a religious philosophy; he reveals man in a world in which the separation of physical fact and spiritual reality has dire consequences.

The main burden of Dostoevsky's vision is to be found in his last five great novels. It is in these that the fundamental meaning of his spiritual art appears with a comprehensive unity of approach and with a maturity of expression and defining significance. And it is in these that his religious metaphysics attains full power and effectiveness. Each novel moves steadily towards crystallizing Dostoevsky's connective view of man and his world, and of life and faith. This movement is at once a dramatic particularization of human and religious themes and an intensifying spiritual synthesis. In their entirety, as both a particularization and a progression of vision, the five novels underline a dynamic creative process in that tradition which Flannery O'Connor discerns when she writes: "The artist penetrates the concrete world in order to find at its depths the image of ultimate reality." Dostoevsky presents his readers not only with a continuous discovery of life but also with an affirmation of meaning in life. Discovery and affirmation cohere in and inspire his total creative process: the first arises out of his imaginative genius, the second out of his metaphysical and theological certitudes. The insistence, then, of some critics on seeing Dostoevsky as a "supreme creator of the world of imagination" is a curiously uncritical view that ignores the moral and religious sources of his picture of the world. Dostoevsky's refusal to divorce elemental reality from ultimate reality marks the triumph of a creative imagination that yields a spiritual art. This refusal is a vindication of "the moral constant" as an indwelling and universalizing principle of art and reality.

*Chapter One*

# SCHISM
## Crime and Punishment

> *The real drama of this century lies in the growing estrangement between the temporal and the untemporal man. Is man, enlightened on one side, to sink into darkness on the other?*
>
> —St.-John Perse

# I

Fyodor Dostoevsky wrote *Crime and Punishment* between September 1865 and December 1866. It first appeared serially in *The Russian Messenger* and then separately in 1867. Containing, as he said, "much that is courageous and new," this novel was Dostoevsky's first major achievement, a "great revelation," and even, according to one claim, "the greatest tragedy about a murderer . . . written since *Macbeth.*" Whatever the validity of its comparison with Shakespeare's work, *Crime and Punishment* not only established Dostoevsky's post-Siberian reputation but also had a far-reaching influence, the magnitude of which Friedrich Nietzsche captures when he writes in his *Twilight of the Idols,* "Dostoevsky . . . was the only psychologist from whom I had anything to learn: he belongs to the happiest windfalls of my life, happier than the discovery of Stendhal."

Critics speak of *Crime and Punishment* as "the ripe fruit of the *katorga,*" a "novel-drama" which depicts "philosophy in action," embodies "the ethical problem," "puts forward problems and riddles," and "illustrates the crisis of Humanism, what its morality leads to, the suicide of man by self-affirmation." "In Dostoevsky the eschatological tension develops into eschatology itself," Eduard Thurneysen observes. "The absolutely final word of his novels is 'resurrection.' Over the dark abysses of the humanity which he depicts there glows from beyond the light of a great *forgiveness*. His men and women confront the problematical nature of their lives questioning, crushed and broken, vexed and shaken. It looms over them like the nearness of death."[1] Indeed, what stands out in *Crime and Punishment* is Dostoevsky's synthesis of artistic technique and religious-philosophical thought to dramatize what he called the "psychological account of a certain crime."

*Crime and Punishment, The Idiot, The Devils, A Raw Youth,* and *The Brothers Karamazov* form, as D. S. Mirsky notes, "a connected cycle," dramatic in construction, philosophic in significance, and tragic in conception.[2] The famous passage of a letter written by Dostoevsky to M. N. Katkov in September 1865, which bears re-quoting, both outlines the plan of *Crime and Punishment* and underscores the dramatic, the philosophic, and the tragic perspectives comprising the artistic and the ideational constituents of this novel:

> A young man of middle-class origin who is living in dire need is expelled from the university. From superficial and weak thinking, having been influenced by certain "unfinished" ideas in the air, he decides to get himself out of a difficult situation quickly by killing an old woman, a usurer and widow of a government servant. The old woman is crazy, deaf, sick, greedy, and evil. She charges scandalous rates of interest, devours the well-being of others, and, having reduced her younger sister to the state of a servant, oppresses her with work.... He decides to kill and rob her so as to make his mother, who is living in the provinces, happy; to save his sister from the libidinous importunities of the head of the estate where she is serving as a lady's companion; and then to finish his studies, go abroad and be, for the rest of his life, honest, firm, and unflinching in fulfilling his "humanitarian duty toward mankind." This would, according to him, "make up for the crime" which is committed against an old woman, who does not know why she is living and who would perhaps die in a month anyway.
>
> ... he is able to commit his crime, completely by chance, quickly and successfully.
>
> After this, a month passes before events come to a definite

climax. There is not, nor can there be, any suspicion of him. After the act the psychological process of the crime unfolds. Questions which he cannot resolve well up in the murderer; feelings he had not foreseen or suspected torment his heart. God's truth and earthly law take their toll, and he feels *forced* at last to give himself up. . . . The feeling of separation and isolation from mankind, which he felt immediately after the crime, tortured him. Human nature and the law of truth take their toll. The criminal decides to accept suffering so as to redeem his deed.

As an artist Dostoevsky is at his best in dramatizing the human soul in torment, in this case the soul of Rodion Romanovitch Raskolnikov, a handsome, debt-ridden, unhappy, intelligent, and idealistic twenty-three-year-old student living in Saint Petersburg in a "little room under the very roof of a tall five-storey building [that] was more like a cupboard than a living-room." From beginning to end, from crime to punishment and its aftermath, the novel recreates Raskolnikov's conflict, which is ultimately a conflict of values. His every thought and action mirror a soul in torment; conscience and hope struggle against an arrogance of intellect and a sense of nothingness; the sacred opposes the profane impulses in man; doubt and disbelief contend with certitude and affirmation.

Raskolnikov can be characterized as one who enacts the truth of Saint Paul's words that "we wrestle not against flesh and blood, but against principalities, against powers, against the rulers of the darkness of this world, against spiritual wickedness in high places." Undoubtedly, Raskolnikov's wrestlings image not only the soul's "shame and fear" but also outer turmoil; the man is viewed in a total process involving himself and others, both his own inner world and the world around him. His wrestlings occur in the awful hours and in the dark days without end in his lodgings, which are about six feet in length, and which are repeatedly compared to a coffin. "It was a tiny cubicle, about six feet in length, which looked most miserable with its dusty, yellowish paper peeling off the walls everywhere" (I,3).[3] Raskolnikov's poverty, his tattered clothes, his confusion, his bitterness, his loneliness, his terror, his restless movements amid the "peculiar summer stench which is so familiar to everyone who lives in Petersburg," further disclose the schismatic nature of his soul.

Petersburg is to Dostoevsky what Paris is to Balzac and London to Dickens. Indeed, he writes in the best tradition of great visionaries and mythopoets of the novel who make use of a particular city in evolving their myths and in giving order to their visions. "The streets," one critic remarks, "are Raskolnikov's contact with life. . . . The real city . . . is also a city of the mind in the way that its atmosphere answers Raskolnikov's spiritual condition and almost symbolizes it."[4] Petersburg contributes to the dissolution of families (the Raskolnikovs, the Marmeladovs) and is the background for identifying states of mind and of isolation. Other external elements also objectify the landscape of a soul in torment. Actions and dialogue of the novel are set against darkness, strange silences, stolen glances, narrow stairways, candlelit rooms, stuffy cafés, frightened whispers presaging dread events.

Not to go unnoticed are Raskolnikov's dreams, which disclose his malaise, a "sickness unto death," to quote Søren Kierkegaard. Dostoevsky's employment of dreams was to anticipate what Carl Gustav Jung speaks of as phenomena in the "nocturnal realm of the psyche" that give us "more than we ask"—"an insight into the causes of the neurosis"—affording "a prognosis as well," an "ineluctable truth," "the utterance of the unconscious," the "secrets of the inner life." Raskolnikov's solitude helps to give birth to his nightmares and reveals concurrently that "there are two sources of solitude and its agony: being cut off from men and being cut off from God."[5] "Solitude," as Nietzsche reminds us, "has seven skins; nothing can penetrate it."

The scene depicting Raskolnikov's murdering Alyona Ivanovna, "the old woman moneylender and widow of a Government clerk," and her half-sister, Lisaveta Ivanovna, "a tall, ungainly, shy, and meek woman of thirty-five, almost an idiot . . . who always seemed to be pregnant . . . a quiet creature, gentle, timid, and acquiescent," provides, in George Steiner's words, "an example of a novelist who must be read with a constant commitment of our visual imagination."[6] It provides, that is, a view of a creative genius in a work of art characterized by "the architecture and substance of drama." The murder scene illustrates Dostoevsky's dramatic mode, his "episodic climaxes," his "unfailing instinct for the dramatic scene," and his "tragico-fantastic" realism vigorously reinforced by his mastery of the Gothic tradition in fiction, with its murders, its other sins, its terrors. In English literature this tradition goes back to Horace Walpole's *The Castle of Otranto* (1764), Ann Radcliffe's *The Mysteries of Udolpho* (1794), M. G. Lewis's *The Monk* (1796), and Mary Shelley's *Frankenstein* (1818); on the continent it appeared in the works of Hugo, Balzac, Schiller, and George Sand, four writers who exerted much influence on Dostoevsky.

The ways in which Dostoevsky dramatizes the two murders testifies to his (often overlooked) powers as a craftsman who insists on giving, in his own words, "all the facts without reflections." Raskolnikov's getting the hatchet; his walk along the street; his careful attention to the time of day; his climbing the stairs quietly and cautiously to the fourth-floor flat of the moneylender: all these are details rendered with imaginative intensity, culminating in his arrival at the door of the flat. The silences, the pauses and hesitations, the interior monologue, the heart-pounding, the pain of decision, the sudden ringing of the bell, the hushed, fearful movements coming from inside, eliciting a fateful note that hangs oppressively over killer and victim alike: these develop the scene with astonishing intensity.

If there is dramatic intensity in the circumstances surrounding the first murder, there is a dramatic momentum in the events that follow, with the sudden "sound of footsteps" heard in the room where the old woman was: "But all of a sudden he distinctly heard a faint cry . . . as though someone had uttered a faint, abrupt moan and stopped." Then there occurs a "dead silence," as we view Raskolnikov "squatting on his haunches by the box and [waiting], hardly daring to breathe." Now, suddenly—with the same element of suddenness that recurs in the novel—"he jumped to his feet, snatched up the hatchet and rushed out of the bedroom." The second murder is committed and the element of suddenness is now complemented by a terrible hush, a rhythmic element recurring throughout. It is Lisaveta, "with a big bundle in her arms, looking petrified at the dead body." Gripped by fear and horror, "her whole body shaking like a leaf and her face twitching convulsively," she is unable to cry out. "She raised her hand a little, opened her mouth, but did not utter a cry. She now began to walk backwards, retreating slowly, looking at him, but without making a sound." The details of how Raskolnikov murders Lisaveta again illustrate Dostoevsky's "unfailing instinct for the dramatic scene":

> He rushed at her with the hatchet. Her lips were twisted pitifully, like those of little children who are beginning to be afraid of something and, without taking their eyes off the object of their fright, are about to scream. And so simple, crushed, and cowed was this unhappy Lisaveta that she did not even lift her hands to protect her face, though that was the most natural and inevitable gesture at that moment, for the hatchet was now raised straight over her face. All she did was to lift her free hand a little, at some distance from her face, and extend it slowly towards the hatchet as though pushing it away. The blow fell straight across her skull. She was hit with the blade of the hatchet, which split the top of her forehead open, penetrating almost to the crown of her head. She just collapsed in a heap on the floor. (I, 7)

Other scenes also achieve a translation of drama into prose fiction. There is the pathetic meeting between Raskolnikov and Marmeladov. There are the three fascinating confrontations of Raskolnikov and the examining magistrate, Porfiry Petrovitch, a lawyer who more than suspects the murderer. And there is the scene in which Raskolnikov meets with Sonia, when he kisses her foot, bowing down "to all suffering humanity," when he terms himself "a great, great sinner," and when she reads to him from the fourth Gospel about the raising of Lazarus—a prophetic episode that discloses the duality of Raskolnikov's very being, his confused groping for redemption colliding with a stubborn refusal to repent.

Dostoevsky's gift for the dramatic is equally evident in his rendering of Raskolnikov's encounters with Zamyotov, the chief clerk at the police station; with Luzhin; with Svidrigaylov. Dostoevsky extracts the maximum effectiveness from the dialogic processes through a subtle blending of scene and language, often packed with tension and irony. Thus, Raskolnikov nearly makes a confession to Zamyotov at the police station and then in a restaurant. When the chief clerk catches him reading newspaper accounts of the murders, his suspicions are sharpened. But Raskolnikov's boldness is too much for Zamyotov as the murderer recreates the details of his crime. "'You're mad!' said Zamyotov, also, for some unknown reason, almost in a whisper, and again, for some unknown reason, he moved suddenly from Raskolnikov."

It suffices to say that the dialogues serve to put us "right into the middle of . . . [Dostoevsky's] people; [hence] we are much closer to them than to people in real life, and consequently we discover characteristics which we scarcely notice in nature. These discoveries are apparently due to our intimate intercourse with the characters."[7] Through these dialogues, likewise, we fathom the peculiar human qualities that distinguish a cross-section of human character: Marmeladov's destitution, Zamyotov's superficiality, Porfiry's artistry, Luzhin's bourgeois machinations, Svidrigaylov's baseness, Sonia's faith and innocence.

Dostoevsky's dramatic sense, therefore, achieves a perfect blend of word and physical detail, with the visual element enhancing the auditory. We hear voices, which we identify with faces and bodies, as if Dostoevsky's people occupied places on a stage: for example, the portraits of Luzhin and of Porfiry that delineate special qualities giving an index to the total personality of each. The following description of Luzhin, Dunya's fiancé, vivifies a "smooth" man of selfish ends who knows how to play the role to the hilt and to make the proper appearance, the right impressions, all the time seeking to control and manipulate and exploit and trap others (the description helps to show why Marxist critics condemn Luzhin as the epitome of "decadent" bourgeois mentality):

> All his clothes had just come from the tailor's, and everything was perfect.... Even his brand-new stylish hat proclaimed it: Mr. Luzhin treated it with too great a deference and held it a little too carefully in his hands. Even the delightful pair of lavender gloves, real Jouvain, established the same fact, if only because he did not wear them, but merely carried them about in his hands for show. As for Mr. Luzhin's clothes, light and youthful colours predominated in them. He wore a most becoming summer jacket of a light brown shade, light summer trousers, the same kind of waistcoat, a fine linen shirt straight from the shop, the lightest possible cambric cravat with pink stripes, and needless to say, it all suited him perfectly. His extremely fresh and even handsome face always looked younger than his forty-five years. His dark mutton-chop whiskers set it off very fetchingly at either side of his shining and clean-shaven chin. (II, 5)

And in the following description of Porfiry we view an alert observer of other men, a brilliant skirmisher, and a "dangerous antagonist." Porfiry is every bit Raskolnikov's mental equal. He knows what questions to ask, how to ask them, and how to weigh responses to them. He is a wise knower and an artist in his own right.

> He was a man of about thirty-five, of not quite medium height, corpulent and even paunchy, clean-shaven, with closely cropped hair on a large round head which bulged out rather peculiarly at the back. He had a chubby, round, and somewhat snub-nosed face of an unhealthy yellowish complexion, but cheerful and even bantering. It would have been good-humored but for the expression of his eyes, with a sort of faintly watery glint in them, covered with almost white, blinking eyelashes, which conveyed the impression that he was strangely out of keeping with his whole figure, which reminded one somehow of the figure of an old peasant woman, and invested it with something much more serious than one would have expected at first sight. (III, 5)

# II

Raskolnikov is Dostoevsky's astonishingly prophetic conception of temporal man who lives in a progressively desacralized world. In *The Sacred and the Profane* Mircea Eliade helps us to comprehend some of the traits of "profane man" who strives to "empty" himself of all religion and all "transhuman meaning" and to become "free" and "pure"; and his words could easily summarize Raskolnikov's own condition, his emerging ethos, his private mythology in all its paradoxes:

> Modern nonreligious man assumes a new existential situation; he regards himself solely as the subject and agent of history, and he refuses all appeal to transcendence. In other words, he accepts no model for humanity outside the human condition as it can be seen in the various historical situations. Man *makes himself,* and he only makes himself completely in proportion as he desacralizes himself and the world. The sacred is the prime obstacle to his freedom.[8]

The philosophical facets of *Crime and Punishment* are thus directly related to the fact that Raskolnikov is an "atheistic humanist" who has rejected traditional religious values; a "superman" who seeks to destroy the "old morality," and who, borrowing here Romano Guardini's phrase, seeks to express *menschliche Selbstbehauptung*, human self-assertiveness. In the opening page Raskolnikov's own thoughts announce the philosophical problem of the novel: " . . . everything is in a man's own hands, and if he lets everything slip through his fingers, it is through sheer cowardice. That's an axiom. I wonder, though, what people fear most. It seems to me that what they are afraid of most is of taking a new step or uttering a new word." Raskolnikov murders for the purpose of becoming a "titan" in spite of his past, his family, his innate humanity and his generosity. His "terrible dream," just before the murders, of how as a boy of seven he protested against the brutal beating of a mare by a heartless and sadistic owner, clearly brings out in his deeper being, his unconscious, humane elements and the spiritual essences that he must override once he chooses to put into action the philosophy of the superman.

Indeed, Raskolnikov's theory and actions dramatize some of the important ideological elements current at the time Dostoevsky was writing and are presented in the idiom of an age that looked back to the eighteenth century, to the Enlightenment and to Rousseau's doctrine of the perfectibility of man, as well as to the nineteenth century with its stress on romantic individualism, on the Byronic hero who defies society, and on the Napoleonic legend. It is precisely against such an ideological background that Raskolnikov must be seen—the Raskolnikov, to recall, whose heart is "unhinged by theories" and who commits his crimes under the influence of "certain odd *unfinished* ideas which are in the air."

Raskolnikov's motives for committing crime must be seen in connection with the assertion of will and with a certain intellectual arrogance. His motives, as he shows, have several ramifications, the Rousseauistic being most apparent on the surface: "For one life you will save thousands of lives from corruption and decay. One death in exchange for a hundred lives—why, it's a simple sum in arithmetic! And, when you come to think of it, what does the life of a sickly, wicked old hag amount to when weighed in the scales of the general good of mankind? It amounts to no more than the life of a louse or a black beetle, if that, for the old hag is really harmful" (I, 6). Initially Raskolnikov's acts are tied to his social and personal protest, to the idealism and the altruism that are seemingly natural to this "Russian Faust" who seeks "salvation in trans-gression." But to see his actions in terms of a Benthamite doctrine that actions are right in proportion to their usefulness oversimplifies Raskolnikov. At much deeper levels his motives are strongly, if not finally, tied to his will, to his intellectual prowess, to his desire to be a "hero" and a "superman."

Intellectual pride pervades Raskolnikov's published essay "On Crime," in which he divides people into two categories, "ordinary" and "extraordinary" (III, 5). The "ordinary" are unimaginative and obedient "and have no right to transgress the law because, you see, they are ordinary." The "extraordi-nary," on the other hand, "have a right to commit any crime," for they "possess the gift or talent to say *a new word* in their particular environment." An "extraordinary" person has a right "to permit his conscience to step over certain obstacles," for the welfare of mankind, even "to step over a corpse or wade through blood." A Kepler or a Newton would have the right to "*eliminate* the dozen or the hundred people" so as to make his discoveries known to all mankind. "Lawgivers and arbiters of mankind" like Lycurgus, Solon, Mahomet, and Napoleon "all shed rivers of blood." Hence, Raskolnikov maintains, "all men who are not only great but a little out of the common ... must by their very nature be criminals." "The first category is always the master of the present; the second category the master of the future. The first preserves the world and increases its numbers; the second moves the world and leads it to its goal. Both have an absolutely equal right to exist. In short, with me all have the same rights and—*vive la guerre éternelle*—till the New Jerusalem, of course."

Raskolnikov thinks and acts according to his theory, the theory of a superman and not of a philanthropist. He acts, that is to say, "*in accordance with the dictates of one's conscience*": "Let him suffer, if he is sorry for his victim. Suffering and pain are always necessary for men of great sensibility and deep feeling. Really great men ... must feel great sorrow on earth." The superman seeks for a limitless "freedom," and his theory, his idea, becomes, as Konstantin Mochulsky states, "his driv-ing force, his *destiny*."[9] He thinks constantly in terms of this destiny: in terms of intellectual power; of a great leader and iron man enunciating a "super-morality" and a new scale of values—a new ethic that, in Nietzsche's words, enjoys the "pleasures of victory and cruelty" and commands men to be "purified" by their triumphs over the elements and over other men and to become finally "the archetype[s] of moral beauty."

The destiny of Raskolnikov must be interpreted on the basis of his intellectuality, his theory, his grand idea. He is the personification and the instrument of the idea. Raskolnikov, hence, is a witness to concepts of history and not to humanity: to stratagems, to campaigns, to large-scale movements and accomplishments, to the supremely impersonal. His dream is of a man of iron: of an Alexander if one returns to the remote past, of a Napoleon if one moves closer to the period of the novel. His vision is of power and of marching armies, of compassionless generals, of expanding empires; his fascination is with dangers and cruel deeds—the achievements of *Sturm und Drang* and the mastery over all personal existence in what Tolstoy calls "the circle of violence." No passage better traces the nature of Raskolnikov's theorizing, or the implicit dangers of an experiment with freedom and strength, than the passage relating to Napoleon:

> A real *ruler of men*, a man to whom everything is permitted, takes Toulon by storm, carries out a massacre in Paris, *forgets* an army in Egypt, *wastes* half a million men in his Moscow campaign, and gets away with a Pun in Vilna. And monuments are erected to him after his death, which of course means that to him *everything* is permitted. No! Such men are not made of flesh and blood, but of bronze! (III, 6)

In committing crime, therefore, Raskolnikov admits to Sonia, "Listen: I wanted to become a Napoleon—that's why I killed the old woman." To Raskolnikov, "the old woman" is merely "a louse," "a useless, nasty, harmful louse." Killing her merely proves the truth of the theory that "he who dares much is right. . . . He who dismisses with contempt what men regard as sacred becomes their law-giver. . . ."

Both psychologically and ideologically Raskolnikov displays, in all his thinking and actions, an arrogant imperialism, or the push for power of the individual. (Later on Henri Bergson described this imperialism as being inherent in the vital urge and at the bottom of the soul of individuals and of peoples.) This individual imperialism was undoubtedly prophetic of precisely that political and collective imperialism that has dictated the course of history, particularly since 1914. Raskolnikov is the epitome of the modernist. He embodies all those ambivalences and paradoxes that have oppressed modern man. That is to say, he is assaulted and trapped by titanic ideas of freedom, progress, enlightenment. As such his imperialism of murder is antecedent to the advanced stage of material, as opposed to moral, civilization as conceived by the modernists. Raskolnikov's driving imperialism is consequentially, as well as representatively, the result of an age of rationalism and of romantic dreaming. His confusion, which comes out in his inner torment, is a symptom of the imperialistic upshot of his actions. In his intellectual conceit, then, Raskolnikov illustrates the imperialistic drive towards the unlimited and the fearlessness before consequences. His admiration of Napoleon is crystallized in his megalomania. Thus, Raskolnikov illustrates, in a prophetic and frightening way, the lust for power and the scorn of wisdom. He is travelling on the road of the modern, unrepentant immoralist, who must ultimately seek fulfillment in the absoluteness of his imperialism.

Raskolnikov's crime must be seen as dependent on a will to power, on the decision to eliminate all obstacles, the kind of deified will that brings to mind Nietzsche's contention that "the whole of history is the refutation by experiment of the principle of the so-called 'moral world order.'" Indeed, we can better understand Raskolnikov's decision to dare in the light of Nietzsche's further observation: "Danger alone acquaints us with our own resources, our virtues, our armor and weapons, our *spirit*, and *forces* us to be strong. *First* principle: one must need to be strong—otherwise one will never become strong." This Nietzschean "*first* principle" catches the ultimate spirit that forces Raskolnikov "to be strong" and that clarifies his response to the daring that Raskolnikov "exultantly" describes to Sonia:

> "It was then that I realized...that power is given only to him who dares to stoop and take it. There is only one thing that matters here: one must have the courage to dare. It was then that, for the first time in my life, I hit on the idea which no one had ever thought of before. No one! It suddenly became as clear as daylight to me that no one, neither in the past nor today, had ever dared, while passing by all these absurdities, to take it all by the tail and

send it flying to the devil. I—I wanted to dare, Sonia, that was my only motive!" (V, 4)

In the end Raskolnikov's crime, his self-doubt, and his confession must be appraised in the light of this "daring." In murdering the old woman, he seeks to confirm the power to achieve freedom of will and conscience that alone permit the "hero" to act as a free agent, answerable to no one and yet answering the "great question":

> "And it was not the money, Sonia, I was after when I did it. No, it was not so much the money I wanted as something else. . . . It was something else that goaded me on: I had to find out then, and as quickly as possible, whether I was a louse like the rest or a man. Whether I can step over or not. Whether I dare to stoop or not? Whether I am some trembling vermin or whether I have the *right*." (V, 4)

In the following remarks to Sonia, Raskolnikov states the reason for his crime and rejects any benevolent impulses leading to the crime—and, in any case, it is a passage that shows that to become a strong man he had at the same time to destroy his philanthropic impulses, to achieve (to use once more Nietzsche's words) "the commanding something, which the people call 'spirit,' which wants to be master over itself and its surroundings to feel its mastery": " . . . I wanted to murder, Sonia, to murder without casuistry, to murder for my satisfaction, for myself alone. I didn't want to lie about it. I did not commit this murder to become the benefactor of humanity by gaining wealth and power—that, too, is nonsense. I just did it; I did it for myself alone . . . " (V, 4). Now in respect to the particular reasons for Raskolnikov's confession of the crime, it needs stressing that "*He did not repent of his crime*," and that he confessed out of a terrible sense of weakness unbecoming to a real superman, a true Napoleon. "It is not remorse which drives him to self-accusation," Julius Meier-Graefe observes, "but partly disgust at himself as well as others, and mainly his nervous condition."[10]

The meaning of repentance, tied as it must be to the spiritual life, eludes Raskolnikov. Without any interior understanding of repentance he can never really grasp the magnitude not only of his crime but also of evil. Raskolnikov does achieve a measure of freedom by the crime he commits, but such a freedom does not really free him from himself; it is an external freedom without depth and hence without an abiding and inner substance. Unconsciously, of course, Raskolnikov seeks for the spiritual freedom that comes from the act of repentance. This search comes out, if only uncertainly, in his relations with Sonia and in his gropings for some form of recovery, or at least for a diminution of the self-doubts that badger him and that make for his schism of soul. In resisting the pangs of remorse Raskolnikov resists the experience of repentance. The burden of his crime and punishment is exacerbated by such a resistance. Repentance, insofar as it presents one with the radical experience of a true understanding of good and evil, is perhaps Raskolnikov's greatest challenge, greater ultimately than the commission of his crime. This is an additional reason why his burden of himself is so overwhelming. Questions of self-justification and self-condemnation obviously occupy a place of importance in Raskolnikov's entire situation. As a comprehensive and unconditional resignation, repentance is a direct threat to one's conditional self. Much more than just a bad memory, it belongs to the highest hierarchy of values connecting time and eternity. It is a mediating experience that alone would assuage, ultimately resolve, Raskolnikov's predicament, which centers in his arrogant conception of the freedom of will. "Repentance culminates in completion only by the condition of absolute sincerity before oneself and before God," writes Sergei Levitzky.[11] For Raskolnikov the repudiation of his actions would constitute the repudiation of the rending forms of the slavery of his titanism: his self-assertion and self-personalization—his "ego." Repentance is antecedent to humility, and humility is both for Raskolnikov and for the multitude of modern immoralists a spiritual substance that must be shunned.

Raskolnikov is essentially an artist, an aesthete to whom disgust comes easily. His sensitivity cannot withstand the ugly aspects of the crime itself or the incongruous structural aspects of the effects of the crime. Hence he cannot cut himself from his conscience and from the life in and around him. In an Augustinian sense, it could be said, he cannot find absolute release from memory, either from the memory of the race or from the vision of God. Memory itself becomes for Raskolnikov a vehicle of grace, even as his dreams prove. Theory, ultimately, cannot overcome his yearning for life, a yearning that appears spontaneously, in his various kindnesses to others, especially his mother and sister, as well as the Marmeladovs. Raskolnikov's dilemma, occasioned by his obsession with cold intellectual theory and his aesthetic propensity, creates too much of a split in him to enable him to capitulate to Euclidean theory and reason. A superman, after all, must be a pure fanaticist, impervious to human frailty. He is lord over empire and death itself. Ruthless, fearless, coldly scientific, he overcomes such puny feelings as guilt, remorse, charity, meekness, pity; he rules the conscious and conquers conscience, and he transcends the tragic dimensions of virtue, the "softnesses" which Sonia exemplifies.

Raskolnikov's sensitivity and his aesthetic predisposition do not allow him the full unbridled power of the profane, the power of the annihilation of humane and spiritualizing elements. When Raskolnikov finally confesses his regrets, his limitations, e.g., that a Napoleon does not crawl under an old woman's bed, or that a Napoleon cannot be "an aesthetic louse," he reveals inner limitations that do not befit a strong man. The dream of the old woman "sitting and laughing" at him is merely another instance of the fact that though he may step over all obstacles, he cannot step over himself, over what constitutes his real self, his human conscience that produces self-disgust and makes him aware of the softer facets of life, such as Sonia. Ostensibly, a superman has no time for Sonias. Surely empires and theories are not the results of *liaisons* with prostitutes, even "pure" prostitutes. By attending to Sonia, Raskolnikov discloses the weakness which must at the same time compromise his theory and ambition.

A superman is above grace and humility. He cannot humble himself, as does Raskolnikov when he bows down and kisses Sonia's foot and when he claims that he "bowed down to all suffering humanity." To be sure, Raskolnikov is not repentant here; he even mocks her for her belief in God and for her effort of prayer, and he considers her mad for claiming that God "does everything." Yet Raskolnikov reveals his mortality by admitting to Sonia that "We're both damned, so let's go together"; that " . . . we must go the same way"; that "I need you, and that's why I've come to you"; that " . . . we must go together along the same road." The fact remains that a strong man has no need for another human being. He must be above sharing pain, or showing sympathy, or fearing damnation. He can only have, in Nietzsche's words, "a trait of cruelty, a tigerish lust to annihilate."

Yet Raskolnikov enjoys the possibility of victory only briefly in the will to do his crime and in the process of it. It is a mechanic victory, for his sense of daring is never sustained or sustaining. He is altogether too aware of the human element, in himself and around him, and he is unable to leap beyond it—to the other side, into the hands of Satan. He is ever susceptible to human reminders which shatter, must shatter, a superman's vision of power. Significantly, Raskolnikov feels his limitations when he stands on the bank of the Neva River contemplating suicide but finding himself unable to commit the act, the act which, as Dostoevsky notes in *The Devils,* makes one equal with God. Raskolnikov's inability to commit suicide shows that he is not to be counted among "the children of darkness" and that he is redeemable. Had he had the courage, the daring, to commit suicide, he would have asserted the "full freedom" that comes, as Kirillov in *The Devils* says, "when it will be just the same to live or not to die." For according to Kirillov, "he who dares kill himself is God."

# III

In *Crime and Punishment* Dostoevsky's tragic vision is preoccupied with the problem of evil and with the passion of suffering on the part of a protagonist "as he sees himself at once both good and bad, justified yet unjustified," as Richard B. Sewall writes in *The Vision of Tragedy.* Throughout, Raskolnikov struggles and suffers within "a structure which shows progression toward value, rather than denial of it, and a relationship between the inner life of the sufferer and the world of values about him." Raskolnikov, in a word, helps us to "see the evil of evil and the goodness of good"; as a consequence, "we are more 'ready.'"[12] In Raskolnikov, a "lost, violent soul," then, we are in the presence of a tragic human being, in a sense a hero who is thwarted by a flaw—the flaw being his humanity, sin, guilt, freedom.

"There are in every man at every moment two simultaneous postulations," Charles Baudelaire asserts, "one towards God, the other towards Satan." In Raskolnikov the pull towards God is seen in all its progressive movement in his relations to Sonia, who represents the redemptive aspect of a soul in torment and epitomizes selflessness and compassion. "Sonia is hope," Dostoevsky writes in his notebooks for *Crime and Punishment,* "the most unrealizable."[13] Childlike and pure, yet defiled by the cruelty and cynicism of life, she is "like a lamb . . . and her voice, too, so meek—she has fair hair and her face has always been so thin and pale." She is " . . . a very small, thin girl . . . blonde . . . with a pair of remarkable blue eyes." Her being a prostitute dramatizes eternal suffering and eternal pity: a dimension of the secular profaning of divine wisdom, and yet its ever-present and sacrificial features of endurance. Not only does she represent "The Gentle Ones and the Great Acceptance," but she also signifies the way of truth and life, as opposed to the hate and darkness and nightmare which pervade the human situation. It should be noted that she is always there for Raskolnikov to turn to, if he will make the effort. In an artistic sense, furthermore, she symbolizes suffering martyrdom. . . . "If we suffer, we shall also reign with Him" (II Timothy 2:12).

Although Western critics have generally misunderstood Sonia's significance in *Crime and Punishment,* L. A. Zander and Romano Guardini have stressed the sapiential facets of her role, that is, wisdom and goodness.[14] To both her father and Raskolnikov she reacts without ever blaming them. She weeps, or she remains silent, or she trembles, but she does not condemn. "Such is the answer," writes Zander, "of purity and innocence to blatant, conscious, insolent evil: indignation which does not find vent in strife (for that would not turn evil into good); horror at the tragedy of evil, at the yawning abyss of evil as such, apart from its results; infinite sorrow for the victims of evil, for those who succumb to it and thus become its embodiment and its servants." That she is spiritual energy accounts for the non-erotic elements in her relation to Raskolnikov. "She is a child of God in the sense that His hand incomprehensibly rests upon her," Guardini writes. "In the world she is defenceless, and yet is protected by the Father." Yet, in spite of being "frightened," "crushed," "accused," "defenceless," she is firm in her position. When Raskolnikov mocks God—"And what does God do for you?" he asks—her reply is uncompromising: "Be quiet! Don't ask! You're not worthy!" When he rationalizes his crime by stating that he merely "killed a louse . . . a useless, nasty, harmful louse," she cries: "A human being—a louse?" Knowing of his crime, she nonetheless refuses to disown him. After the requiem service there occurs this revealing scene that epiphanizes Sonia's spiritual strengths:

> After the service Raskolnikov went up to Sonia, who suddenly took hold of his hands and pressed her head against his shoulder. This brief, friendly gesture took Raskolnikov by surprise; it struck him even as exceedingly odd: good Lord, not the slightest feeling of horror and disgust for him? Not the slightest tremor of her hand? . . . Sonia said nothing. Raskolnikov pressed her hand and went out. . . . If at that moment he could have gone away somewhere and remained there entirely alone, even for the rest of his life, he would have thought himself blessed indeed. (VI, 1)

Raskolnikov's descending movement towards Satan appears in his relations to the voluptuary Svidrigaylov, an evil figure who has menacing, demonic powers. The notebooks record of this man: "Svidrigaylov is despair, the most cynical . . . conscious of mysterious horrors within himself which he will tell no one but lets slip out as facts. He has convulsive, animal-like urges to rend and kill; coldly passionate. A wild beast. A crawling reptile. A tiger." Svidrigaylov, undoubtedly, serves as Sonia's contrary and as Raskolnikov's alter ego. What remains potential in the young student, what would be the end of all his theory and his crime, the inevitable dead-end, is ascendant in Svidrigaylov. As Philip Rahv says, Svidrigaylov is a subordinate but crucial character.[15]

Artistically, the circumstances and milieux in which Svidrigaylov appears emphasize his evil, his innate depravity, his darkness, his menace to life. He is seen in the blighted areas of Petersburg where he moves about in cellars and in filth. The blackness of night seems always to hover about him. Flies and mice, in his dreams and in his wakeful hours, seem to be his companions. (Dostoevsky often makes use of lower forms of animal life—flies, beetles, cockroaches, spiders, snakes, tarantulas, scorpions—to suggest demonically dissolute characters.) The beauty and iridescence of the natural world fade in his presence. His creatureliness seems to profane the world itself. Characteristically, Svidrigaylov hates the light, and the sun, and the beauty of the earth and the sea: "I've been abroad before, and I always got sick of it . . . the sunrise, the bay of Naples, the sea—all that makes you feel so damnably depressed" (IV, 1).

A former nobleman who served two years in the cavalry, a card-sharper, and now a widower, he has come to Petersburg "for the sake of women." He exhibits a devouring passion for carnal pleasures, and he seeks for "a whiff of the familiar smells" in the familiar dens of vice. "I like my dens to be dirty," he admits. Understandably, then, does Raskolnikov speak of Svidrigaylov as "that dirty villain and voluptuous roué and scoundrel." His outward appearance, however, is delusive, for he wears a mask. He is a rather handsome, dandified man of fifty, but he looks younger than his years:

> It was a peculiar kind of face, which looked like a mask: white, with red cheeks, with bright-red lips, a light, flaxen beard, and still very thick, fair hair. His eyes were, somehow, a little too blue, and their expression was, somehow, too heavy and motionless. There was something repulsive in his handsome and, to judge by his age, extremely young face. Svidrigaylov's clothes were smart, of light summer material, and he seemed to be particularly proud of his fine linen. One of his fingers was adorned by a huge ring with a valuable stone. (VI, 3)

If Sonia stands for light, Svidrigaylov stands for baseness, for the satanism that in biblical terminology is "like a roaring lion, seeking whom it may devour"; for Svidrigaylov human dignity and reverence for life are meaningless. Only vice is natural and permanent, he says, "something that is always there in your blood, like a piece of red-hot coal." He has seduced young girls and married women; he caused the death of his own wife, whom he married only because she promised to pay his gambling debts and whom he continually and flagrantly dishonored by his behavior. It is implied, too, that the death of Philip, his servant, was the result of Svidrigaylov's abusiveness and meanness. Even worse, he drove a deaf-and-dumb girl of fourteen or fifteen to commit suicide after he had violated her. Svidrigaylov's appetite for young girls is unquenchable. This particular craving leads him to become engaged to a sixteen-year-old: "I put her on my knees yesterday, but I suppose a little too unceremoniously—she flushed all over, and tears started to her eyes, but she did not want to show it, she was on fire herself." Even his nightmares relate to his molesting girls. Stephan Zweig terms Svidrigaylov a "calculating tactician of debauchery."[16] "As an example of sexual behavior," R. P. Blackmur observes, "Svidrigaylov is incredible. Sex is Dostoevsky's symbol of a diabolic, destructive power, which he can sense but cannot measure, and which he cannot otherwise name."[17]

Svidrigaylov is inevitably bored by life: "I feel rather," he says, "like joining an expedition to the North Pole; for drink makes me miserable, and I hate drinking and there's nothing left for me to do except to get drunk" (IV, 1). He harbors a complete, impregnable cynicism: "But you can never be sure of anything that may take place between a husband or wife or a lover and his lass. There's always a little corner which remains hidden from the rest of the world and which is only known to the two of them" (IV, 4). Particularly revealing is his concept of eternity: "We're always thinking of eternity as an idea that cannot be understood, something immense. But why must it be? What if, instead of all this, you suddenly find just a little room there, something like a village bathhouse, grimy, and spiders in every corner, and that's all eternity is. Sometimes, you know, I can't help feeling that's probably what it is" (IV, 1).

Admittedly, Svidrigaylov has a certain "atrophied grandeur" about him, as one commentator has remarked. This is to be seen, for example, in his financial help to the Marmeladovs, his willingness to bear Mrs. Marmeladov's funeral expenses, his efforts to place the three children in orphanages, even his plans to assist Sonia. But these ostensible acts of kindness do not indicate either a humane or a heroic predisposition. They are, in fact, acts prompted by a devouring passion for Dunya; they are avenues of approach to her and overtures that are impelled by far-reaching designs. They are acts that bring to mind Saint Tikhon of Zadonsk's warning that Satan "frequently offers evil under the semblance of good, like poison steeped in honey." His generosity is also closely related to his "boredom of non-being"; he does what he does because he is bored. His are kind deeds with a price, not at all magnanimous outbursts. For Svidrigaylov always knows that he is playing with life. He is a "calculating tactician of debauchery," to recall Zweig's words, a man who, Raskolnikov thought, "was always full of all sorts of plans and projects." When Svidrigaylov's advances are denied by Dunya, who even fires a revolver at him, we see him as a defeated fiend whose mask has been stripped away and whose ego has been defeated. His failure with Dunya is of paramount importance, for it is his cynicism and not his conscience that is dealt a blow. Life, we are glad to see, does not always cringe before brute will or fall into a pattern of cynical expectation. His only recourse is suicide, a perverse form of courage to a Man-God. Svidrigaylov's death, as Mochulsky observes, comes from a "mean-spirited" feeling and not from "remorse."

When Raskolnikov admits to Svidrigaylov that "I can't help feeling that in some way you are very like me," we can readily comprehend the truth of Mochulsky's contention that Svidrigaylov "is placed next to Raskolnikov to serve as his dark and sombre double. . . . Svidrigaylov is Raskolnikov's 'devil.'" For Raskolnikov there is a choice between Sonia with her message of regeneration and affirmation of life that has "taken the place of dialectics," and Svidrigaylov with his limitless freedom of negation. Svidrigaylov stands for a complete impasse of nothingness. Sonia stands for the effort of hope. "Go at once," she says to Raskolnikov, "this very minute, and stand at the cross-roads, bow down, just kiss the earth which you have defiled, and then bow down to all four corners of the world—and say to all men aloud, I am a murderer! Then God will send you life again" (V, 4). She stands for the balm of love, a final saving force without which there can be nothing but a denial of all human meaning and the existence of what is "something like a village bathhouse, grimy, and spiders in every corner"—that is, an eternity of debasement.

"Evil is multifarious and fragmentary," writes Simone Weil in *Gravity and Grace,* "good is one; evil is apparent, good is mysterious; evil consists in action, good in non-action, in activity which does not act."[18] No words could better describe the two forces that pull at Raskolnikov, as seen in the persons of Svidrigaylov and Sonia, and that depict the descending and the ascending movements of a soul in torment.

# IV

When, at last, as seen in the Epilogue, Sonia's love for Raskolnikov begins to turn the tide, "now their hands did not part." This act is symbolic of the regenerative power of wisdom and light. Significant, too, in the Epilogue, is the vision that Raskolnikov, now a prisoner in Siberia, has early one morning while he is sitting on the bank of a river. Before this vision he was merely perturbed by a "wounded pride" and viewed his predicament in terms of his "blunder"; moreover, he detested and was detested by the other prisoners, who attacked him as an atheist and who said he "ought to be killed." The rending sense of isolation that he experiences in Siberia—"the terrible unbridgeable gulf that lay between him and all those other people"—brings to mind Dostoevsky's words in one of his letters: "To transform the world, to recreate it afresh, man must turn into another path psychologically . . . but first we have to go through a period of isolation." During Holy Week Raskolnikov is overtaken by illness. In delirium he sees the whole world swept by pestilence. It is a prophetic dream with a message of disaster and speaks in what Martin Buber calls "the language of history":

> Whole villages, whole towns and peoples became infected and went mad. . . . Each of them believed that the truth only resided in him. . . . They did not know whom to put on trial or how to pass judgment. . . . Men killed each other in a kind of senseless fury. They raised whole armies against each other; but these armies . . . began suddenly to fight among themselves, their ranks broke, and the soldiers fell upon one another . . . bit and devoured each other. . . . And they began to accuse each other, fought and killed each other. Fires broke out. Wholesale destruction stalked the earth.

In his vision of evil, Raskolnikov demonstrates the ultimate consequences of negation. But, as it has often been pointed out, affirmations sometimes come out of denials. The possibility of a "break-through," a word that figures prominently in the prophetic idiom, is always present as long as there is a Sonia to oppose a Svidrigaylov. This "break-through" in *Crime and Punishment* occurs directly after Raskolnikov's vision of evil, after he has failed to see Sonia, who has "been taken ill and was unable to go out." The news of her illness upsets him, but later she writes him a note that she is better and will see him soon: "His heart beat fast when he read that note." His reactions must be counted as significant, for Sonia represents the possibility of light, "pointing beyond, hinting at something inexpressibly great and distant," as Thurneysen puts it. Sonia, thus, provides the means of a "break-through" to affirmation—she provides, in other words, apocalyptic hints, "a tremor of bliss, a wink of heaven," to quote T. S. Eliot's phrase.

At last the prophecy of despair gives way to the prophecy of hope, as we find Raskolnikov early one bright morning working on the bank of a river and looking at its "wide, deserted expanse." A new vision and new voices come to him and point to a "break-through"—to the capacity for perception—that is directly related to rebirth:

> From the steep bank a wide stretch of the countryside opened up before him. Snatches of a song floated faintly across from the distant bank of the river. There in the vast steppe, flooded with sunlight, he could see the black tents of the nomads which appeared like dots in the distance. There there was freedom, there other people were living, people who were not a bit like the people he knew; there time itself seemed to stand still as though the age of Abraham and his flocks had not passed.

This passage, with its emphasis on open spaces, on serenity, on sunlight, on freedom, on people not enslaved by theory, has a restorative effect, augmented at this point by the sudden arrival of Sonia, who holds out her hand. Marmeladov's words in the early part of the novel, "For every man must have at least somewhere to go," come to mind here, for Sonia personifies this "somewhere to go," without which life is directionless, anarchic. And it is only now that Raskolnikov begins to achieve the "break-through" to repentance and redemption: "How it happened he did not know, but suddenly something seemed to seize him and throw him at her feet. He embraced her knees and wept."

This episode has profound meaning, for at no point hitherto has Raskolnikov openly or knowingly allowed his innate feelings, his humanity, to rise above his adherence to theory. In terms of dramatic art it is only now that we view Raskolnikov's growing awareness of the fate of a "strong individual" who seeks to free himself from God and who succeeds at the price of his being reduced to "sheer demonism." "As pitilessly as might crushes," Simone Weil warns, "so pitilessly it maddens whoever possesses, or believes he possesses it."[19] And Nicolas

Berdyaev notes in this respect that "he who does not bow before that higher will destroys his neighbour and destroys himself. That is the meaning of *Crime and Punishment*."[20] In the Epilogue, which has often been scored by literary scholars as a kind of artistic forcing of a particular point of view, it is precisely a "break-through" that occurs, a prophetic "break-through" so beautifully seen in this passage describing Raskolnikov and Sonia:

> They wanted to speak, but could not; tears stood in their eyes. They were both pale and thin; but in those sick and pale faces the dawn of a new future, of a full resurrection to a new life, was already shining. It was love that brought them back to life: the heart of one held inexhaustible sources of life for the heart of the other. They decided to wait and be patient. They still had to wait for another seven years, and what great suffering and what infinite joy till then! And he had come back to life, and he knew it, and felt it with every fibre of his renewed being, and she—why, she lived only for him.

In every way Dostoevsky is a great prophetic novelist who bears "the troubling and unloved responsibilities of prophecy."[21] As such he can be considered a modern artist and seer who continues an ancient tradition that goes back to the great prophets of the Old Testament. The prophetic novelist's theme, E. M. Forster declares, "is the universe, or something universal, but he is not necessarily going to 'say' anything about the universe; he proposes to sing, and the strangeness of song arising in the halls of fiction is bound to give us a shock."[22] If a prophetic artist "speaks forth" of disaster, he also speaks of hope, for hope too is an implicit part of prophecy. That there "will be an evil time," that "the soul that sins shall die," is never without the prophet's attendant promise that "ye shall find rest for your souls."

The ending of *Crime and Punishment* places Dostoevsky in the prophetic tradition of spiritual art. "I have my own view of art," he wrote to N. N. Strakhov in 1869, "and that which the majority may call fantastic and exceptional is for me the very essence of reality." For Dostoevsky the "fantastic" and the "exceptional" are the special, hierophantic properties of spiritual art, rendered as drama and revealed as prophecy.

*Chapter Two*

# TERROR
## The Idiot

> *Man's estrangement from his essential being is the universal character of existence.*
>
> —Paul Tillich

## I

Hermann Hesse calls *The Idiot* (1868) "this terrifying book" *(dieses erschreckende Buch).*[1] At first glance such a description seems paradoxical to apply to a novel in which Dostoevsky seeks to create "a truly perfect and noble man." Goodness, after all, is not usually associated with terror, and the experience of goodness, it is hoped, transcends or precludes what is terrifying. It is the experience that leads to what is, or should be, gratifying and redeeming in human life. *The Idiot* is not only Dostoevsky's most personal but, in some ways, his most profound novel. The profundity entails the kind of metaphysical radicalism that has no boundary and that passes from the realm of the predictable into the realm of the unusual and exceptional, without concern for accepted norms. Indeed, Dostoevsky's fictional world, always to the irritation of his pragmatic interpreters, is never normative, no more normative than reality. Dostoevsky, particularly in *The Idiot,* must be accounted a radical visionary artist whose rendered view of life knows no categorical demarcations or imperatives. Man, as he unceasingly shows, is ever the prey of "double thoughts." On the other side of hope he saw despair. In the presence of belief he knew disbelief. Tenderness can lead to cruelty. The incorruptible easily becomes corrupted. *Pro* and *contra* characterize

47

all social discourse and intercourse. Everywhere life proves consistent only in its contradictions and enigmas, around which universal truth Dostoevsky's art revolves. In ever confronting the truth of such a reality, Dostoevsky looks terror in the face, and in his second major novel he portrays goodness not in its commonplace but in its metaphysical essences. When goodness is metaphysical, and thus even incomprehensible and inaccessible, it indeed brings terror to the heart and the mind. Expecting the good to be good but harmless, and finding it filled with brambles and snares must inevitably lead to something radical, so staggering in its ultimate implications that terror alone remains the primary communicated response.

But by no means must this terror be accounted as a negative, reductive experience, as Dostoevsky's *oeuvre* discloses. For Dostoevsky terror is an important spiritual element, a religious emotion akin to other religious emotions, though recreated on another aesthetic plane, like love, or suffering, or longing, or rapture. That is, terror could be both transportive and transactional as, initially, an aesthetic force or agent. Ultimately, it is another doorway to the holy, through which one travels from a profane to a sacred world, that *other* world which Prince Myshkin alone sees and offers as a new reality and that makes him, in the eyes of most men and women, the enemy. Such terror makes for entrance into the "mystic way," and, as a numinous element of energy or urgency, to adopt here Rudolf Otto's terms, aids in the transcendence of self. Terror has theopathic and determinate powers that help awaken the self to consciousness of Divine Reality and then purge the self in the anticipation of divine illumination. Terror, in this religious and special emotional sense, as it is conveyed in *The Idiot,* is one of the fundamental numinous properties of the *"mysterium tremendum."* It is, likewise, part of a process of the total religious experience, or passional consciousness, that inheres in and comprises the very phrase *mysterium tremendum,* nowhere more definitively described, in all of its conundrums and animadversions, quantitatively and qualitatively, empirically and metaphysically, than in Otto's words:

> The feeling of it may at times come sweeping like a gentle tide, pervading the mind with a tranquil mood of deepest worship. It may pass over into a more set and lasting attitude of the soul,

continuing, as it were, thrillingly vibrant and resonant, until at last it dies away and the soul resumes its "profane," non-religious mood of everyday experience. It may burst in sudden eruption up from the depths of the soul with spasms and convulsions, or lead to the strongest excitements, to intoxicated frenzy, to transport, and to ecstasy. It has its wild and demonic forms and can sink to an almost grisly horror and shuddering. It has its crude, barbaric antecedents and early manifestations, and again it may be developed into something beautiful and pure and glorious. It may become the hushed, trembling, and speechless humility of the creature in the presence of—whom or what? In the presence of that which is a *mystery* inexpressible and above all creatures.[2]

*The Idiot*, both in its form and in its metaphysic, shows Dostoevsky to be one of our greatest novelists of terror precisely in the sense that Otto delineates. Perhaps no other scene in the novel better crystallizes the terrifying essences than the two occasions when there are references to Hans Holbein's famous painting of "The Dead Christ in the Tomb" (1521) at the Basel Gallery. In 1867 Dostoevsky and his wife had viewed the picture while in Switzerland. The picture so distressed and horrified her that she had to go into another room, whereas, she later recalled, Dostoevsky was so "agitated" that he remained before it, "as though transfixed," for fifteen or twenty minutes. "His face had the kind of frightened expression that we had had occasion to note before his attacks of epilepsy."[3] The events and the very world of *The Idiot* must be viewed against the backdrop of Holbein's remarkable but almost revolting picture, which Dostoevsky himself said could smash one's faith. On the first occasion Myshkin is visiting Parfyon Rogozhin's ancestral house in Saint Petersburg— "a large, gloomy, three-storied house, of a dirty green colour." A dark shroud seems to hang over the house, and Myshkin comments particularly on the heavy darkness of the study. "You dwell in darkness," he tells Rogozhin. It is over the door of one of the rooms that Myshkin spies a copy of Holbein's picture, "of a rather curious shape, about five feet wide and no more than ten and a half inches high. It showed our Saviour, who had just been taken from the cross." Rogozhin tells Myshkin that he likes looking at Holbein's picture, to which remark Myshkin replies: "'At that picture! Why, some people may lose their faith by looking at that picture!'" (II, 4).[4]

On the second occasion it is the tubercular youth Ippolit Terentyev who describes (in the course of reading his manuscript, "A Necessary Explanation! Epigraph: *Après moi le déluge*") his own visit to Rogozhin's house ("it is like a graveyard"), during which he, too, was disturbed by the same Holbein picture "over the door of one of the gloomiest drawing-rooms of the house." The graphic and the aesthetic aspects of the picture are given in far greater, even terrifying, detail this time, as Ippolit goes on to note that in it there is not the usual trace of extraordinary beauty, "even in his moments of greatest agony," that one finds in most painters' works depicting Christ: "...the face has not been spared in the least; it is nature itself, and, indeed, any man's corpse would look like that after such suffering." That Christ's body on the cross was fully subject to the laws of nature is made emphatically clear: "In the picture the face is terribly smashed with blows, swollen, covered with terrible, swollen, and blood-stained bruises, the eyes open and squinting; the large, open whites of the eyes have a sort of dead and glassy glint." Dreadful terror prevails as Dostoevsky, through Ippolit, states, not only in the physical details depicting a tortured man, but also in the frightening questions that such a corpse must necessarily arouse in Christ's disciples and followers, and even in Christ Himself ("if, on the eve of the crucifixion, the Master could have seen what He would look like when taken from the cross"). Surely the meaning of the Resurrection is sabotaged by such a depiction, for "Here one cannot help being struck with the idea that if death is so horrible and if the laws of nature are so powerful, then how can they be overcome?" The very meaning and substance of religious faith must totter before the irrevocable power of nature:

> Looking at that picture, you get the impression of nature as some enormous, implacable, and dumb beast, or, to put it more correctly, much more correctly, though it may seem strange, as some huge engine of the latest design, which has senselessly seized, cut to pieces, and swallowed up—impassively and unfeelingly—a great and priceless Being, a Being worth the whole of nature and all its laws, worth the entire earth, which was perhaps created solely for the coming of that Being! The picture seems to give expression to the idea of a dark, insolent, and senselessly eternal power, to which everything is subordinated, and this idea is suggested to you unconsciously. (III, 6)

"The Dead Christ in the Tomb" emblematizes the organic nature of the terror one experiences in reading *The Idiot*. It is a terror that chills the soul and strikes at the heart. The accursed questions that Dostoevsky wrestled with are at the very center of Ippolit Terentyev's words. And the agonizing significance of the picture, especially in terms of its effect on the meaning of belief, of the ground of religious experience itself, seems to remain constant, referentially and ideationally, in the entire novel. Whether it is, then, a tortured body or a tortured mind, the picture both contains and consumes the problematic issues of the novel, even as it sums up in the most universal way the unending warfare between naturalism and supernaturalism. Holbein's picture shows the symbolic whole of existence, the final question and the deepest crisis. No wonder Dostoevsky stood transfixed before the original painting in Basel. For him the picture epitomized a terrifying ultimacy in the meaning of human existence. This ultimacy connoted, existentially, either abject surrender to terror and thus the acceptance of a final life-negation—acceptance of the temporal world—or the metaphysical transcendence of the pain of terror, bringing with it spiritual recovery and belief—acceptance of the world to come. *The Idiot* is in this respect the most terrifying of Dostoevsky's novels, as Hesse believed, for it is the least protective or comforting of his major novels. No utterly redemptive figure here appears to cushion spiritual contradictions, ambiguities, doubts, ambivalences, shocks. The situation is not only irrevocably problematic but also fluid and dialectical. One never forgets the memory of Holbein's painting and the disturbances it evokes; the ensuing pressures are immense and profound and are "solved" only in idiocy or in madness. Neither is there an easily posited Godward path in this novel, for there is no easy resolution of what Holbein so remorselessly depicted in the stark terror of "The Dead Christ in the Tomb."

If in his other major novels Dostoevsky generally provides divinized human props which are sympathetic and conducive to religious transfiguration, in *The Idiot* he provides no such material help. For here the experience of terror is superior even to Myshkin, who is preëminently Dostoevsky's most Christ-like symbol. Here it is the interior condition of terror that predominates, and it is, consequently, with the world, that world of the power and the glory with which Satan strove to tempt Christ in the desert, that one struggles with and against. What makes *The Idiot* so terrifying is that this experience of terror must be undergone by anyone who comes into contact with the world of this novel. No one escapes the feelings of fear and dread that constitute this terror. The sound of death and a ceaseless, irreversible movement of life in all of its passion and intensity further exacerbate this terror. The fate, and faith, of religious man is what is at stake as one struggles with terror, a struggle that is no less tremendous than a spiritual wrestle. Terror, as Dostoevsky reveals it, determines the movement of faith, particularly when faith is confronted with those tremendous conflicting forces fighting for the expression of affirmation or of negation, as embodied in Holbein's painting. In a deep sense, then, the world of *The Idiot* is a static world for those who live and act in it, insofar as they never escape its eternal power of nature that enforces its will, that prescribes and circumscribes the conditions of existence, spatially and temporally. In this world nothing avoids humanness, and what remains incontestably certain in it is the unending rhythm of the laws of nature. The people of *The Idiot* remain the unredeemed witnesses to the way of the world, which is the final *stasis*.

Dostoevsky's aesthetic (or poetic) purpose, however, is far from *static* in this novel. In confronting the reader with such a terrifying world of body, as it were, Dostoevsky is at the same time trying to reach a spiritual ground of recognition. The state of terror in *The Idiot* is a terror *de profundis,* a metaphysical as well as a temporal terror. Metaphysical terror signifies a dying to the world of sinfulness, the sinfulness that inheres so densely and immitigably in *The Idiot*. This higher, spiritualizing terror is simultaneously and closely related to suffering, which, as Pascal notes, "is the natural state of the Christian, just as health is that of the 'natural' man." Through this terror one grasps more fully his religious situation and incurs, as Kierkegaard would have it, a movement of faith as it crystallizes in a moment of decision when the individual realizes that he needs assistance. From this standpoint *The Idiot* can be judged as Dostoevsky's most religious novel, for in no other does he show so penetratingly just how solitary and terrifying is one's existence without supernal assistance. No view of what happens in *The Idiot* can escape the fact that man, if he is not to be victimized or arrested by the temporality of terror, requires help. The ever-present nearness of death, consummated in the scene of murder at the close of the novel, emphasizes the full significance of the terror of suffering. But, again as Kierkegaard puts it, "That is the road we all have to take—over the Bridge of Sighs into eternity."[5] To attain this eternity, Dostoevsky maintains, one must enter the crucible of terror, both situationally and religiously. Unlike *The Brothers Karamazov,* or even *Crime and Punishment, The Idiot* makes no promises, contains no portents, proffers no operative spiritual prefiguration or transfiguration. The brute experience of this novel is antecedent to and ancillary of faith, but not in the sense that, as Hesse also declares, "'This is what you must become.' It is something different, but fully as significant: 'We must pass through this. This is our Destiny.'"[6] The religious man's belief inevitably entails satisfying the severest criterion of belief. The *via solitaria* is never easy, as Dostoevsky reveals.

*The Idiot* is Dostoevsky's most terrifying novel because it reaches into the deepest recesses of the soul. Now, *The Devils,* too, contains terror, but it is the terror that one associates with the social fabric and with the corporate life. And it demands that attention be given to the body politic as its foundations totter in the wake of ideological nihilism. In a biblical sense, *The Devils* points to the consequences of "the sword without," *The Idiot* to the "terror within."[7] The "terror of God," we know, can fall like a plague upon the cities, and the results make for a common experience that is, nevertheless, assuaged by being a common travail. Inner terror, by virtue of its solitariness, is a far greater individuating travail when one, as in death itself, stands alone before God. No longer can one take comfort in identifying with others, either more or less fortunate than he. The religious experience here is hardly primordial or invidious and can have no comparative human referents or indices. This is what makes the terror of *The Idiot* invariably awful; appropriately, therefore, as it has been observed, the form of this novel is like a whirlwind. There is no alleviating vision. Only terror prevails in the form of this novel, " . . . the form of the elementary explosion with which the world responds to this existence: it is scandal at its paroxysm," Guardini states.[8] In confronting this world, one confronts what is irreconcilable with the demands of the life of belief. The realms of the natural and of the supernatural prove exclusive here, and from this qualitative exclusiveness is born terror as an element of religious experience. Terror of the "wholly other" is, in the end, the most positive, and, indeed, the most hopeful sign of this experience. For Dostoevsky, the metaphysics of terror, as it informs the form and content of *The Idiot,* is a numinous antecedent to leaping forward into faith.

As a novelist Dostoevsky was a master of the aesthetics of terror; he had learned well the psychic forms that terror could take in modern fiction. But as a prophetic and apocalyptic writer he had purposes that went far beyond purely aesthetic techniques and values. The excitation of terror had, for Dostoevsky, a category of value that had religious signification. His art evolved as a metaphysics of art and, beyond this juncture, as a spiritual art. His uses of terror illustrate this process, of which *The Idiot* is a remarkable example. His sense of terror, hence, becomes religious in its intensity; it culminates, in Berdyaev's phrase, in "holy terror." Terror absorbs and is absorbed by the world of *The Idiot,* and as such it is an immediate element that is poetically captured and evoked as an aesthetic form and function. But Dostoevsky, of course, was a spiritual artist who was well aware of the metaphysical heights he was scaling. For him the problem of art was the problem of man. And the problem of man was a moral problem. Terror of itself, as part of the subjective world, was not enough if it failed to coalesce with the religious sense. Dostoevsky's burden of vision was much heavier than just that of conveying formalistic artifacts and, like Turgenev, of endowing his work with a beautiful symmetry. In gauging the constituents and the effects of what makes *The Idiot* so terrifying, it is first necessary to comprehend this novel—and all of Dostoevsky's major novels—in relation to art as spiritual art. This is why the phrase "metaphysics of terror" is used here to designate both the refining and the qualifying aesthetic differences. Aesthetically, terror can be for one a freezing experience when fear arrests all action and reaction. The feeling of dread and horror can be overwhelming. It can also be, as it is in *The Idiot,* an essence of spirit and a fundamental theurgic experience. This terror is a spiritual and purifying form of revelation that goes by the name of φόβος: the numinous perceptualization of awe and reverence in an experience of the holy.

# II

A major cause of this terror actually derives from the main figure of this novel, Prince Leo Nikolayevich Myshkin, who serves as a constant point of severe contrast, as our spiritual "double," so to speak. The entire novel dramatizes precisely this comparative process. The astonishing immensity of his role in the novel, even of his "idiocy," is such that we cannot avoid or ignore it. From beginning to end, from his first appearance during a train ride from Warsaw to Saint Petersburg, Myshkin has a commanding presence heightened by his extraordinary characteristics: he is a prince and an idiot simultaneously igniting attention. So extraordinary, so radical and provocative, so different and non-human is he, that one must ask, "Who is this man and what is he doing in this world?" To say that he is non-human is to say that he is of spiritual and of metaphysical essences of the most refined and the most pristine kind. In this respect he is Dostoevsky's most religious theandric creation. "There is a natural body, and there is a spiritual body," Saint Paul writes to the Corinthians (I, 15:44). Myshkin is precisely this "spiritual body" among "terrestrial bodies." John Middleton Murry, more than any other Western critic, comes closest to the mark when he writes in this connection: "Myshkin descends into life a spirit. He is perfect man, but this perfection is a denial of humanity."[9] Perhaps another, possibly better, way of placing Myshkin in literature is to describe him as a "seraphic" being, that expression of spirit in human form which, as G. Wilson Knight has shown, impinges on our present society from beyond. These seraphic persons, Knight stresses, "are close to, and yet independent of, sexual instinct; they bisexually symbolize the fusion of all opposites; though human, they link us to spirit-spheres."[10]

Myshkin is Dostoevsky's supreme metaphysical creation. He is beyond poetic symbol, beyond the world and the pivotal problem of personality.[11] We can hear his voice throughout the novel, but we cannot touch his body; the image of the Prince is, as Mochulsky believes, *chiaroscuro*.[12] And even the voice itself, like the body, is pure spirit, nowhere better heard or more spiritually epitomized than in Myshkin's reply to Ippolit's question concerning the best way for the latter to die: "'Pass by and forgive us our happiness'" (IV, 5). Throughout the novel, as Allen Tate notes, Myshkin has an astonishing detachment, a receptivity, and a profundity of insight into human motives that nobody but Dostoevsky has ever succeeded so well in rendering dramatically.[13] These qualities further emphasize the kind of metaphysical energy, the spirit-powers, that Myshkin possesses. Unlike most of Dostoevsky's characters, Myshkin is not embroiled in the personal experience relating to basic questions of self-respect and dignity. Indeed, he is not in the least a spiritual hero, who must find, prove, and elevate himself in respect to the world and to others. He is not a driven, idea-haunted man preoccupied with the problem of life or death, or of recovery or death; he is not one who must confront the crisis of soul as Raskolnikov must. Nor has he come to save the world; his is not in the least a mission of redemption. Rather, his is a compassionate presence. All this, however, should not imply that Myshkin incarnates spiritual passivity or that blank kind of quietism that Aglaya Yepanchin accuses him of, at one point, when she declares: "'Whether one showed you an execution or a little finger, you'd be quite sure to draw highly laudable conclusions from either, and remain happy and contented, too. To live like that is easy'" (I, 5).

The basic theory behind Aglaya's accusation leads one critic, Murray Krieger, to treat Myshkin in a severely limiting relation to "the curse of saintliness" and to see his "involvement" in the lives of the other characters as divisive and damaging in its consequences.[14] Such an empirical view fails to fathom Myshkin's seraphic being that transcends even those tragic elements that are central to Dostoevsky's other major works. This seraphic spirit-power is what enables him alone to see Nastasya Filippovna Barashkov's suffering in all of its ramifications. The source of this power comes from a deeper connection, at once spiritual and religious in that greater sense that Myshkin underlines when he tells Rogozhin that "the essence of religious feeling has nothing to do with any reasoning, or any crimes and misdemeanors or atheism; it is something entirely different and it will always be so" (II, 4). Myshkin's entire worth must be assessed according to this religious complex. Or, to put it another way, Myshkin's presence in this novel is quintessentially spiritualizing, passive precisely because it has no material need for an active sensibility; hence, it is eternal. This spiritual presence is numinous, filled with signs of what must be, from a divine standpoint, inexpressible and indescribable. "He never disturbs the boundaries of the last things," Thurneysen writes of Myshkin, "and never shortens the eternal distances. But he guards them. He is always seeking with all the power of his soul that ultimate point where everything has its end and its beginning in God, that ultimate point which is comparable only with death and birth."[15]

Myshkin is the pure spirit of innocence. In a profane and profaning world, which the other people of *The Idiot* represent in all degrees of profanity, any encounter with innocence must needs be terrifying. (Dostoevsky's aesthetic sense is, in this connection, invariably keen.) Contact with Myshkin is lightning contact with the eternal, and readers of the novel can never be the same afterward, even as all the other characters in *The Idiot* are not the same again. Innocence in any way or form surprises us; that is, it is something alien to our mortality, dramatizing as it does our fallen state: our imperfection, our capacity for evil, our vulnerability to the world. The human situation, as Dostoevsky perceives it in *The Idiot,* is both unprepared for and resistant of such an encounter. If it does occur, the immediate human reaction is one of fascinated disbelief. It will be noted that Myshkin arouses in even the most insensitive people "most violent indignation," yet at the same time much fascination. Certainly only what is pure and innocent can do this. ("Scoundrels love honest men," Ganya tells the Prince at one point; "Don't you know that?" I, 4.) The troubling consequences of the encounter with Myshkin are not at all "inverted," as has been suggested, and therefore rightful cause for rejecting him. What needs to be recognized is the terrifying fact that the outer life has built up its defense strongly. The terrestrial, or the juridical, condition, as it might be called, knows what action and gesture it must adopt, if only to protect its special province of being and to maintain its equilibrious state of disequilibrium. It knows, in its peculiarly perverse way, the Unknown, which must be kept at a safe distance, since it has compelling and relentless powers against which no doors can be permanently locked. *The Idiot* is very much, and finally, the experience of the unlocking of doors: the sudden, terrifying apprehension, somehow, of the interchangeableness of temporal and eternal. Inversion is not, after all, without benefit in the realm of spiritual creativity.

Critical attitudes towards the novel as a whole and towards Myshkin in particular are generally commonplace.
Characteristically, the novel is seen as mere exploration of "an
epileptic mode of being" and Myshkin as the embodiment of
"ontological predicament."[16] Repeatedly commentators dis-
miss the spiritual depth of the novel as an example of mysticism that is baseless and false, "born of its author's peculiar
desire to transcend normal feeling, and [that] leads to anarchy."[17] Dostoevsky's metaphysics of art becomes identified
with a preoccupation with the abstract and, hence, becomes a
"case" for psychopathology. Cynicism contributes in large
part to such attitudes, particularly whenever metaphysics is in
question. Critical distortion is likewise a factor that leads to
misrepresentation. Yet passional consciousness is as real to
Dostoevsky as to any other great modern novelist, including
D. H. Lawrence. But for Dostoevsky the passions must achieve
their hierarchy in the total scheme of things. His metaphysics
is, in fact, a rendition of what Kierkegaard writes about in his
Epilogue to *Fear and Trembling:* "Faith is the highest passion
in a man." Dostoevsky's mysticism must be judged by these
words, as also must Myshkin's innocence. The passions that
are at war in *The Idiot* are precisely those that distinguish the
corporeal from the metaphysical. Distinctions and discriminations, especially on the spiritual plane, have a way of terrifying
our modern relativists. In this respect Dostoevsky was one of
the most discriminating of novelists. His art, most notably *The
Idiot,* is the achieved creation of spiritual discriminations.
Prince Myshkin is his most ambitious refinement of this discriminating process. Through him the reader passes through
the farthest frontiers and enters the country of the spirit. Man's
natural fear of such a journey could perhaps be overcome only
by a metaphysics of terror as employed in *The Idiot.* Critical
discriminations, though vital, must be measured, in the end,
against something more permanent and demanding: Spiritual
Discrimination.

Myshkin is a qualitative figure in the novel, and one must
not expect from him the specificity of the aggregate. That is to
say, we must not expect from Myshkin concrete forms and
works, whether on a human or on a superhuman level. Indeed,
in Myshkin transcendental religion *per se* is missing. But this
absence in no way diminishes Myshkin's presence in the novel,

nor, in fact, the need for his presence in not only a fictive but also a metaphysical sense. As indicated earlier, Myshkin's image is *chiaroscuro,* a fact that must not be forgotten in any critical appraisal of his role and importance. To speak of Myshkin in relation to "the ethics of image" rather than to "the ethics of deeds" is a way of further delineating the magnitude of his metaphysical dimension.[18] In any case, Myshkin's shadow-like presence, far from being a shadow of the impalpable and intangible, has a rendered metaphysical validity and a spiritual meaning; it has the concrete metaphysicality that makes *The Idiot* an astonishing work of genius. There is nothing obscure about Myshkin's fictive form. He is Dostoevsky's greatest metaphysical creation in poetic form. Myshkin, as such, must not be viewed as merely an idiot, or a saint, or a mystic; to see him as just one or as a composite of these is to oversimplify Myshkin as the creation of a spiritual artist. Myshkin has a unique significance, which is best captured by the word "witness" and by the special religious meaning that Kierkegaard attaches to this word when he writes that "the true knight of faith is a witness, never a teacher."[19]

As a religious guide Myshkin is a failure, of which Dostoevsky was to be as much aware as his severest critics. His contact with life does very little to assuage the physical disorder and the spiritual aridity that prevail in *The Idiot.* Outside of his harmonious relations with the children whom he knew in a Swiss village, where he lived for three years, his relations with grown-up people are never satisfying and even hectic and damaging, because, as Myshkin explains, "I don't know how to behave with them." This inability often leads to most painful consequences, and even, in the end, to death. But the world of *The Idiot,* more than that of any of the other major novels, is more terrifying because the whole of it is in disarray. It is a fallen world, beyond all hope for salvation. Myshkin is a witness, the only witness, to this overwhelming, immobilizing fact. He arrives on the scene in man's darkest hour, so to speak. He brings with him no promise of rescue, no spiritual panacea, no sacramental system. Those persons whom Myshkin now meets, and even those whom he wants to love, simply cannot understand the testimony of the prince. Their treatment of Myshkin is tinged with cynicism and contempt. " . . . you are a regular holy fool, Prince, and such as you God loves," Rogozhin says. " . . . he's a perfect child and one could have a game of blind man's buff with him," General Yepanchin notes to his wife. These are typical reactions that underline the grim condition of the men and women of *The Idiot*. Negation epitomizes this condition and consummates the extent and depth of their fallen nature. Under the circumstances Myshkin can hardly begin to establish any spiritual connection with such people; his overtures are dismissed as the rantings of an epileptic fool, "God's fool" *(Yrodivy)*. Is it any wonder that Myshkin's only spiritual communion is limited to children or that his only spiritual victory is in improving the attitude of the children of the village towards the pitiable consumptive Marie, who had once been seduced by a French commercial traveler?

It will be noticed throughout that Myshkin does not judge others. Innocence and compassion constantly inform his presence, which is always in contrast with the endless hate and cynicism that characterize the others. Again and again, even when he is humiliated, he testifies steadfastly to the belief that humility is a terrible force. His humility remains as constant as the painful truth of Ippolit's observation that "men are created to torment each other." Myshkin's humility seems powerless before this fact of life. The novel is all the more terrifying when one views the unrelenting power of the pharisaism that Dostoevsky re-creates. In this particular respect, *The Idiot* is possibly the bleakest of Dostoevsky's religious statements, no matter what importance he was to attach to the figure of Myshkin. For against the power of the world he is helpless; that he is reduced to epilepsy and idiocy has here its informing referent. Even when, at times, some of the characters seem to like Myshkin, their attitude is ultimately as hard and selfish as his is selfless. Not one character really comes round to adopting Myshkin's spiritual meaning, for the people of this world are impervious to all spiritual possibility. When, at times, they pay tribute to Myshkin, the tribute is composed of merely empty words. Spiritual substance is found ever lacking. Myshkin's presence (and mission) is thus ultimately scorned insofar as it is seen to be a threat to the ways of the world that the other people in *The Idiot* embrace and represent. Myshkin is not admired or loved but simply tolerated. Repeatedly there are scenes when Myshkin's movements are closely followed by Rogozhin's eyes. This phenomenon is fraught with a stern warning: The spiritual life must remain on the periphery or else face annihilation. No matter what Myshkin does, then, he is never able to alter the actual, material life and attitude of the people around him. Non-spiritual life proves invulnerable in a profane, secular world.

There are two antithetical and irreconcilable worlds in *The Idiot*: the world of experience and the world of revelation. The first contains men and women who are oblivious of grace. It is the world of time and of history, not of eternity. The second contains the solitary, delicate figure of Myshkin, the "Prince-Christ," as Dostoevsky describes him at one point. In a Blakean way he can be pictured as a child of vision. These two worlds are in perpetual confrontation: The world of fact refuses to make the passage into the world of revelation. (For this miracle one must wait for *The Brothers Karamazov*.) Under the circumstances, Myshkin is relegated to "the cloud of witnesses";[20] he can testify to eternal truths, but in the end he stands condemned to his testimony. If meekness is, as Dostoevsky often says, a terrifying force, so is intransigent disbelief. Terror in *The Idiot* has a double edge, which makes it all the more terrifying. The only connection between the two worlds is that of darkness, beginning with the opening sentences (" . . . the end of November, during a thaw. . . . It was so damp and foggy that it was a long time before it grew light, and even then it was difficult to distinguish out of the carriage windows anything a few yards to the right and left of the railway track") and ending with the darkness of night in the death scenes with which the novel concludes. Myshkin continually finds himself in a "dark world." He is always in danger, nowhere better epiphanized than in the scene when one day, reaching his hotel as a thunderstorm erupts, Rogozhin attempts to knife him on a dark staircase. Myshkin is spared only because he has a sudden epileptic attack.

Sensuality occupies a central place in *The Idiot*, complementing and heightening the mental anguish and the disorder that prevail generally. Representative of this sensuality is Rogozhin, whose lustful pursuit of Nastasya Filippovna brings to a head some of the major conflicts. Early in the novel Myshkin's insight into Rogozhin is prophetic: "He might marry her to-morrow and, perhaps, murder her a week later." In Rogozhin sensuality triumphs to the point of murder.

His predecessor, in *Crime and Punishment,* is Svidrigaylov; his royal successor, in *The Devils,* is Stavrogin. He stands, in his way, for the terrible power of nature, just as Myshkin stands for the terrible power of humility. Dostoevsky does not portray Rogozhin in terms of disgust or of pathos. There is no wallowing in the portrayal of Rogozhin's sensualism, which is an elemental force of enormous consequence in the world. His sexuality has a symbolic significance of the destructive power of the world, which can neither be thwarted nor converted. Rogozhin is, to borrow a word of depth psychology, Myshkin's "shadow"—Myshkin's original sin, as Steiner declares.[21] "They are Body and Soul," to recall John Middleton Murry's words. "They are the divided being of the Christian Dispensation, the spirit which must mortify the flesh, and the flesh which must kill the spirit."[22] Rogozhin is element, Myshkin essence. Dostoevsky accepted both, but how to reconcile them was a problem impossible to solve.

This tension generates religious experience. Myshkin and Rogozhin embody the totality of this experience; or, better, through them Dostoevsky explores it. But before this religious experience can be attained, Myshkin and Rogozhin have to annihilate each other. What makes religious experience terrifying is the process of this annihilation, which *The Idiot* dramatizes. For Dostoevsky the process has the spiritual value of purgation that ultimately brings illumination. It is the dark night of the soul that one experiences in this novel: a period of crisis. And yet *The Idiot* is not a rendition of the *via mystica;* Rogozhin's active presence throughout insures against such a one-dimensional possibility. Spirit cannot be, in any of Dostoevsky's fiction, a rarefied form; all his people, not only Myshkin, are witnesses to this existential truth. Concern with life is pronounced in the novel, in which the making, the getting, and the keeping of money, for instance, underscore this concern. (That, on one occasion, some of the characters play a parlor game in which each confesses his worst action is equally revealing and symptomatic.) One must never lose sight of the large-scale assembly of people with whom Myshkin comes into contact, nor of the ever-present fact that these are normal people who live in a normal world, at least by our standards. "It is not easy," Prince Sh. tells Myshkin, "to achieve heaven on earth . . . heaven is a different matter,

Prince, much more difficult than it seems to your excellent heart" (III, 1). Myshkin is, during his journey in the world, a "visitor from Heaven" though also an "impotent redeemer."[23] Nastasya Filippovna certainly intuits the kind of innocence, even the religious life, that Myshkin represents, when she tells her guests at her birthday party: "The prince means a lot to me, for he is the first man I've ever come across in my life in whom I can believe as a true and loyal friend. He believed in me at first sight, and I believed in him" (I, 14).

Nothing could be more terrifying than to comprehend Myshkin's fate. He, too, is a dead Christ, whose world is a tomb and whose epilepsy is the stigma of a tortured, broken body. Through his experience of the world one experiences, in the deepest religious sense, the hostility of the world that led to Christ's curse when He excluded the world from His prayer: "I pray not for the world. . . . I have given them thy word; and the world hath hated them, because they are not of the world, even as I am not of the world" (John 17:9, 14). Myshkin's own final breakdown occurs simultaneously with the breakdown of all virtues, of relation to the good. He, too, passes from the world when the world reaches its apex of blasphemy. Indeed, it can be said that Myshkin is the victim of the spirit of blasphemy that at one time or another permeates the lives of the inhabitants of the world that Myshkin confronts. Here blasphemy must be accounted along with the other heinous sins of the novel, including evil thoughts, adulteries, fornications, murders, thefts, covetousness, wickedness, deceit, betrayal, lasciviousness.[24] The young nihilists' reviling of Myshkin defines the nature of blasphemy; and of these nihilists, it is Ippolit who speaks the language of blasphemy at its shrillest when he shouts at Myshkin: "' . . . I hate you more than anyone and more than anything in the world—you jesuitical, treacly soul, you damned idiot, you philanthropic millionaire, you! I understood and hated you long ago, when I first heard of you; I hated you with all the hatred of my heart'" (II, 10).

In choosing to revile Myshkin these characters choose not to see what is positive in religious meaning. Selfhood enshrines their blasphemy throughout. To employ here Blakean terminology from *Jerusalem* helps in penetrating one of the crucial problems of *The Idiot:* Myshkin's religion is the religion of continual self-annihilation and hence of forgiveness; that of the others (as, no doubt, accounts for the brutal way in which Ippolit condemns Myshkin) is the religion of selfhood. As a result the gulf between these two forms of religion is immense. Unregenerate selfhood, of the kind that the young nihilists preach and that Rogozhin seeks to glorify in his passions alone, at any price, makes for war. The war that is actually taking place throughout *The Idiot* is the war that is the condition of men's lives. It is in the very midst of such war that Myshkin must suffer what William Blake calls "terrors of self-annihilation" and out of what comes the condition of forgiveness, the experience of eternity. It is this latter which is the quintessence of religious experience that one discovers through Myshkin and that makes *The Idiot* spiritual art. The people whom Myshkin confronts are in what Blake terms "the state of Satan"; hence they are unable to discover the Eternal Moment, or that "highest moment," as Myshkin describes it, which he experiences just before an epileptic fit: "His mind and heart were flooded by a dazzling light. All his agitation, all his doubts and worries, seemed composed in a twinkling, culminating in a great calm, full of serene and harmonious joy and hope, full of understanding and the knowledge of the final cause" (II, 5).

Myshkin's epilepsy is a heightened epiphanal terror of self-annihilation that distinguishes Myshkin's religious state, "an ecstatic and prayerful fusion in the highest synthesis of life." As prisoners of selfhood, the other characters cannot aspire to such a consummate religious awareness. They cannot see anything beyond themselves; they are their own slaves. Their ambiance, consequently, is a nullifying gross materiality, which is rarely vital, or creative, or regenerative, and which weighs them down and makes them heavy with the burdens of the world and with the concerns of selfhood. Such an ambiance precludes divine vision that both annihilates and liberates the self from itself—and from despair. A self-annihilating moment of this vision occurs, signally, early in the novel as Myshkin recounts his first impressions of Switzerland. The incident which he describes is small and humble enough in itself. He tells of his illness and of his anxiety, his despair, and particularly his feelings of alienation, the latter brought on by his presence in a foreign land. But he also recalls how one evening, at Basel, he was roused by the braying of a donkey in the market-place. "Ever since I've been awfully fond of donkeys," he continues. "I feel a sort of affection for them . . . and came almost at once to the conclusion that it was a most useful animal—hard-working, strong, patient, cheap, and long-suffering" (I, 5). The shock of seeing the donkey, he concludes, made him like everything around him.

What we have here is a forerunner of the kind of epiphanies that James Joyce later made major use of in his novels. The donkey is, in any event, a manifestation of spirit, a sudden revelation of otherness; it points to a dimension of life to which Myshkin's listeners, the Yepanchin women, are blind. "A donkey?" Mrs. Yepanchin asks and then goes on to comment in a tone fraught with derision: "That's strange. Still . . . there's nothing strange about it. I shouldn't be surprised if one of us fell in love with a donkey. It happened in mythology" (I, 5). Her reaction is not in the least unusual. Here we have the voice of the world. Irreverent, unbelieving, scornful, selfish, it is precisely that voice that makes its shrillness heard throughout *The Idiot*. In his reaction to the donkey, on the other hand, Myshkin speaks in a reverent voice. He steps back, as it were, and exemplifies an elementary virtue that the other persons in the novel are incapable of comprehending, so caught up are they in their self-concerning ways and attitudes. Dostoevsky's epiphany of the donkey epitomizes that dual process of self-annihilation and of forgiveness that exemplifies Myshkin's journey in the world and that effects his passage from time to eternity and from eternity to time. His total religious and life-attitude is contained in his recollection of the donkey. It is not at all surprising that Myshkin is not understood by those who meet him and who refuse to make the kind of surrender that Myshkin makes again and again. For Myshkin the process of self-annihilation is instinctively experienced as a law of life. For him there is no separation between natural and supernatural. The donkey is symbolic of Myshkin's special capacity to annihilate and to create at the same time. In this capacity is to be found the religious core of his significance.

*The Idiot* can be likened to a duologue in which Myshkin's voice cries out against the voice of the world. His voice is compassionate, the voice of virtue; the world's is rasping and hateful, the voice of irreverence. Myshkin speaks in a voice that knows of a greatness greater than itself. His antagonists continually speak in a voice that respects only its own authority. The tonal contrast in the two voices readily identifies each speaker's inner condition, his spiritual nature. Myshkin's reaction to Nastasya's affliction, that is to say, her tormenting sense of having been sexually violated and exploited since the age of sixteen by the *roué* Totsky, is singularly expressed in the language of reverence, that reverence which culminates in reverence for the holy. Myshkin, to recall, has offered to marry Nastasya, "Rogozhin's slut," as she describes herself. "And how can you be thinking of marriage," she cries to him, "when you want a nurse to look after you yourself!" Here, indeed, is an example of how the holy provokes man's rebellious spirit, which endows language with mockery and blasphemy. Myshkin's reply, "in a trembling, timid voice, though at the same time with an air of profound conviction," is couched in the language of reverence in which God Himself exists and operates: "You're quite right, Nastasya Filippovna; I know nothing and I've seen nothing, but I—I think you'll be doing me an honour, and not I you. I'm nothing, but you've suffered and emerged pure out of such a hell, and that is a great deal." Dostoevsky's great dramatic talent is vividly evidenced in this scene in some of the sneers of the others, as their reactions underline that irreverent world with which Myshkin must contend. Thus, Myshkin's words are also met by this reaction: "At his last words Ferdyshchenko and Lebedev could be heard sniggering, and even the general cleared his throat with a sort of feeling of great displeasure. Ptitsyn and Totsky could not help smiling, but restrained themselves. The rest just gaped with amazement" (I, 15).

It is true, as Dostoevsky himself admitted, that Myshkin's place in the novel is problematic: His works, when measured in terms of any spiritual progression, amount to very little, outside of his influence on the children. There is nothing remarkable about him, and even for those who believe in his spiritual meaning there are times when their belief is shaken almost to the roots. To the very end he remains "that worthless little idiot," "not quite right," "a sheep," "nice, but a little bit too simple," "an innocent simpleton," a "clown," an "invalid," "a knight-errant, a virgin." He is certainly not a man of action, not a man of power, not a man for the modern world. He represents precisely those transcendent virtues that a secular and technic age has completely rejected, and has been rejecting with furious rapidity for at least four centuries. That Myshkin is likeable to some hardly means that he is acceptable; and if he is likeable it is his oddity that often dictates such a response. A critical sentimentality too often glorifies Myshkin's niceness, his gentleness, his quixotic personality and mystery. This critical attitude is, in the last analysis, one that believes in safety: in safely isolating and containing Myshkin's spiritual essences. And behind all this condescension to Myshkin, both in the novel itself and in critical estimations, lies a deep and fearful suspicion of what he ultimately stands for.

Lebedev, one of Dostoevsky's most "fantastic" and corrupt opportunists, clearly comprehends Myshkin's threat to the established social order, of which Lebedev is himself a wily representative. Nowhere is this brought out better than in the scene of the planned wedding one evening, of Myshkin and Nastasya, when a large crowd gathers at the church. Rogozhin, who suddenly appears and whose eyes Nastasya has caught, seizes her and carries her away. Some members of the crowd, as well as invited guests, now follow Myshkin to the house, where heated disputes take place regarding the unusual happenings, including Myshkin's passive acceptance of Nastasya's flight from him (" . . . in her condition—it might have been expected"). Here is an episode that reveals some of Myshkin's hidden inner power, for he manages to pacify the disputants and even to gain their respect. It is one of the few times that Myshkin is resourceful in an active, social sense. "The prince answered everyone with such simplicity and cordiality and, at the same time, with so much dignity and so much confidence in the decency of his guests, that the indiscreet questions petered out by themselves." To Lebedev, Keller, one of Myshkin's loyal admirers, now confides: "'You and I would have made a row, started a fight, disgraced ourselves, and dragged in the police, but he made some new friends and— what friends! I know them.'" Lebedev's reply is brief but pregnant with significance: "'Thou hast hid these things from the wise and prudent, and hast revealed them unto babes,' I said so about him before, but now I'll add that the Lord has preserved the babe himself and has saved him from the abyss, He and all His saints'" (IV, 10).

These words contain an inherent recognition of Myshkin's power, albeit an underlying fear is what must prompt and inform them. For, though Myshkin's power is not worldly, it has a metaphysical, a religious, power that his role constantly attests to. His power surpasses and transcends the world around him, as not only Lebedev fearfully realizes. So all-encompassing is this power that when, as one commentator observes, darkness conquers Myshkin in the end, "virtue goes out of everybody" and the novel "closes on a lower, an almost cynical note."[25] Humility is at the center of Myshkin's power. It will be noticed that his humility constantly battles with the kind of arrogance that the other characters epitomize. Their language, and the tone of their language, abounds with desecration, precisely that desecration which easily transposes into blasphemy. In a sense theirs is the secular language of power, lacking any controlling measure of contrition, of the interiority that Myshkin discloses when he speaks, especially as the novel moves in its later stages. Their language has a destructive, dehumanizing edge and is motivated by struggle for dominion. Subject to instinct and inclination, it defies all constraint and restraint. Predominant in it is the selfhood that negates compassion. In such language the absence of God is made visible; in His absence verbal cruelty and abuse are necessarily ascendant. A joyless world lives in such language, in which we hear the voice of Satan. This language is a veritable part of man's prison.

The profane, secular nature of this language, which stands in such sharp opposition to reverence for the holy words, bursts forth with unparalleled savagery at the end of the novel. The scene in which all this takes place marks the triumph of evil in the world; indeed, it is a triumph of the world. One evening Myshkin and Aglaya go to visit Nastasya, who is with Rogozhin. The scene that ensues, though it involves both men, particularly Myshkin, is an excruciating confrontation between the two women, who are rivals for Myshkin's love. Nastasya's face has "an obstinate, hard, and almost hateful look." Aglaya is pensive; "there was a distinct expression of disgust on her face, as though she were afraid of contamination in this place." From the beginning the scene is acrimonious, Godforsaken; the atmosphere is fraught with a hatred that will easily communicate itself in the language of hatred. "One of these women," Dostoevsky's narrative reads, "so despised the other one at that moment, and was so anxious to tell her so . . . that however fantastical the other one was, with her disordered mind and sick soul, she would not have been able to stand up against the malevolent purely feminine contempt of her rival, whatever her original intentions might have been" (IV, 8). The two men merely look on, Myshkin with a bewildered expression, Rogozhin with an ominous smile. It is clear that the exchange between the women signals a crisis in the lives of all four persons and that this crisis will lead to breakdown and death. The beginning of the end thus occurs, in a scene the bitterness of which lives in the memory and touches all in the sense that Saint Paul depicted in his words to the Romans: "Their throat is an open sepulchre; with their tongues they have used deceit; the poison of asps is under their lips: Whose mouth is full of cursing and bitterness" (3:13-14).

One of the issues in the confrontation concerns three wild and strange letters that Nastasya has written to Aglaya and in which she underlined her love not only for Myshkin but also for Aglaya, who, she claims, is the embodiment of innocence and perfection. Partly out of a feeling of rivalry and partly out of an instinctive and haughty detestation of Nastasya, Aglaya is ruthless in her condemnation of "that woman." "All you are able to love is your dishonour and the constant thought that you have been dishonoured and humiliated," Aglaya cries out, "as she watched with malignant eyes their effect on Nastasya Filippovna's face, distorted with agitation." The scene is charged with brutal, unforgiving contempt; the compassion that Myshkin has pleaded for in human relations is totally disregarded as the women argue. Arrogance conjoins with cruelty, as Aglaya continues her attack: "And what about your letters? Who asked you to be our matchmaker and to persuade me to marry him?" She goes on to ask why Nastasya has not married Rogozhin, "who loves you so much and who has done you the honour of offering you his hand? Oh, that's plain enough, isn't it? If you marry Rogozhin you wouldn't have any grievance left, would you?" Aglaya, Dostoevsky is careful to note, "is absolutely carried away instantaneously by her emotion, just as though she were falling over a precipice, and she could not restrain herself from the dreadful delight of revenge." She trembles with hatred when she detects that Myshkin understands the "look of great suffering" on Nastasya's face. Through speech people commune. Such is not the case here. Aglaya uses words for the sake of their power to insult and injure. She is unable to remain silent and withdraw into the realm of reserve. Her words are impassioned, and every emotion is exposed as she cries out: "If you wanted to be an honest woman, why didn't you give up your seducer Totsky simply— without any theatrical scene?" Nastasya's retort is equally impassioned, and the exchange between the women that continues at this point dramatizes in the most horrifying way how language is not only destructive but also self-destructive. Clearly, the situation is hopeless, as the following passage reveals:

"What do you know of my position that you dare to judge me?" asked Nastasya Filippovna, with a start and turning terribly pale.

"I know that you didn't go to work, but went away with a wealthy man like Rogozhin in order to pose as a fallen angel. I am not surprised that Totsky tried to shoot himself to escape from a fallen angel!"

"Don't!" Nastasya Filippovna said with disgust and as though deeply hurt. "You have understood about as much as— Darya Alexeyevna's parlour-maid who sued her fiancé for breach of promise recently. She'd have understood better than you. . . ."

"I expect she's an honest girl who works for her living. Why do you speak with such contempt of a parlour-maid?"

"I don't speak with contempt of work, but of you when you speak of work."

"If you'd wanted to be an honest woman, you'd have taken in washing."

Both got up and were looking with white faces at one another.

"Aglaya, stop it!" the prince cried, in great distress. "This isn't fair!"

Rogozhin was no longer smiling, but listened with compressed lips and folded arms.

"Just look at her," said Nastasya Filippovna, shaking with anger, "look at this young lady! And I took her for an angel! Have you come to me without your governess, Miss Yepanchin? And do you want me—do you want me to tell you frankly—without mincing words, why you came to see me? You were afraid—that's why you came!"

"Afraid of you?" asked Aglaya, beside herself with naive and arrogant amazement that this woman should dare to talk to her like that.

"Yes, of me, of course! You are afraid of me, or you wouldn't have decided to come and see me. If you are afraid of a person, you don't despise him. And to think that I've respected you up to this very moment! And shall I tell you why you are afraid of me and what you are so concerned about now? You wanted to make quite sure yourself whether he loved me more than you or not, because you're awfully jealous—"

"He has told me already that he hates you!" Aglaya could just bring herself to murmur. (IV, 8)

These voices deny hope, resist conscience, and, above all, affirm death. The scene is portent and prelude. It prepares us for the most rending consequences: for that final drama of terror and of death. If dark passions hover in the words that Aglaya and Nastasya speak, in the final scene passion is pushed to its darkest limits, and we grope in darkness. The focal point of experience now becomes one of unalleviating anguish and of collapse. Once more, with Myshkin, we find ourselves in the tomb-like interior of Rogozhin's house, and we cannot help thinking of Holbein's "The Dead Christ in the Tomb." The final scene of terror and death constitutes another test of faith. It is night, another dark night of the soul. In this scene, unlike the wild, screeching exchange earlier between the two women, Myshkin and Rogozhin speak hesitantly and in whispers. Their whispered conversation is composed of questions and answers: "But—where is—Nastasya Filippovna?" the prince asks. "'She's—here,' Rogozhin said slowly, as though pausing for a fraction of a second with his answer." Their conversation is often punctuated by silent intermissions, which sometimes last for five minutes. In this silence true knowledge is attained. Myshkin is repeatedly described as trembling, gripped by terror. The scene takes place in Rogozhin's study, which has now undergone a change, for a heavy green damask curtain stretches across the whole length of the room and divides the study from the alcove, where Rogozhin's bed stands. The atmosphere is one of darkness, even though there is a full moon. The men are like silhouettes: "It is true, they could still see each other's faces, though not very distinctly. Rogozhin's face was pale, as usual; he stared intently and fixedly at the prince with his glittering eyes."

This last scene can be compared to a vigil of watching and waiting, a vigil of lamentation. Rogozhin takes hold of Myshkin's hand and makes him sit on a chair, opposite his own, so that their knees are almost touching. A little to one side, a small round table is between them. All the intensity that has been building up, especially since the scene between Aglaya and Nastasya, seems too heavy to bear any longer. Intensity and fear unite in terror. It is as if all passion has been spent and revelation is at hand. The last event or act has come. For Myshkin and Rogozhin this ending has an immediacy of the recognition of despair and death. Again Myshkin asks about the whereabouts of Nastasya, and even in his words there is almost a detection of a bleak understanding of finality. Inevitability colors the exchange, as Rogozhin motions toward the curtain, which he lifts, and then invites Myshkin to come in. Darkness does not deter Myshkin from seeing the bed to which he draws near: " . . . someone lay asleep on it in an absolutely motionless sleep; not the faintest movement could be heard, not the faintest breath. The sleeper was covered from head to foot, with a white sheet, but the limbs were, somehow, only faintly visible." A white silk dress, flowers, ribbons, even glittering diamonds lay in disorder all around. Dostoevsky's narrative detail now seems to move with a kind of horrible momentum to a hopeless moment, submerged as it is in "the works of darkness."[26] For at this moment Myshkin sees, as if through a veil, the dead body of Nastasya, whom Rogozhin has killed out of passions that have gone mad with frenzy. Myshkin sees and knows that a life has now gone beyond his pity, as Rogozhin whispers to Myshkin's "Was it you?" that he is responsible for the murder of Nastasya, whom he has killed, he later admits, with the same knife that he had earlier almost used against Myshkin.

> At the foot of the bed some sort of lace lay in a crumpled heap, and on the white lace, protruding from under the sheet, the tip of a bare foot could be made out; it seemed as though it were carved out of marble, and it was dreadfully still. The prince looked, and he felt that the longer he looked the more still and death-like the room became. Suddenly a fly, awakened from its sleep, started buzzing, and after flying over the bed, settled at the head of it. The prince gave a start.

What a violently trembling Myshkin views here is truly a hopeless moment; beyond this it is Dostoevsky's own terror of his vision. Myshkin and Rogozhin agree to stay the night here,

together, with Nastasya lying beside them. Rogozhin points
out that he has taken the precaution to cover Nastasya's body
with "good American cloth" and a sheet on top of that. He has
also placed there four uncorked bottles of Zhdanov disinfec-
tant. Having decided that the two of them should lie side by
side, he had managed to make, with some cushions, a bed, to
which he leads Myshkin. Dostoevsky renders here the absolute, agonizing immediacy of a temporal moment. An ending of
measured time *(chronos)*, in the presence of death, is the central
experience of this scene. Terror is written throughout, and
prevails, quintessentially, in the silence that is violated eventually by Rogozhin's screams.

> Rogozhin lay motionless, and did not seem to see or hear his
> movement; but his eyes glittered brightly in the dark and were
> wide open and staring fixedly. The prince sat down on a chair and
> began looking at him with terror. Half an hour passed; suddenly
> Rogozhin uttered a loud and abrupt scream and began laughing
> at the top of his voice, as though forgetting that he had to talk in a
> whisper.

The scene now takes on the semblance of a vigil as Myshkin
begins his night watch, so to speak. He waits, and *watches*, and
watches over, a stricken and fallen man: a murderer. "Blessed
are those servants, whom the lord when he cometh shall find
watching," Saint Luke writes (12:37).

> The prince jumped up from his chair in new terror. When
> Rogozhin grew quiet (and he grew quiet suddenly), the prince
> bent over him gently, sat down beside him, and began looking at
> him closely with a violently beating heart, breathing heavily.
> Rogozhin did not turn his head to him, and indeed seemed to have
> forgotten all about him. The prince looked and waited; time was
> passing, it began to get light. Now and again Rogozhin began to
> mutter suddenly, loudly, harshly, and incoherently; he began
> uttering little screams and laughing; then the prince stretched
> out his trembling hand and gently touched his head and his hair,
> stroking them and stroking his cheeks—he could do nothing
> more! He began trembling again himself, and again his legs
> suddenly seemed to give way under him. Quite a new sort of
> sensation was oppressing his heart with infinite anguish. Mean-
> while it had grown quite light; at last, he lay down on the cushion,
> as though in utter exhaustion and despair, and pressed his face
> against Rogozhin's pale and motionless face; tears flowed from
> his eyes on Rogozhin's cheeks, but perhaps he no longer noticed
> his own tears and knew nothing about them. . . . (IV, 11)

Myshkin's vigil has no comparable or more astonishing parallel in modern literature.

# III

The foregoing scene is one of Dostoevsky's greatest apocalyptic scenes. That is to say, the temporality of the episode, ending with Rogozhin being sentenced to hard labor in Siberia for fifteen years, and with Myshkin, now suffering a complete breakdown, returning to Dr. Schneider's Swiss clinic, transposes into a moral moment when ultimate and thus religious concerns, relations and interrelations must be examined. Catastrophe is the immediate consequence and condition of this drama of terror and death. Dostoevsky has penetrated to the heart of human affliction; nothing could be more terrifying than to comprehend the human meaning of this drama. Sorrow and suffering are shown as the fundamental conditions of human existence. We are faced, as from the beginning, with Holbein's painting, with the distress and dread of nothingness when faith in and promise of redemption have been shattered by the crushing power of a temporal moment. It is a problematic situation that recurs in Dostoevsky's *oeuvre* precisely because it is the situation of man himself. But this situation is both conditional and preliminary: It belongs exclusively to the finite world. It is necessarily within the province of spiritual, or sacred, art that ultimate concerns must be aroused and heightened—must be confronted, as they continually are in Dostoevsky's major novels. Through its aesthetic form *The Idiot* discloses the power of expressing some aspect of ultimate concern. This particular power is designated apocalyptic because it is one that, relating to man's *telos*, presses a moral urgency which helps to define ultimate concern, which Paul Tillich associates with the power of threatening and saving our being, with that power, in short, which determines our being or not-being. Aesthetically and spiritually, conjoining in a metaphysics of terror, *The Idiot*, when it comes to an end, transfigures what is preliminary into what is ultimacy. It forces the question of being or not-being. In forcing such an ultimate question it belongs to the spiritual art of ultimate concern in that peculiarly religious sense that Tillich delineates in his

*Systematic Theology* when he writes: "The unconditional concern is total: no part of ourselves or of our world is excluded from it; there is no 'place' to flee from it. The total concern is infinite: no moment of relaxation and rest is possible in the face of a religious concern which is ultimate, unemotional, total and infinite."[27]

Myshkin's paradox of fate must be viewed against the much larger and transcending paradox of faith. He must be seen at the vortex of the movement of the novel towards that ultimate concern that Tillich depicts. Through Myshkin, again aesthetically and metaphysically, Dostoevsky renders the terror that reaches a crisis of decision between being and not-being. Myshkin more than anyone and anything in the novel has the final power of threat and salvation. He contains both the drama and the release of those tensions that must resolve themselves in the religious exigencies that the novel presents. Myshkin epitomizes the religious question. To view him only in terms of either the triumph or the failure of aesthetic form is to subscribe to an incomplete view made even more incomplete when one accepts Dostoevsky's tragic vision. The preliminariness of art, under such circumstances, becomes itself the absolute of incompletion, which the modern world has so relentlessly glorified. This view, too, must suffer from the limits of selfhood. But *The Idiot* is an example of art that goes beyond such a spatial and temporal limit-situation and that renders the ultimate concern in search of transcendence. This search grows out of the predicament of man that *The Idiot* singularly re-creates not only in the apocalyptic scene involving Myshkin and Rogozhin but also in the very last scene of the novel—the "Conclusion"—in which the *survivors* are still groping about in their predicament. With the exception of Aglaya, who has married a fraudulent *emigré* Polish Count and has become a Roman Catholic, it is Mrs. Yepanchin who crystallizes the extent of this predicament as a limit-situation *par excellence* when she utters the final words of the novel: "And all this, all this life abroad, and all this Europe of yours is just a delusion, and all of us abroad are a delusion."

*The Idiot* poses deeper critical problems than merely the recognition of a competent but nevertheless limited and reductive discovery of Dostoevsky's allegorizing tendency and allegorical imagination, and the conclusion that his fable is demoniac.[28] Such an empirical conclusion severely restricts the multi-dimensional, the universalizing, reaches of Dostoevsky as a religious poet who never loses sight of the spiritual unity of power and of life and who never separates life from spirit. *The Idiot* is a novel in which body and spirit are inextricable and interdependent. Myshkin's presence is a guarantee of this relationship, to which Dostoevsky's novels always testify. Could it not be said that Myshkin's breakdown is the breakdown of spirit in life? Once Myshkin disappears, or is ousted, from life, a certain abject hopelessness becomes the ascendant human condition. His demise is part of the de-spiritualizing process that characterizes the modern world, precisely the Europeanism that Dostoevsky indicts in Mrs. Yepanchin's last words. The pain and the consequences of this de-spiritualization are the stuff of *The Idiot*. It is a story that, in its impelling spiritual constituents and criteria, revolves around the moral problem. Myshkin's embodiment of the dimension of spirit itself contains what is problematic, at least from a pragmatic situational point of view. Yet, as Tillich observes, "there is no straight and certain way to the norms of action in the dimension of spirit. The sphere of the potential is partly visible, partly hidden. Therefore, the application of a norm to a concrete situation in the realm of the spirit is a venture and a risk. It requires courage and acceptance of the possibility of failure."[29]

Tillich's words help to clarify, if not to define, the problematic aspects of Myshkin's spiritual significance, as well as of the unintelligibility with which his place in *The Idiot* is often greeted. What makes his role in the novel—and the novel itself—terrifying in the special sense that Hesse speaks of is the magnitude of the spiritual peril to the temporal world that Myshkin brings in all his encounters with those who make up and fashion the *ethos* of the world. The realm of these encounters is one in which estrangement and meaninglessness typify the human predicament. Dostoevsky's re-creation of this predicament is existentialistic; his art is an existentialist reading of the life of man. As Father Georges Florovsky stipulates: "He interpreted current events, but always in the perspective of the ultimate. All his writings were 'situation-conditioned' and need historical commentary."[30] Myshkin's answers to the questions of this predicament are religious; they arise from the depths of theological necessity, as Tillich would have it. His answers, in other words, are grounded in forgiveness and compassion, and not in the dead-end of pessimism. Myshkin's significance in the novel belongs to the finite. It could be said of the other characters that their conscious or unconscious awareness of this fact is what colors and distorts their actions. Not death but time—time as *chronos*—is their enemy. In murdering Nastasya, Rogozhin tries to murder time itself: he seeks a victory in the world of flesh and of time. His answer originates in demonic power, or, to apply to him Tillich's words: "His existential unwillingness to accept his temporality makes time a demonic structure of destruction for him."[31] These words also help to explain why there is throughout *The Idiot* a profound, active resistance to Myshkin, of which Rogozhin's sexual appetite is a symbolic force.

From a spiritual viewpoint Rogozhin's resistance to Myshkin can be seen as the refusal of grace. This refusal brings about the spiritual disintegration that one feels to be an irremediable condition at the end of the novel. Loss and emptiness are the feelings one has when viewing the state of estrangement at this point. As long as Myshkin remains a dynamic force in the novel, even within the particular limits that he himself must create, there always remains a sense of understanding, which attests to the spiritual unity that his person both essentializes and potentializes. In him there is spiritual presence and hope, until the murder scene. Somehow all the fragments—and this is, surely, Dostoevsky's most fragmented novel; it could not be otherwise in its metaphysical framework—attain a coherence of unity around him. The destructive or, as Dostoevsky would have it, the nihilistic spirit is kept in an uneasy abeyance as long as Myshkin appears. In this respect he embodies theological necessity, the repudiation of which can lead only to the spiritual atrophy that the world of *The Idiot* increasingly assumes as "a structure of destruction."[32] Despair, the name of what is without hope and without possibility, is certainly the overarching consequence of all that happens in *The Idiot*. To see Myshkin and Rogozhin together at the end is to grasp the full and most terrifying significance of Dostoevsky's vision. His vision is not only tragic but also prophetic of man's predicament. In *The Idiot* this predicament is at its most fragmented state. Yet, as Dostoevsky is trying to say in the murder scene, Myshkin and Rogozhin are inseparable life-conditions and life-entities insofar as they encompass the totality of man's predicament. Once again it is William Blake who comes to mind here in rendering the poetic contexts of "contraries which mutually exist." And again it is Paul Tillich who clarifies one of the major theological necessities that Dostoevsky struggles with in *The Idiot*, quintessentially in that encounter between Myshkin and Rogozhin. "For the negative," writes Tillich, "can be experienced and spoken of only in union with the positive. Both for time and for eternity one must say that even in the state of separation God is creatively working in us—even if his creativity takes the way of destruction. Man is never cut off from the ground of being, not even in the state of condemnation."[33]

*The Idiot* must be approached in the light of the accumulating crisis of modernism. It is Dostoevsky's most modern novel, especially if the modern element is seen as one in which spiritual values are challenged and displaced by the ever-changing values of a new cosmology and a positivistic empiricism. Myshkin's fate in the modern world is constantly influenced, and surrounded, by the materialistic *ethos*, which judges actions not from a dialectical and dynamic perspective. In *Crime and Punishment* this materialistic *ethos* is pictured in its ascendant stages; in *The Idiot* it is rampant and powerful. The possibility of spiritual goals in Dostoevsky's first major novel always exists, even in the most dangerous of circumstances. In *The Idiot* the final movement from skepticism to the "new" metaphysics of disorder, of fragmentation of the soul and of life, has taken place. (Dostoevsky examines the political ramifications of this fragmentation in *The Devils*.) A post-historicism, it could be said, prevails in the form of a universal spiritual death which touches everyone and everything. As a result Myshkin's isolation is incontrovertible. His antagonists in (and outside of) the novel are incapable of rising above themselves; each is a slave of his own personality, which, in another, perverse way, becomes the modern collective consciousness. The fragmented and disintegrative character of this process is inherent in the levels of the value-experience of the people who make up this world in *The Idiot*, and in which man's own perception of his position in the realm of being has disappeared. The driving force behind this picture of life is both diagnostic and unsentimental in this most diagnostic and unsentimental of Dostoevsky's novels.

Some of the surrealistic elements (and effects) that he employs, in what André Breton calls "the perpetual rambling in the depth of the forbidden zone,"[34] underscore the various forms that this "end" takes in the novel. Myshkin personifies the crisis of spirit in a modern world that has neither limits nor center. It is in the nature of such a crisis that Myshkin must constantly be put on the defensive and must become a stranger in a world in which he has no place. Within the total economy of the novel, it is worth noting, Myshkin stands at a pivotal point. His spiritual significance and value dictate such a position. But throughout the novel his place is also under attack, and in the end he is removed by the forces of the disoriented modern consciousness. His fate is thus dictated by a progressive, ruthless displacement in the kind of warfare that accompanies "the shaking of the foundations." Myshkin's encounter with the world is, then, an encounter with the mounting dangers of the modern world. It is an encounter with the demonic, when both the experience and the possibility of self-transcendence of life are impossible. Through Myshkin, Dostoevsky gives his prophetic vision of a modern world in which belief in a life ordered by Revelation and the ability to experience the world in a religious way are lost. The impoverishment of religious sensibility is one of the central characteristics of the conditions of modernism that Dostoevsky prophetically captures. In the modern world Myshkin is an irrelevance; or to be more exact, his virtues, his values, can have no place in an empirical situation.

The beleaguerment and the breakdown of Myshkin are indicative of the emptying process of a new age in which spiritual values must accede to the kind of pagan and neutral society that is ascendant in the twentieth century. The moral and ethical flabbiness of Myshkin's antagonists underline the transvaluation of spirituality, as well as of the consequences of this ultimately emptying process. Rootlessness and disorientation are two primary conditions that describe not only the end of *The Idiot* but also "the end of the modern world" that Dostoevsky prophetically announces here. A sense of crisis thus pervades the novel, as would be appropriate to any apocalyptic statement. Dostoevsky was to see beyond the crisis of modernism *per se* in *The Idiot*. That is, he was to capture and re-create the schismatic, disoriented consciousness that reached a perilous point in the nineteenth century. But he was also to catch a prophetic glimpse of the terrors beyond it: in short, to see human existence in its *meta*-modernism, of which *The Idiot* is its images of terror in the ascendant stages of demonization. The immediacy of this demonization is registered everywhere in the stuff of the novel; the prophetic vision is an implicit property of Dostoevsky's metaphysics of art. *The Idiot* is, in this respect, a bridging of these two dimensions as they converge towards spiritual art. In the first Dostoevsky displays a radical artistic genius; in the second he affirms the tempering supports of religious belief not only as "an answer to all human problems" but also as "a challenge to all human answers."[35] An understanding of *The Idiot* must succeed in direct relation to a willingness to accept the religious paradox.

For Myshkin the last scene is his last day, which has far more than merely dramatic significance. Everything in the novel has been building up and leading to this scene, in which the element of lastness translates into a spiritual significance that draws nearer and nearer to what is hidden. The eschatological quality of Dostoevsky's art is here at a high point of tension. His prophecy of the end of the modern world, or even of the end of history, attains it most startling quintessence, both its meaning and its consequence, at this climactic point. It constitutes and is subsumed in the final moment of crisis, like the "break-through" in *Crime and Punishment*. In order to hear that "other voice," Hesse writes, "this death must be died, this hell must be traversed before the other, the heavenly voice of the master, can really reach us." And what one hears in this prophetic voice is a different element from death, a different reality, and a different essence, which Hesse distinguishes in this way: "Let human life be all war and suffering, baseness and horror—in addition to that there is something else: man's conscience, his ability to put himself in opposition to God."[36] Myshkin personifies, in his dramatic and metaphysical contexts, the pain of conscience; as such, despite all of his ambiguities, which are the ambiguities of life, he points to the eternal. He manifests, in Tillich's phrase, the "negation of the negative."[37]

*The Idiot* is a story of the human predicament. In it beats a steady rhythm of breakdown, of disconnection and separation, of cynicism and lostness. The human situation is characterized not only by its ambiguity but also by its inadequacy. Sickness and despair are, in fact, the novel's most consistent and centralizing conditions. It is impossible to escape from them: they are imaged in crowded train compartments, long streets, dark stairways, and shadowy rooms. The infectious disease that permeates human life in this novel is bodily and spiritual. It is Myshkin who contains the healing power needed to combat this disease and to "cast out the devils."[38] But he himself is by no means free of disease, as Dostoevsky takes pains to show. His own electrifying glimpses of the sickness in himself enable him to understand just how fatal the sickness is in the world around him. Thus, Myshkin's experience of this world, within the spatial and temporal limits of his role, is really an encounter with the "mystery of evil," to be more exact, that evil which Gabriel Marcel sees as being invincible in history.[39] This invincibility is certainly made evident at the end of *The Idiot*. Myshkin faces evil head-on and in the process Dostoevsky shows what evil is, what its demonic powers consist of and bring about in a world that itself becomes a god. Dostoevsky's concern with evil as a condition of life is unflagging; his novels are the rendered variations of this concern. His consequential aim, in the light of his metaphysical and aesthetic roots, is that of forcing one to probe one's inner consciousness of evil, to become aware of one's self. The terrors of the recognition of our body of death form a basic and impelling part of *The Idiot*.[40] In the end this self-recognition, even self-accusation, becomes religious experience.

Myshkin is our consciousness not only of our human predicament but also of our personal dilemma of good and evil. And in this capacity is to be found the reason why he is such an overwhelming figure in the novel, both to read about and to appraise. He finally serves as communicated religious insight, which saves the novel from the exigencies of existential despair. It is in this respect that his presence has a hidden greatness. Not all the evil of the world can destroy this greatness even if it does destroy Myshkin himself. For the religious insight that he excites by virtue of all that he is and suffers points far beyond the changing events of the story in which he appears. With and through Myshkin we attain insight into life as predicament and as dilemma, and this insight is healing and liberating. But, above all, Myshkin penetrates the ground of our temporality and helps us to see beyond the immediate world, beyond its problematic conflicts, into a new depth. He is the only transcendent dimension of the novel that frees us from the bondage of time, from the illusion of the world's self-sufficiency, and allows us the shock of recognition and forces us to look deeper into others and into ourselves. Even Myshkin's antagonists are unable to resist completely the power of his greatness, which has its jarring effects even on the most inveterate of the deniers of spirit. His greatness of spirit is invariably pitted against the power of the world; the whole world opposes Myshkin and resists what he signifies. He is to be seen, therefore, in the midst of warfare. That his antagonists use every conceivable weapon against him is significant of what has been called Myshkin's hidden greatness.

Insight and compassion are the essence of Myshkin's spiritual significance, as well as the root of his religious passion. These two words also best define the nature of his mission in the novel. Myshkin is a very passionate figure, though not for the reasons most critics cite. That is, he should not be judged in terms of his erotic victory or failure in his relations with Aglaya or Nastasya. His passion must be viewed on a much higher level than that of mere self-interest. Contravening the fallacy of self-interest, Myshkin penetrates the depth of passion. And he who knows about depth knows about God.[41] The immediate, the human and surface depth, as Dostoevsky shows, is one of passion; here this is a destructive depth. With Myshkin we step into the "deep things," into "the ultimate depth of the Divine Ground," to use Tillich's phraseology.[42] This is a spiritual, a religious depth. Myshkin has transcendent meaning, and it is in this light that his religious passion must be interpreted. He is, to use a phrase common to some religious thinkers, God in search of man. His meaning is infinite, and infinite meaning has depth. If Myshkin defies critical categorization, it is because the experience of his meaning is a transcendent one. "Transcendence can never be an object of possession or of comprehension," Rabbi Abraham J. Heschel reminds us. "Yet man can relate himself and be engaged to it."[43] Myshkin is thus the experience of religious depth.

Existence without transcendence poses one of the most torturous problems of *The Idiot;* it accounts, in short, for the human predicament and the personal dilemma that the novel renders. The world of this novel is inexorably submerged in nature, in passion. The characters are caught up in the schemes of passion, which they seek to possess for the sake of its perpetrating temporal power. Myshkin alone exposes and challenges this goal; he is their penultimate encounter with transcendence, and as such he is their final crisis. Embodying the transfiguration of passion, he posits for them the transcendent need that completes man's meaning and clarifies the mystery of being. Without Myshkin *The Idiot* would be the story of the nothingness of passion; through him, passion achieves its spiritual depth and transcends its nothingness. Myshkin is not the denial of passion but rather its ultimate fulfillment through transcendence. In him the finite becomes infinite; he is a revelation of the holy. More than any other of Dostoevsky's creations Myshkin presents the greatest and most perilous challenge to all whom he encounters, for he tests their ability to witness the holy and to acknowledge transcendence. In *The Idiot,* more than in any other of his novels, Dostoevsky plunges deeply into the religious "underground": so deeply that he himself was to be aware of the limitations of his "miscarried" art form. Not only the question of God but also the question of man constituted for him the inescapable experience of that underground, of which *The Idiot* is a total exploration and Myshkin its most gravitating "historio-sophical" center of reflection.[44]

*The Idiot* is Dostoevsky's fearless venture "down to the depths." No other of his major novels was to be more free of a conscious denial of the negative, of "the shadow side," "the dark side in life." This side of existence, both physical *and* spiritual, gives to this novel its most acutely modern dimension. In other words, the problematic human situation, and personality, is not suppressed. The tormenting question of what constitutes "good," as it is embodied in Myshkin, particularly emphasizes Dostoevsky's radical view of absolutes— a view that is religious but not necessarily orthodox and has led, in part at least, to the contention that in his novels Dostoevsky "neglects the mystery of Golgotha."[45] But Dostoevsky, whatever the degree of his "anthropological" emphasis on

Incarnation and Transfiguration rather than on Resurrection, never abandons the roots of his religious vision. His concern with theological necessity remained strong. Or, to put it in another way, his concern with a religious metaphysic is what initiates, impels, and governs his vision. *The Idiot* must be seen as an example of Dostoevsky's metaphysics. It could be asserted that in this novel Dostoevsky, as a poet and a seer, provides what José Ortega y Gasset terms "some lessons in metaphysics" (*unas lecciones de metafísica*), particularly as these are relevant to the situation of the modern world. Ortega notes that metaphysics consists of the central fact that man searches for a basic orientation in his situation: "But this assumes that man's situation—that is, his life—consists of a basic disorientation."[46] *The Idiot* is the poetic reaction to and revelation of these words, which also help define the basic contexts of Dostoevsky's metaphysics.

Dostoevsky's metaphysics must be seen in modern contexts: in terms of crises—the crisis of consciousness, the crisis of faith, the crisis of culture. *The Idiot* is a poetic diagnosis of crisis; it provides no prescriptive or remedial alternatives of a "new ethic." It does not seek for the enlargement of personality but for the comprehension of personality, with all its sides and angles. Myshkin is the *pneuma,* the spiritual soul, of *The Idiot,* and the dark and light sides of all that happens in the story attain their meaning in direct relation to all that happens to him. The novel constantly calls our attention to this fact. Dostoevsky's art is radicalizing in its technical autonomy; in its metaphysics it is religious insofar as it is not an art of integration but of meditation. The significance is enormous. What we see in this novel is the extremity of human limits set against the delimitation of the religious lessons implicit in Myshkin. His goodness is absolute in its simplicity. This is perhaps the single most important critical derivation that must be drawn from Dostoevsky's religious metaphysic. Once this is seen, much that is complex or unclear in the novel is made clear. Myshkin is Dostoevsky's witness to the "basic disorientation" in the human situation. He also provides a clue to what can be done to diminish the problem of man's "fundamental dislocation." As an assertion of humility, his entire response to the human situation is an act of moral courage. It instances the need to affirm spiritual criteria, without which breakdown occurs and grows. Myshkin's presence is in this respect the presence of standards, which are not ascetical but disciplinary. Their absence, as the novel shows, leads to a debased human condition. Myshkin's humility, as a reverent discipline, is an antidote to the abyss.

Myshkin stands for the good that saves man from chaos. He embodies a religious principle metamorphosing into religious experience as "a living sense of God."[47] In this Myshkin is another manifestation of Dostoevsky's search for God; Myshkin's "good" contains Dostoevsky's glimpse of harmony. To be sure, *The Idiot* is a novel of discord and despair; yet it is also about Myshkin, about good. This "double" theme gives the novel its heightened perspective, which in turn is clarified by Dostoevsky's own words: "The Holy Spirit is a direct conception of beauty, a prophetic consciousness of harmony and hence a steadfast striving toward it."[48] This statement must be kept in mind in approaching all his novels. It defines the spiritual content of his burden of vision as it is dramatized by the specifics of terror in *The Idiot*. The experience of this novel is, in some ways, purgatorial. Through Myshkin there is a striving toward harmony; through his pain Dostoevsky gives us a hint of eternity. Myshkin's final breakdown in some ways elicits forgiveness, and in the concluding paragraph of *The Idiot* we read: "Mrs. Yepanchin wept bitterly when she saw the prince in his sick and humiliating condition. Evidently all was forgiven him."

Spiritual victory, however, cannot be the theme of *The Idiot,* a novel in which Dostoevsky's awareness of antinomies and anomalies reaches the outermost boundary. The human process attains no measurable spiritualization, and Myshkin's own contribution is decidedly qualified. Dostoevsky's vision of the world is not at all ennobling in this novel and indicates at times a stoic acceptance of the world that Myshkin confronts. Here the emphasis is everywhere on man's affliction and deprivation, not on man's realization of spirit. Dr. Schneider's Swiss clinic, to which Myshkin returns, is a fit symbol of man's unceasing travail. *The Idiot* is Dostoevsky's glimpse of damnation; there can be no doubt that what he saw terrified him and also helps to account for the spiritual agony that permeates the novel and that, understandably, continues and expands on other levels in *The Devils*. Can spiritual life survive in the world of *The Idiot?* This is one of the central questions that Dostoevsky asks, and it is necessarily succeeded by others. And the answer to this question is not reassuring when one considers Rogozhin's murder of Nastasya. It is Myshkin who is also murdered. The pressure of a collective evil is paralyzing. That Myshkin, as the spirit of good, will not be able to overcome it is known from the beginning. The element of futility permeates the entire story and challenges the value of spirit.

With respect to the critical response to *The Idiot,* Dostoevsky writes: "All those who have spoken of it as my best work have something special in their natural formation that has always struck and pleased me." It is a novel that no doubt meant a great deal to him and into which he poured much of himself and of his vision. The movement of Dostoevsky's vision, both downwards and upwards, was always excruciating, but particularly in *The Idiot.* Dostoevsky wanted to touch and to hold all that is good and pure in and through Myshkin, who represents a constant aspect of the novelist's vision. But this was an immensely ambitious hope—and a vulnerable undertaking. *The Idiot* fully, if not brutally, assaults the sanctity of this quest. Seeking to find redeeming spiritual perfection in life, Dostoevsky was to reveal things "frightful, sheer, noman fathomed."[49] The final meaning of the vision of *The Idiot* is terrible and terrifying. Any total understanding of this novel must first rest on this predication. But for Dostoevsky the discovery and the revelation of the terrible and terrifying were not oppressive, not damning, not catastrophic. Terror had for him a religious cast. It contained a positive religious experience and posited a spiritual value in reminding all those who watch and wait that "To every purpose there is a time and a judgment" (Ecclesiastes 8:6). *The Idiot* dramatizes Dostoevsky's vision of the abysses of human existence, which he yet sees in constant relation to man's religious situation. His concern is with the state of this crisis-situation, which he sees in terms of terror. But for Dostoevsky terror is much more than a mere technical virtuosity or ingredient as a "stem of stress" in how and what the poet communicates.

As a novelist Dostoevsky created a metaphysics of art. The place and nuances of terror in *The Idiot* must be judged from the vantage point of this literary perspective. Hence, what stands out in this novel is that, in grasping the terrible things

of the world, terror also contains and interrelates sacred energies, inner numina. It revolves around religious principles,
even when these principles are threatened by doubt. Myshkin
embodies an entity governed by these higher principles; he
manifests intangible things caught in the sharpening conflict
between skepticism and perfectionism. He is a witness to the
modern mind in a faithless age. In this novel one is never far
away from distress and dread, death and strife: the symbols of
not-being appear and press everywhere. On an aesthetic level,
terror becomes a kind of visionary sensation of these laws of
life. The inexorability of these laws, as they affect the whole
life-rhythm and life-ethos, is one of the most frightening features of the novel. Fires raged endlessly in Dostoevsky's furnace of doubt. But behind, beyond, and above these fires, terror
in *The Idiot* is a prolegomenon to philosophical shock. With
special poignancy and intensity it makes for an awakening to
religious mystery and truth. It becomes an actualization of the
spiritual. Through terror Dostoevsky was to perceive the continuous warfare between God and Satan. *The Idiot* underscores
Dostoevsky's preoccupation, even his obsession, with the consequences of this warfare, which he could never simplify or
reduce to a formula. Terror is part of the pain of affirmation:
*The Idiot* is thus a landmark in Dostoevsky's spiritual art,
which is consummated in *The Brothers Karamazov*. Without
Myshkin Dostoevsky could not give us Father Zossima.

Terror begins with fear and ends in struggle. In *The Idiot* it
is an active, winnowing process for both body and soul that
had already started on a smaller scale in *Crime and Punishment.* Terror for Dostoevsky can be likened to a "spiritual
exercise" that is in turn part of a spiritual pilgrimage. This
exercise must be experienced in all its severity: The road to
faith is filled with treachery. Against an ever-present treachery Myshkin posits value of spirit; but he also exemplifies the
pain of revealing it, the difficulty of attaining it, the anguish of
sustaining it. Around him gather all the forces of life that make
his presence and meaning no less terrifying than the conditions that these forces exude. Terror proliferates in *The Idiot* as
value and non-value collide. Nothing is more terrifying than to
view the energy consumed, and consuming, in this collision.
Everything, everyone is assaulted; nothing remains sacro-
sanct, nothing is revered. What Myshkin must face, above all

else, is the enraged power of the finite as it seeks to determine and maintain the province of its being. In effect he has to face sin, hardships, resistance, insults, enemies, betrayal. He faces, that is to say, the terror of the power of the world. And yet in terror Dostoevsky was to find the gift and challenge of grace: "My grace is sufficient for thee: for my strength is made perfect in weakness," Saint Paul writes (II Corinthians 12:9). In Dostoevsky's art there is no impassable distance from the "terror of God" to the "grace of God." If Prince Myshkin is a witness to the human plight, with all its darkness and mystery, he is also Dostoevsky's Paraclete who calls us to good that is hard.[50]

*Chapter Three*

# SATANISM
## The Devils

ἀλλὰ ῥῦσαι ἡμᾶς ἀπὸ τοῦ πονηροῦ.

Matthew 6:13

# I

In Dostoevsky's vision of evil the figure of the devil assumes a powerful role and brings to mind the contention that a writer's obsessive concern with the devil can result in "indelible burns" and "incurable wounds." In a trenchant essay, "The Devil in Contemporary Literature," Claude-Edmonde Magny declares that an artist who has too strong a desire to look the devil in the face may even seek "to vie in cunning with him." "Once the mere thought of evil is present in the mind," she goes on to observe, "it loses no time in invading the imagination; then the soul, which has taken delight in the thought, makes a movement towards it, and ends by consenting to it."[1] In a more realistic and conciliatory vein, Friedrich Schleiermacher has remarked that the poetic use of the devil is to be accounted the least harmful, and "no disadvantage is to be feared from an emphatic use of this idea in pious moods."[2] André Gide, in his *Journal des Faux-Monnayeurs,* has also expressed a keen interest in this subject (though from another angle of aesthetic vision), pointing out that the devil is best served when he is unperceived. The devil's securest hiding place, Gide stresses, is behind any approach that dismisses him as *une puérile simplification,* that argues his non-being according to *explications rationnelles,* and that relegates him to *l'hypothèse gratuité.*[3]

Indeed, no less an authority than Saint Ignatius Loyola, in his *Spiritual Exercises* ("Discernment of Spirits," R. 13), has vigorously asserted, "Unmask Satan and you vanquish him."

Perhaps in no other novelist has the figure of Satan been as conspicuous or inexorable as in Dostoevsky. Indeed, the whole range of life depicted in his novel *The Devils* (1873) must be regarded as fundamentally a product of satanic activity when, as Dostoevsky quotes from Pushkin in one of the two epigraphs to the novel,

> We've lost the way,
> Demons have bewitched our horses,
> Led us in the wilds astray.[4]

In this work Satan is supremely active in human experience. "Like a roaring lion, seeking whom he may devour" (Ephesians 6:11-12), Dostoevsky's devil has in a very large and true sense "gone round about the earth and walked through it" (Job 1:7). The meaning of human existence seems irremediably violated to the point that "the very laws of the planet are a lie and the vaudeville of devils" *(samye zakony planety lozh i diavolov vodevil'),* as the God-tormented Alexey Nilitch Kirillov has direly concluded. In *The Devils* in general and in the person of Nikolay Vsyevolodovitch Stavrogin in particular, Dostoevsky tremblingly but relentlessly confronts Satan as the Evil One, the Adversary, the Accuser, the Tempter, the Liar, the Murderer, the Tormentor, the Prince of this World, the Prince of Darkness. This confrontation is achieved with extraordinary artistic success, and for Dostoevsky the medium of art thus becomes the frightening reality of struggling with that infinitely diabolical phenomenon whose *raison d'être* is best expressed by the Greek word ὁ Πονηρός. Surely, it was not accidental that Dostoevsky entitled his novel *Besy—The Devils.*

Dostoevsky's use of Satan must be seen in a decidedly different light from that of artists like Milton, Goethe, Shelley, Byron, Hugo, Carducci, and Baudelaire. It must be seen as transcending the applicability of H. G. Wells's statement in *The Undying Fire*: "Satan is a celestial *raconteur*. He alone makes stories." For Dostoevsky, Satan was not a literary device or problem. Nor, in his portrait of Satan in the figure of Stavrogin, was he striving for aesthetic effects *per se,* such as the invocation of a Radcliffian terror or the evocation of the weird, the macabre, the startling, the grotesque, the gloomy, or the terrifying. What he was attempting was chiefly motivated by Christian values and a Christian consciousness; his response and vision were preponderantly religious and moral. Stavrogin must not be approached in the Miltonic framework of a creature "majestic though in ruin," endowed with and admired for his "heroic energy." Neither is he to be coupled with Lord Byron's "fatal" man, that mighty outlaw lingering on the misty borders of vice and virtue. Stavrogin, it will be seen, is in severe contrast to any romantic archetype of Satan as a fiery rebel or a composite of a Typhon and a Prometheus, defying divinity for the sake of an oppressed humanity. He is Dostoevsky's vision of evil and of the innermost reality of sin. The Russian writer does not try to show the origin of this evil, but rather its alluring and hideous aspects, above all its *present* existence as an actual fact, as a "falling away." The total scheme of *The Devils,* Dostoevsky seems to bring out, is justified theologically and poetically because it not only gives the truth about evil, but also induces an examination of conscience, a profound spiritual experience, and a thirsting and hungering for God.

Appraisals of Stavrogin are consistently and overwhelmingly timid and irresolute. Conclusions to the effect that to "settle on any prototype would be hazardous" and that Stavrogin is "a complex amalgam of many literary characters" summarize precisely the approaches of most critics.[5] To them Stavrogin is a kind of disenchanted character—he is beset by boredom; he is a tragic figure; he is a man with a curse on him, his "greatness nullified by his split personality"; he is a divided, Russian Luciferian type, perhaps an offshoot of a Speshnev or a Bakunin; he is "a typically modern personality haunted by the 'demon of irony'"; he is a "victim of romantic *ennui*"; he is the "most complete development of the romantic, 'Byronic,' egoist"; he is the victim of a "hopeless solitude."[6] "Wrapped in indifference, lost in an egotism he does not value, he passes by, simple but deadly, as if he were the inhabitant of another planet, spreading around him, impassively, a miasma as he goes."[7] There seems to be almost common rhetorical agreement that Stavrogin cannot be categorized either as a man or as a *homo fictus.* He has become an enigma fascinating to behold and explore, a wonderful opportunity for clever critical exercises and semantics—clever, that is, as long as critics disregard moral value judgments, religious awareness, and definite ethical and theological elements, without which, as T. S. Eliot has well noted, literary criticism remains incomplete. The proper, more adaptable critical approach to Dostoevsky, as one eminent comparatist has phrased it in a collection of essays, is "to avoid the fierce commitments of the Russians [e.g., Merejkowski, Ivanov, Berdyaev, and Zander[8]], to make compromises, to combine approaches, to suggest shadings of meaning."[9] But the results of such an attitude are, to say the least, all too apparent in the excessively secularized critical pronouncements of the skeptic, the aesthete, the formalist, the rationalist, the positivist—for such comprise the gang that has continually made of Stavrogin everything and nothing.[10]

It would, of course, be a presumption to deny Dostoevsky's debts to the Western literary tradition and the profound influences made on him by such writers as Balzac, Dickens, George Sand, Hugo, Sue, E. T. A. Hoffmann, Byron, Schiller, Racine, and Corneille. That Dostoevsky borrowed and adapted freely from other writers is quite obvious; yet, as Charles E. Passage has noted in his interesting study, Dostoevsky was a creator, not an imitator. Hoffmann's *Die Elixiere des Teufels*, for instance, persisted as an inspiring influence in much of the Russian's work, but as Passage also brings out, "It is of silver; Dostoevsky turns it into gold."[11] The claim, furthermore, that Dostoevsky is, as artist and thinker, in the stream of Western thought and literature, though not essentially inaccurate, fails far too often to take an informed or sympathetic view of Dostoevsky's obligation to "Orthodox culture" *(Pravoslavnaia kul'tura)*, to the philosophical and spiritual realities of which Dostoevsky had been exposed since his early youth and from which he was unable and unwilling to separate himself throughout his life and work. What needs to be insisted upon, in the face of the increasing attempts to make Dostoevsky into just another commodity for the consumption of Western readers and more grist for Western critics, is that Dostoevsky's greatest and primary debts were to "Orthodox culture" and that before his art and the people of his cosmos are understood readers will have to have some idea of what constitutes an

Eastern Orthodox milieu and metaphysic. "In Dostoyevsky," as Zenkovsky has very aptly declared, "... we see philosophic creativity *growing out* of the womb of the religious consciousness."[12]

In the Eastern Orthodox tradition the devil is the personification of a fierce evil that besieges human life. Every measure must be taken to keep him away. When we consider "The Office of Holy Baptism" and "The Prayers at the Reception of Catechumens," as found in Eastern Orthodox rites, we can ascertain how formidable and threatening the figure of the devil is. For example, in the First Exorcism there appears this typical passage, as the devil is adjured: "Fear, begone and depart from this creature, and return not again, neither hide thyself in him, neither seek though to meet him, nor to influence him, either by night or by day; either in the morning, or at noonday: but depart hence to thine own Tartarus, until the great Day of Judgment which is ordained."[13]

Satan is able to assume human attributes that enable him to descend upon man "in a mighty rage" (Revelation 12:12). He is not only a κοσμοκράτωρ but also a δύναμις that must be constantly reckoned with and fought: a disturbing force that ceaselessly harasses man by day and by night. He is an "unclean spirit" (Revelation 16:13) with a "deceitful tongue" (Isaiah 14:13, 14), seducing, subverting, frustrating, destroying life at every opportunity—"a murderer from the beginning." Often he "disguises himself as an angel of light" (II Corinthians 11:14) who, in the words of Saint Tikhon of Zadonsk, "offers evil under the semblance of good, like poison steeped in honey."[14] "The angel of the bottomless pit," he afflicts, infects, and maims life. He incessantly emerges from the abyss to become a prowler in life. Even when he takes human shape, Satan represents a completely unregenerate humanity, a humanity that has "known the 'deep things' of Satan" and has died, never to wear the "crown of eternal life." Ultimately, too, Satan must transhumanize himself and return to his domain of darkness, despair, and impiety. He stands outside of time and is exempt from responsibility; he is that "lawless one" and everlasting κατήγορος.

If some of his critics have been deluded by the person of Stavrogin, Dostoevsky at any rate was not. In his portrayal of Stavrogin, the Russian novelist was actually participating in the unending conflict with evil and concurrently resisting it and acquiring "patient endurance" (Revelation 2:1, 2). For Dostoevsky a profound lesson was to be learned in this confrontation, a lesson which is nowhere more simply and poignantly phrased than in the words of James (4:7), "resist the devil and he will flee from you." Stavrogin illuminates perfectly the immense difficulties of viewing satanism in its various enigmatic guises. In this respect, Dostoevsky indicates that the powers of Satan are not mere theories or explorations, not mere questions and answers, but rather manifestations that must be directly encountered, seen for what they are, judged, and resisted. In *The Devils*, then, Dostoevsky is firmly committed to waging a battle with the devil and with the evil that the devil perpetrates. In it he also discerns the epiphenomena of the warfare that one must enter into with πειρασμός, not merely with the devil as a personality but with the devil as the embodiment of those terrifying energies, "principalities and powers" which assail and brutalize life. "For we wrestle not against flesh and blood," Saint Paul reminds us, "but against principalities, against powers, against the rulers of the darkness of this world . . . against the prince and power of the air" (Ephesians 6:12). Dostoevsky fiercely probes these powers and energies, neither sentimentalizing nor romanticizing them. And the implicit, unwavering moral judgments of his novel indicate the deepest religious convictions of the artist, in spite of the nagging doubts, insecurities, and tensions of faith that periodically burst into the whole of his art and message.

The stress on the irreducible in Stavrogin and the persistent attempts to enigmatize and humanize him have failed to perceive the dimensions of the evil he represents. All too often Stavrogin's activity is not seen in the light of the impelling value that he has made of evil; rather it is subordinated to what must presumably remain as an absurdity or a riddle. Both the dimensions and the intensity of Stavrogin's crimes remain unexplained, and serious omissions relating to Dostoevsky's own intentions as a religious artist result. Yet, to explain evil merely as what is inexplicable in life abrogates religious faith itself and moral responsibility. One of the most constant demands exacted by Dostoevsky's novels is that evil should be apprehended in its exterior and interior forms. Dostoevsky's approach to evil is a profoundly vital one, resting firmly on the belief that, in contrast to the good-natured Tolstoian attitude of nonresistance, evil must be confronted and challenged. It should be stipulated that in his depiction of evil Dostoevsky does not preach an eschatology of vengeance and torment, does not fail to bring out the mysterious, unending interpenetration of the clean and the unclean. His recognition of human error and frailty and the acuteness of his vision itself are far from being narrowly moralistic, and his art affirms that man, through penitence and purification, can recover the image of God.

Just as Dostoevsky discloses a strong optimism in his belief in "the perfection of the human soul" and in the redemption of humanity through Christ, he also recognizes the existence of limitations in the doctrine of divine economy. His portrayal of Stavrogin reveals the limitations of compassion and charity in this doctrine. In a sense, it can be asserted that Dostoevsky is at times groping in his delineation of Stavrogin's character. His steadfast belief that under rough exteriors there is to be found some gold comes to the surface time and again, perhaps even to salvage Stavrogin, perhaps to diminish the implacability of his sins, perhaps to find some niche for him in God's infinite mercy. However, when we consider the Eastern Orthodox concept of evil, we can comprehend not only just how steeped Dostoevsky was in its doctrine, but also how it enabled him to see through and unmask "the spirit of error, the spirit of guile, the spirit of idolatry and of every concupiscence." The figure of Stavrogin accentuates the whole truth of this, for he is precisely the unmitigating evil that is synonymous with satanism. Above all he illustrates the absence of goodness and the consequent darkness and disintegration that fill the realm of hell and Satan. John of Damascus in his *Exposition of the Orthodox Faith* (II, iv) makes note of this absence in words that could easily serve as an epigraph to the whole of Dostoevsky's art and message: "For evil is nothing else than absence of goodness, just as darkness also is absence of light. For goodness is the light of the mind, and similarly, evil is the darkness of the mind." Stavrogin's diabolism is attested to by his inability to appreciate what Kirillov speaks of as "moments of eternal harmony" *(minuty vechnoĭ garmonii)* and by his own admission that "from me nothing has come but negation, with no magnanimity and no force. . . . Everything has always been petty and lifeless" (III, viii).[15]

# II

The biblical statement "My name is Legion: for we are many" (Mark 5:9) is especially applicable to Dostoevsky's "sons of disobedience" in *The Devils.* Stavrogin serves as an archetype of the various satanic disguises, shapes, and images. Indeed, so incredibly sly and clever is he that there is even the tendency on the part of readers to sympathize with him, to forgive his well-nigh unmentionable sins and crimes, and to ignore his moral depravity, his "brutal conduct," his outrages against society, his disdain for all spiritual values. Stavrogin, in the light of such a response, should be neither judged nor condemned. He merely personifies the paradoxes of the burden of mortality; he is man cruelly trapped by his doubts, conflicting loyalties, questionings, anxieties, ambivalences; he is a mirror of poor mankind's frailty and plight and fatefulness. He is that pitiably and helplessly *human* element. Such an approach to Stavrogin not only deemphasizes moral and spiritual responsibilities, but also encourages an indifference and a rationalizing that lead to an escapism of the most serious consequences. This not uncommon response to Stavrogin renders one defenseless to the many "wiles" and "snares" and "devices" employed by the devil, whose central aim is to debase all human significance and to bring death to the soul. "For he is insatiable," Saint Gregory Nazianzen observes; "he grasps at everything. He fawns upon you with fair pretences, but he ends in evil; this is the manner of his fighting" (*The Oration on Holy Baptism,* X).

To Dostoevsky satanism is not only the absence of goodness and of magnanimity, but also of impelling, active love, which recalls Father Zossima's words in *The Brothers Karamazov:* "What is hell? I maintain that it is the suffering of being unable to love."[16] It is in such a "hell" that Stavrogin finds himself, for if there is one quality he lacks throughout, it is love. Unlike a Svidrigaylov, who seems to be furiously groping in his depravity so that he may satisfy his "insect-lust," Stavrogin is (in Zweig's memorable phrase) "the cal-

culating tactician of debauchery."[17] Stavrogin has come to a
full stop: he neither questions nor answers what is evil. He
*knows* that he lives and is evil: "Indignation and shame I can
never feel, therefore not despair, either" (III, 8). He is the evil
that ultimately has transcended all distinctions and has
passed beyond the morality and immorality of this universe
into the amorality and conscienceless being of a satanic realm.
Stavrogin has "decayed and corrupted children," has made
"no distinction in beauty between some voluptuous and brutish act and any heroic exploit, even the sacrifice of life for the
good of humanity" (II,1, 7). He has leaped beyond all boundaries of compassion and the charity of divine largesse. His
calm, his indifference, his composure, his pride, even his
boredom are the consequences of a satanism that wallows in
the abyss. "Oh, you never walk at the edge of the abyss, but
precipitate yourself over it boldly, head downwards," Shatov
says to Stavrogin (II, 1, 7), and his words underline the true
condition of the satanic. Dostoevsky, in his delineation of
Stavrogin, ventures into the abyss, but his purpose is not of
alliance with its infernal creature but of spiritual warfare,
which Saint Macarius the Great describes as "The most important work in spiritual struggle is to enter the heart and there to
wage war with Satan; to hate Satan, and to fight him by
opposing his thoughts."[18]

On numerous occasions Stavrogin is called "Prince," but
the title, like the name Stavrogin, which comes from the Greek
word for cross (σταυρός), is grimly ironical. Dostoevsky's
peculiar use of the word "Prince" (ἄρχων) compares with the
traditional treatment of Satan as the prince of demons, as the
ruler of this world, as the prince of the power of the air.
Stavrogin is the artistic counterpart of the "fallen Lucifer," the
"awful Aristocrat," the creature who as lightning fell from
Heaven (Luke 10:18). He, too, contains a certain element of
charm and of grandeur, an aristocratic appearance, a handsome and glittering exterior that have traditionally been associated with Satan and that led Dante to the depiction of Satan
as the "paragon of all creation." On one occasion Stavrogin
is imaged as "a diamond on the filthy background of . . . life"
(I, 5, 6). Even Shatov once admired him: "You, you alone could
have raised the banner!" (II, 1, 7). And like the biblical Satan,
Stavrogin is very much the aristocrat surrounded by mystery

and spoken of in fear and awe. Dostoevsky's description of Stavrogin in the following passage is certainly in line with that of the "fallen Lucifer":

> . . . his hair was just a little too black, his light-coloured eyes a little too calm and clear, his complexion a little too tender and white, his colour a little too dazzling and pure, his teeth like pearls, his lips like coral—he would seem to be a paragon of beauty, yet at the same time there was something hideous about him. People said his face reminded them of a mask; there was, by the way, a great deal of talk about his amazing physical strength. (I, 2, 1)

The atmosphere generated by the presence or actions of Stavrogin is unmistakably one of murkiness and putrefaction, heightening and deepening the titanic evil which he contains and which blasphemes majesty (Jude 8). When Stavrogin appears, when he encounters other figures, when he is related to episodes of the past and present, when he conjures up the future, it is hideousness and fear that permeate the scene. Ugliness and decay become, in association with him, recurrent images. Often, too, references to him have the effect of linking him with the lowest animal life: he is imaged as a wild beast showing its claws, a monster, a serpent, a spider, a vampire. His presence incites the consciousness of evil, of instinctive fear of contact with the demonic. This consciousness becomes evident when Marya Timofyevna Lebyadkin says to Stavrogin: "As soon as I saw your mean face when I fell and you picked me up—it was as if a worm had crawled into my heart" (II, 2, 4). On one occasion, when Captain Lebyadkin leaves a gathering, he accidentally collides with Stavrogin in the doorway: "The Captain somehow suddenly cowered before him and stopped dead in his tracks without taking his eyes off him, like a rabbit in front of a boa-constrictor" (I, 5, 6). One night, when Stavrogin goes out, Dostoevsky describes the scene in these words: "The wind howled and tossed the almost denuded tops of the trees, and the little, sand-covered paths were soggy and slippery" (II, 1, 4). And when Stavrogin arrives to talk with Kirillov he is "covered with mud." Entering the room, he sees Kirillov playing with an eighteen-month-old baby held by a woman. "The child, catching sight of him, clung to the old woman and went off into a prolonged childish cry; the woman at once carried it out of the room" (II, 1, 4). Toward the end of the

novel, in a letter to Dasha, Stavrogin expresses a desire to leave
Russia and to live in the canton of Uri in Switzerland: "The
place is very dull, a narrow valley, the mountains constrict
both vision and thought. It is very gloomy" (III, 8). Stavrogin is
inevitably identified with darkness, and with him we make the
descent into the abyss.

Stavrogin communicates the experience of hell itself; his
presence, directly or indirectly, engenders a relentless spirit of
destructiveness, terror, and hideousness. Often he is not even
on the scene, but his dark shadow seems to fall on all the other
characters and on all the other episodes of the novel. He seems
to stand fixed in the center of a universe, and yet he also seems
to propel the fate of those whom he addresses, touches, or looks
at. The mystery and fear that immediately emerge in relation
to him are no doubt the projection of what is sinister and
woeful. It is obvious that his stagnancy is of the most perverse
form and cannot hide the realization that the evil in him is
supreme and powerful to the degree that it automatically
overflows into all avenues of human activity. Stavrogin is thus
the chief source of the poison that brings contamination and
death. His very nature stands in direct opposition to the creative and the beautiful. Stavroginism, then, signifies the inability to suffer or love or feel. Consistently he refuses to make
any positive struggle or decision for the good. His woeful
effortlessness, consequently, is conducive to a state of soul in
which, to use Buber's sage words, "Intensification and confirmation of indecision is decision to evil."[19] Stavrogin embodies
the brutal entity of whatever is malevolent and beyond hope,
and this accounts for the fact that he is receptive to no expression or action kindled with human passion. "His malice was
cold, calm, and, if one may put it that way, *rational,* which
means that it was the most abominable and most terrible kind
of malice" (II, 5, 8). His whole existence revolves around this
malice—it is his only world, his only nourishment. We recall
Byron's Lucifer crying to Cain: "Mortal! My brotherhood's
with those who have no children."[20] Everything must pale and
recoil before the infernal spirit, which remains ageless and
unmoved in its evil. Even as we happen to cross his path,
arouse "his faint smile," or hear his "gentle, melodious voice,"
we can discern "strange screams of death" and "the smoke of a
great furnace" as it blackens the sun and air. To know

Stavrogin is to know "the torment of a scorpion." Very likely it is the terrifying knowledge of this truth that grips Varvara Petrovna Stavrogin when she chances to see her son as he sleeps:

> His face was pale and stern, but it looked completely frozen and immobile; his brows were slightly drawn together and frowning; he certainly looked like a lifeless wax figure. She stood over him for about three minutes, hardly daring to breathe, and suddenly she was seized with panic; she tiptoed out of the room, stopped for a moment at the doorway, hurriedly made the sign of the cross over him, and went away unobserved, with a new heavy feeling and with a new anguish. (II, 1, 4)

When Dmitri Karamazov cries out to his brother Alyosha, "The awful thing is that beauty is mysterious as well as terrible. God and the devil are fighting there and the battlefield is the heart of man,"[21] he expresses a belief that pervades the totality of Dostoevsky's thinking. The devil is integral to Dostoevsky's artistic and moral vision, and the Russian novelist continuously converses and clashes with him. When the devil appears, he can do so *in persona*, mysteriously but distinctly visible to a particular figure, as in the case of Ivan Karamazov, or within another character, as in the case of Stavrogin in *The Devils*. In the first, Satan takes the form of a nightmare; in the second, he is an ontological reality. Combined, these two manifestations embody a complete picture of satanism. Whereas the devil is *with* Ivan, pulling him, tugging at him, lacerating him, he is *in* Stavrogin, commanding him, regulating him, impelling him.

Ivan epitomizes the satanic element which leads to the ultimate self-betrayal of the soul. Ivan's devil coexists with a rending inner yearning for deliverance in a man who embodies an agonizing "riddle." Dostoevsky's Christian view of sin is also brought out in his characterization of Ivan, for evil is not inherent in this man but is the result of a corruptive, pervasive process of wrong-doing and the tyranny of a "Euclidean earthly mind." The devil encountered in Ivan's nightmare is eloquent, witty, affable, clever; both in speech and form he contains the most sophisticated elements which Dostoevsky equated with "rational egoism." Certainly, the description of the devil sitting on Ivan's sofa "against the opposite wall" reinforces the "idea" of a Satan endowed with gentility and sophistication:

> This was a person or, more accurately speaking, a Russian gentleman of a particular kind, no longer young, *qui faisait la cinquantaine*, as the French say, with rather long, still thick, dark hair, slightly streaked with grey and a small pointed beard. He was wearing a brownish reefer jacket, rather shabby, evidently made by a good tailor though, and of a fashion at least three years old, that had been discarded by smart and well-to-do people for the last two years. His linen and his long scarf-like neck-tie were all such as are worn by people who aim at being stylish, but on closer inspection his linen was not over clean and his wide scarf was very threadbare. The visitor's check trousers were of excellent cut, but were too light in colour and too tight for the present fashion. His soft fluffy white hat was out of keeping with the season.[22]

Ivan's devil wanders in the secret recesses of the mind and heart in search of a refuge, a victim. "I suffer," he tells the distraught Ivan, "but still, I don't live. I am $x$ in an indeterminate equation. I am a sort of phantom in life who has lost all beginning and end, and who has even forgotten his own name." Of course, Ivan wants the devil to be a "dream, not a living creature," and he thus hopes to equate him with *l'hypothèse gratuité*, to recall Gide's words. The devil, however, stubbornly clings to Ivan exactly because the latter has all along been advancing the theory that "all things are lawful." Ivan's assumption, then, embodies an inviting shelter to the satanic, extends a welcome to a "visitor" who is always willing to "enter into the world" and to take a seat on a sofa, "to keep his host company at tea," "ready for any affable conversation as soon as his host should begin it." Satan's central aim is to give living reality to this theory from the very moment it is entertained. To promulgate such a theory, the devil will adopt diverse guises, indulge in all sorts of charming postures and gestures ("I lead you to belief and disbelief by turns, and I have my motive in it. It's the new method"). Nevertheless, his final aim is unmistakable and his unflagging cynicism overshadows all outward amicability. Even a deracinated Ivan cannot help perceiving the devil's real goal. He suddenly snatches a glass from the table and flings it at the devil, who, quoting Ivan's own past utterances, ends with these words:

> There is no law for God. Where God stands, the place is holy.
> Where I stand will be at once the foremost place . . . "all things are
> lawful" and that's the end of it! That's all very charming; but if
> you want to swindle why do you want a moral sanction for doing
> it? But that's our modern Russian all over. He can't bring himself
> to swindle without a moral sanction. He is so in love with truth.

This quotation is particularly important, for it not only
adumbrates a conspiracy of feelings in Ivan, but also, by way
of contrast, indicates how in Stavrogin evil is *the* condition of
existence, "without a moral sanction." Contrary to Ivan Karamazov, Stavrogin is not plagued by an "earnest conscience"
or torn by a division of soul. In him there is absent "the anguish
of proud determination" which we find in Ivan. The satanic is
an inextricable condition of Stavrogin's existence, and its
power over and in him is as unquestioned as it is unyielding.
Stavrogin has totally resigned himself to his lostness, his
cynicism, his denial of God. He is a creature who no longer
resists Satan but has abjectly surrendered himself to him. He
represents a defeat concurrent with the triumph of deception
and denial. "To cook a hare—you must catch it, to believe in
God—you must have God" (II, 1, 7). This, we are told, is one of
his favorite sayings. Stavrogin's condition, furthermore, has
passed beyond the ramifications of struggle between a Cham-
pion and an Oppressor. The aridity of disbelief is his "infinity
of endless ages": "If Stavrogin believes in God, then he doesn't
believe that he believes. And if he doesn't believe, then he
doesn't believe that he doesn't believe" (III, 6, 2). No wonder he
is an alien in the human realm: "I have nothing to keep me in
Russia—everything is as foreign to me there as anywhere else"
(III, 8). No wonder that Lisa Tushin, after spending a night
with him, senses how barren he is of human feeling, of love: "I
always imagined that you would take me to some place where
there was a huge, wicked spider, as big as a man, and we should
spend the rest of our lives looking at it and being afraid of it.
That's what our love would be wasted on" (III, 3, 1). No wonder,
finally, that Varvara Stavrogin must wail, "I have no son!"
(III, 7, 3). Companion of Satan and denizen of hell, Stavrogin is
the epitome of dismemberment from God and from life, and he
must suffer the fate of those whom Father Zossima has so well
described in one of his "exhortations":

Oh, . . . there are some fearful ones who have given themselves over to Satan and his proud spirit entirely. For such, hell is voluntary and ever consuming; they are tortured by their own choice. For they have cursed themselves, cursing God and life. They live upon their vindictive pride like a starving man in the desert sucking blood out of his own body. But they are never satisfied, and they refuse forgiveness, they curse God Who calls them. They cannot behold the living God without hatred, and they cry out that the God of life should be annihilated, that God should destroy Himself and His Own creation. And they will burn in the fire of their own wrath for ever and yearn for death and annihilation.[23]

The last two chapters of the third and final part of *The Devils* show the depth of the horrifying void in Stavrogin. It is especially seen when we compare Stepan Trofimovitch Verhovensky's last days of life with Stavrogin's. In the death of Stepan, Dostoevsky evinces a deep note of compassion for human loss, and an implicit sense of forgiveness resounds in the course of Stepan's sickness and death. What starts off with his almost comical decision to reject Varvara Petrovna's charity and "luxurious provision," and to hold aloft "the standard of a great idea and . . . to die for it on the open road," ends up as an inherently spiritual pilgrimage, achieving a sense of redemption and even nobility. Stepan, in the course of his "last wandering," is imaged as a sick man freed from the devils and now come to sit "at the feet of Jesus." As he approaches his end, he is more and more the picture of a pilgrim who has suddenly felt bright rays of light shining warmly on him. Stepan has at last confronted decision and has, as a result, gained insight into his heart and mind. "The hardest thing in life," he says to the gospel woman, Sofya Matveyevna, who cares for him during these last days, "is to live without telling lies . . . and without believing in one's lies" (III, 7, 2). At this point, above all, Stepan is juxtaposed to Stavrogin. He now radiates the innate humanity and warmth and magnanimity which are totally absent in Stavrogin. There is a positive note in Stepan's utterances, especially in his affirmation of life, and he dies blessing life and the mystery of existence: "Every minute, every instant of life ought to be a blessing to man . . . they ought to be, they certainly ought to be! It's the duty of man to make it so; that's the law of his nature which always exists even if hidden" (III, 7, 3). Stepan indicates the power of renewal and belief that girds him in the presence of much pain. And this paradigmatic power stems from a realization of human limitations:

> The one essential condition of human existence is that man should always be able to bow down before something infinitely great. If men are deprived of the infinitely great they will not go on living and will die of despair. The Infinite and the Eternal are as essential for man as the little planet on which he dwells. My friends, all, all: hail to the Great Idea! The Eternal, Infinite Idea! It is essential to every man, whoever he may be, to bow down before what is the Great Idea. (III, 7, 3)

In contrast, Stavrogin, as the end approaches, reveals his desperate aloneness and lostness, his betrayal of life. "One may argue about everything endlessly," he confides to Darya Pavlovna in a letter, "but from me nothing has come but negation, with no greatness of soul, no force. Even negation has not come from me. Everything has always been petty and spiritless" (III, 8). At the core of Stepan there is an indwelling power that allows him to rediscover the kinship with and the necessity of "the Eternal, Infinite Idea" (*Vechnaia, bessmertnaia Mysl'*) that lies in all persons. In short, he acknowledges in the most reverent terms a community of feelings that all men must share in the end, in spite of the obstacles and misfortunes of "cruel history." Whereas Stepan speaks from the depths of his heart and from an overpowering love and a religious need, necessarily and finally surmounting all hatred and despair, Stavrogin, through his suicide, reveals the inner desolation of his heart and the false pronouncements of his soul.[24] Stepan dies in reverent affirmation of life; Stavrogin hangs himself, the only witness to his own isolation in the loft: "The citizen of the canton of Uri was hanging there behind the door. On the table lay a piece of paper with the words in pencil: 'No one is to blame, I did it myself.' Beside it on the table lay a hammer, a piece of soap, and a large nail" (III, 8). Self-murder is for him the final act and the final death, the quintessence of his satanism, his Hell—that Hell which, as Berdyaev writes, "is continuous dying, the last agony which never ends."[25] In destroying himself, Stavrogin simply discloses his separation from life and his denial of what Dostoevsky often spoke of as its "gladness."

# III

Stavrogin's decision to go to Bishop Tihon and to confess his sins brings into focus Dostoevsky's severest testing of the doctrine of divine economy. A mere surface view of the meeting of sinner and holy man will perhaps tend to induce compassion for Stavrogin as he utters some "wild and incoherent" disclosures "with unaccustomed frankness." His inner sufferings, his terrifying hallucinations, his expression of love for the monk, his sense of transgression, even his recognition of God— all of these would tend ostensibly to suggest a repentant, guilt-stricken nature in Stavrogin, as well as a feeling that he bears within him seeds of redemption. It is the picture of the persecuted, not the persecutor, that we supposedly have. With that remarkable aesthetic distance and objective vision which pervade his art, Dostoevsky strives to give a dispassionate depiction of a man in the agonizing act of confession. But the revelations and dialogue, especially as they evolve from Stavrogin himself, ultimately speak for themselves, and the feeling that we are in the presence of a "liar," a "misanthropic demon" (in the words of Justin the Martyr), becomes indisputable. Slowly we grasp just how complete Stavrogin's separation from and renunciation of God and life are, how much he is frozen in his abysm. "I don't invite anybody into my soul," he snarls at one point; "I do not need anybody, I can shift for myself."[26] His meeting with Tihon confirms the magnitude of his violations of life and of his mania to pervert truth. The informing response to this entire scene and to Stavrogin himself is crystallized in a little-noticed incident occurring in the course of Tihon's reading of the pamphlet documenting the confession: "Meanwhile, Stavrogin stopped at the writing-table, and taking up a small ivory crucifix, began to turn it about in his fingers, and suddenly broke it in half." This is a profoundly meaningful happening, which accents the discrepancy between Stavrogin's words and actions and further shatters any image of him as an erring human being. The incident also illustrates both a conscious and an unconscious condition of a creature of evil that ruins everything with which it comes into contact, and we are duly reminded of Denis de Rougemont's comment in his work concerning Satan: "Everything he annexes to himself he destroys."[27]

What we especially find in Stavrogin during his visit to Tihon is the fully developed evil that "shows different faces and assumes different characters, and yet is always the same." His decision to go to the monastery is a facet of this definition, another instance of the role and power of Satan as the Tempter and Tormentor. Stavrogin is not at all sincere, repentant, or humble, but wholly blasphemous and cynical throughout his talk with Tihon. It is significant that Dostoevsky's narrator interprets Stavrogin's purpose in having Tihon read the document relating his crimes as one that seeks to "exchange one kind of suffering for another. ... Indeed, in the very existence of such a document one senses a new, unexpected and irreverent challenge to society." The document, "vile, crawling and abominable," forcefully underlines the irreversibility of Stavrogin's crimes, the self-centeredness and self-absorption of all his actions and dissimulations. The picture of Stavrogin on these pages is a confirmation of evil; from it we are able to grasp how restless and unsatisfied is his yearning to subvert and harm life. It is the "criminal energy" of Stavroginism that we see here, and its scourge is both inversionary and perversionary. Stavrogin's violation of the twelve-year-old Matryosha validates this "criminal energy" and discloses a diabolic scorn of all human decency. His actions, too, are always the product of his free will, of his choice of and responsibility for evil: "I was in full possession of my faculties, and ... consequently I was not a madman, and ... I am responsible for everything."

When Stavrogin admits, even after Matryosha has hanged herself, that "I was able to master my memories and ... became callous to them," the satanic element in him becomes absolutely clear. Later on, while traveling in Germany, he dreams of the "Golden Age," but the vision is the fleeting and inconsequential one of a man who has already suffered the "death of the soul" and who has abandoned all hope and given up the struggle. Such a dream cannot really comfort or renew a man who has moved beyond the frontier of religious vision and affirmation. The truth of this conclusion is measured by Stavrogin's own cynical, despairing response to the dream as a "lofty illusion," as "the most improbable of all visions, to which mankind throughout its existence has given its best energies, for which it has sacrificed everything, for which it has pined and been tormented, for which its prophets were crucified and killed, without which nations will not desire to live, and without which they cannot even die!" Ironically, this dream is immediately followed by an apparition of "Matryosha, grown haggard and with feverish eyes, precisely as she had looked at the moment when she stood on the threshold of my room, and shaking her head, had lifted her tiny fist against me." He admits that this image of Matryosha, especially with her "threatening gesture," stabbed him with "a maddening pity." But he also admits—and the significance of this admission can hardly be overstressed—that the fundamental reason for his pity and remorse is not a humane one at all, but one that is interlinked with his overweening pride ("the beginning of all sin"). It is Stavrogin's sadism and shamelessness that are predominant here; and to Tihon, at one point, the confession smacks of arrogance and insincerity:

> Even in the very intention of this great penitence there is something ridiculous, something false, as it were . . . not to speak of the form, which is loose, vague, unsustained because it is weakened by fear, as it were. Oh, don't doubt but that "you'll conquer." . . . Even this form . . . will avail, if only you will sincerely accept the blows and the spittle, if you will endure it! It was always thus, that the most degrading cross became a great glory and a great power, if only the humility of the act was sincere. But is it? Is it? Will it be sincere? Oh, what you should have is not a challenging attitude, but measureless humility and self-abasement! What you should do is not despise your judges, but sincerely believe in them, as in a great Church, then you would conquer them and draw them to you and unite them in love. . . . Oh, if only you could endure it.

Stavrogin's central aim in his confession is not to evoke forgiveness. His aim stems from his boundless egoism, his titanic pride, his obsession with self-glorification and self-blessing. "Listen to me, Father Tihon: I want to forgive myself. That's my chief object, that's my whole aim!" He categorically refuses to "wash" his heart (Jeremiah 4:14) and he makes a mockery of "confession" itself. The entire incident should be imaged as a flagrant desecration of the sanctity that Tihon represents. What Saint Athanasius writes of the devil in his *Life of Antony* is appurtenant to Stavrogin's encounter with Tihon: "Let us then heed not his words, for he is a liar: and let us not fear his visions, seeing that they themselves are deceptive." The meeting of Tihon and Stavrogin is, as Mochulsky has noted, an intense struggle between belief and disbelief, the collision of the two greatest forces in the world, God and the devil, embodied in two personalities: the mystic Tihon and the atheist Stavrogin.[28] Throughout the meeting, Stavrogin's behavior accords with the mold of his character and attitude, into which the poor cripple, Marya Timofyevna, has amazing prophetic insight. He is, in her words, "an owl and a shopkeeper," a "mask," an "imposter," a "pretender," a "grishka Otrepyev," anathematized in seven cathedrals. No, Stavrogin's confession must not be misconstrued as an act heroic in scope and noble in gesture. For he is mocking and profaning the Λόγος of God (to the point, in fact, that even the kindly and naive Tihon is fooled or outwitted). Like Satan he refuses to "hate the evil" (Amos 5:15) in his heart and to embrace the meaning of the Psalmist's injunction, "Stand in awe, and sin not" (Psalm 4:4). His confession embodies the uttermost limits of impiety (ἀσέβεια) and moral deception, and like Satan he ultimately deceives himself. In the brilliantly perceptive words of Guardini,

> He is the poorest of all men. One feels great compassion for him, yet Satan truly has no majesty! What modern apologists for satanism and for moral transvaluations say about the greatness of evil is simply not true. For Satan is the one who is being cheated, cheated by himself. He is absolutely empty. He is not great in anything. He is the wretched "simius Dei."[29]

It needs to be reemphasized that Stavrogin is always composed, unenthusiastic, cold. Above all else, he lacks tenderness and reverence, those particular graces of kenotic religion that are embodied in the Russian word *umilenie.* He can hardly share Kirillov's love of children and nature, or Shatov's faith in the "God-bearing" people of Russia. His marriage to a poor cripple, "after a drunken dinner, for a bet, for a bottle of wine," and his silence in permitting a little girl to be punished after being wrongly accused of stealing his knife, which he knew he had misplaced, also clearly bring out his sadistic impulses. The inexhaustible presence of Satan in Stavrogin is especially to be seen in the latter's lack of compassion. The puny extent of his concern for other human beings is captured in the course of his meeting with Captain Lebyadkin. Having come to the

Lebyadkin lodgings to talk with Marya Timofyevna and having conversed with the Captain (her brother) for a time, Stavrogin tells him to go out while he speaks in private with Marya Timofyevna. Because it is raining, he tells the Captain to take his (Stavrogin's) umbrella:

> "Your umbrella? But, sir, am I worth it?" the Captain said ingratiatingly.
> "Every man has a right to an umbrella."
> "You've defined the minimum of human rights in one short sentence, sir." (II, 2, 2)

There is no doubt that Stavrogin shows "unnatural strength," both in his physical prowess and in his social relations with other figures. In this respect, he embodies the strength and cunning inevitably associated with the "evil spirit" and its cosmic power. Though he is often "quiet, listless, and rather morose," looking even "abstracted," he is constantly "watching and listening." In him we are made aware of the coalescent principle and obtrusiveness of evil. To generate itself in God's creation, the "evil spirit" must fulfill itself in an outer substance, achieve a peculiar fullness of being in an external body. Stavrogin's relation to Pyotr Stepanovitch Verhovensky illustrates such an hypostatization. Pyotr is the exteriorized evil that Stavroginism inspires and breeds: an actual, identifiable force and entity in life. "You're my leader," he cries out to Stavrogin; "you're my sun, and I am your worm" (II, 8). He is the fleshly, substantive body of evil ("a scoundrel and a sophist," "a filthy human louse," "a rogue," "a political seducer") as it appears in a particular time and place. There is nothing abstract about Pyotr, and his goals are tangible ones. He plots to cripple the physical body of life—"to level mountains," to create "political disturbances," to cause such "an upheaval that the foundations of the State will be cracked wide open," to inaugurate a new system of "monstrous, disgusting vice which turns man into an abject, cowardly, cruel, and selfish wretch":

> "The thing we want is obedience. The only thing that's wanting in the world is obedience. The desire for education is an aristocratic desire. The moment a man falls in love or has a family, he gets a desire for private property. We will destroy that desire; we'll resort to drunkenness, slander, denunciations; we'll resort to

unheard-of depravity; we shall smother every genius in infancy. We shall reduce everything to one common denominator." (II, 8)

Stavrogin stands for the death of life. Pyotr, whom Stavroginism torments and actuates, is the murderer of life. Totally "absorbed in his sensations," Pyotr personifies the cruelest bestiality of evil. Even in the midst of treachery and killing, this executioner must satisfy his appetite with a beefsteak. Who can ever forget the picture of Pyotr, accompanied by another conspirator, Liputin, eating heartily in a restaurant:

> Pyotr Stepanovitch did not hurry himself; he ate with relish, rang the bell, asked for a different kind of mustard, then for beer, without saying a word to Liputin. He was pondering deeply. He was capable of doing two things at once—eating with relish and pondering deeply. Liputin loathed him so intensely at last that he could not tear himself away. It was like a nervous obsession. He counted every morsel of beefsteak that Pyotr Stepanovitch put into his mouth; he loathed him for the way he opened it, for the way he chewed, for the way he smacked his lips over the fat morsels, he loathed the steak itself. (III, 4, 2)

From the beginning to the end of the novel, Stavrogin's actions and thoughts lead in the direction of utter breakdown, chaos, and death. In him there is no sense of aspiration at all, no ascent of the "living soul" (Genesis 2:7). He fears nothing, he doubts everything. Ἀγάπη, πνεῦμα, πίστις — those eternal verities that provide a sense of direction and that stand for the victory of belief over disbelief—are to him senseless and unattainable. His character shows a complete lack of positive development, not because of any structural deficiencies or artistic failures on Dostoevsky's part, but because of the kind of creatureliness and evil that Stavrogin must represent and re-create. Stavrogin can travel in only one direction, out of a primordial past into a primordial chaos, evincing the total denial of the possibility of *new life*. It could be said that his very existence is a cyclical one, inasmuch as he refuses to appeal to transcendence, to reach out for or to desire what is above him. It is an existence that reacts only to what lies around it, to what can be manipulated and grasped from immediate levels. Stavrogin cannot *respond to* or *commune with* others; he can merely appear as an aspect of evil that is incarnated in a Pyotr Verhovensky or in a Kirillov.

Irremediably "dwelling in evil things," Stavrogin is unable to find a "place of rest." In his terrible restlessness and dissatisfaction, he seems to be a tormented wanderer, in constant flux and turmoil. For him there can be no inner peace or outer stability. Plagued by demonic impulses and hatred, he is in everlasting pursuit of hostage and victim. He travels in the Orient; he goes to Mount Athos and stands through interminable night services; he visits Egypt, moves on to Jerusalem, stays in Switzerland, journeys as far as Iceland, attends the University of Göttingen for an academic year. And yet for him there is no surcease, no content, no "gladness," no destination. Whether he is in Russia or abroad, he is unhappy, possessed, loveless. And whether he is a student, a soldier, a traveler, or a rebel, he must needs be the irreconcilable enemy of life and of man. His existence metamorphoses into a demonism that is destined to make him homeless and hopeless. Not all the power in the world can save him from his admission to Dasha that "Nothing comes to an end in this world" (II, 3, 4). But, then, the satanic as found in Stavroginism has bound itself to a wheel of sin which never stops turning. Evil feeds on life: its appetite is endless: its thirst quenchless. Stavrogin dramatizes, in effect, the burden of sin, of impenitence, of negation.

By no means must Stavroginism be assessed as a desperate "search for values."[30] To make such a claim, as unfortunately so many critics do, is to ignore the satanism of a figure who blandly realizes that he cannot even "play at magnanimity." "I know that it will be another delusion again," he confesses, "a delusion in an infinite sequence of delusions" (III, 8). The desire of some critics to excuse Stavrogin may very well be prompted by an optimism and a charity which, though commendable, are essentially misguided and illusionary. This desire may also arise from a preëminently relativistic appraisal of evil and from a belief that the satanic element in life is an insignificant element or an ancient superstition which can no longer harmonize with the modern scientific world.[31] The figure of Satan and the problem of evil remain real and adamant in life, as real and adamant as Dostoevsky's Stavrogin. Surely, it is grievous to believe that in Stavrogin lies the story of a "spiritual adventure."[32] It is grievous, too, that modern man refuses to acknowledge the real Satan till he must feel him at his own throat. "The fire is in the minds of men and not in the roofs of houses," Dostoevsky writes at one point in *The Devils* (III, 2, 4). The fact remains that for the great Russian novelist art was a theurgical function interdependent with the state of the soul. In this connection, his recognition of evil must at once be witnessed as a charismatic quality of a visionary artist who, with Saint Cyril of Jerusalem, clearly realized that God suffers the devil to wrestle with men that they who conquer him may be crowned (Lecture VIII, 4).[33]

*Chapter Four*

# PURGATION
## A Raw Youth

> *But when some spirit, feeling purged and sound,*
> *Leaps up or moves to seek a loftier station,*
> *The whole mount quakes and the great shouts resound.*
>
> —Dante, *Purgatorio* xxi, 58-60

> *. . . my ending is despair,*
> *Unless I be relieved by prayer,*
> *Which pierces so that it assaults*
> *Mercy itself and frees all faults.*
>
> —William Shakespeare, *The Tempest,*
> Epilogue

> *This world is the closed door. It is a barrier, and at the same time it is the passage-way.*
>
> —Simone Weil

## I

*A Raw Youth* (1875) is a novel about personality. It depicts the realization of personality, which in turn is identified by the interiorization of a discriminating consciousness. This existential process of identification, transcending the biological and societal states of what is merely individual, is two-dimensional and consubstantial, involving the experience of break-

113

down concurrent with the struggling recognition of the life of value and spiritual essence. "The personality is a spiritual category," Berdyaev points out in *Solitude and Society;* "it is the spirit manifesting itself in nature. The personality is the direct expression of the impact of the spirit on man's physical and psychical nature."[1]

For the integrating force of this spiritual expression of personality, effort and suffering are inescapable. The drama, and mystery, of personality is all-inclusive and consuming. The confessional form of *A Raw Youth* has, not unlike what mystics call "internal conversations," the special quality of probing and illuminating the inward terrain of personality, so that its essences are distinguished from objective fact. As such this drama of personality is an unfolding and not a functional process; it presages revelation—the revelation of Spirit. The prophetic properties of Dostoevsky's great novels are never compromised; his prophetic element remains constant. *A Raw Youth* thus contains his prophetic vision of personality, at once problematic and absolute in the sense of which Berdyaev shows a profound awareness when he writes:

> The personality is the realization within the natural individual of his *idea,* of the divine purpose concerning him. It therefore supposes creative action and the conquest of self. The personality is spirit and, as such, it is opposed to the thing, to the world of things, to the world of natural phenomena. It reveals the world of man, the world of living beings, who are concrete by virtue of their relationship and of their existential communion.[2]

Personal, individuating experience is depicted in its depths. And, as is seen progressively, the pain of disorder and the search for order—chaos and harmony—are locked in fearful combat, with each individual grasping for some special self-object of concern, one that provides a measure of release. In the end the consequence of all that happens in *A Raw Youth* is dramatized in the most rending supra-personal contingency. If *The Devils* instances Dostoevsky's piercing view of the cumulative process of assault against the whole social fabric, as embodied in unrestrained satanic impulses and invasions, *A Raw Youth* instances Dostoevsky's sympathetic view of people struggling at the very center of their lives with those inner and outer forces that determine the fate of personality. A tragic optimism has its moment of vision in this novel, as satanism is arrested. Dostoevsky's vision in *A Raw Youth* is somewhat ambivalent, though not in the least ambiguous. Spiritual momentum seems to have caught up with the demon of personality. The hell of *The Devils* is not as impregnable as one would think. Schism, terror, satanism are, to be sure, compositely present in the frenzy of each personality in *A Raw Youth*. But there are also some courageous interludes of respite, when each personality must find rest in discovering itself. Self-perception of personality is the keystone of *A Raw Youth,* which carries with it a positive factor that anticipates *The Brothers Karamazov.*

In Dostoevsky's great quintet, *A Raw Youth* occupies a middle ground. It serves as a bridge. Or, to put it in another way, it makes possible for pilgrim and non-pilgrim alike the terrifying journey from hell to paradise, from satanism to saintliness. In *A Raw Youth* the moments of respite are tantamount to moments of purgation, for personality is not only explored but also cleansed and refined. Spiritual preparation defines the experience of personality, and ascent rather than descent gains momentum by the end.

Though Dostoevsky remained always aware of the temptations and brute realities of the "second self," the self that acts senselessly, godlessly, the variations of which actions are portrayed in all his novels, he was equally aware of the aspirations of one's spiritual self: the desire for self-transcendence, for what Dostoevsky specifically images in this novel as "the gift of tears" and as "the resurrection to the new life." Naturalism and supernaturalism attain their symbolic quintessence in Dostoevsky's novels; they exert the full weight of his burden of vision as it takes shape. With *A Raw Youth* Dostoevsky moves closer to an understanding of the spiritual reaches of his vision. The irremediable destructive spirit of the preceding novels, particularly of *The Devils,* abates as the human personality, consciously and unconsciously, confronts a greater power and law, much greater than itself, that the holy man, Makar Ivanovitch Dolgoruky, posits when he declares: "It's impossible to be a man and not bow down to something; such a man could not bear the burden of himself, nor could there be such a man" (III, ii, 3).[3]

Makar's words epitomize the problematic aspects of personality. Both the spiritual and the intellectual development of personality must acknowledge the imperativeness of these words. Human fate revolves around the reaction to Makar's declaration. Personality, and the novel itself, achieve their idiosyncratic forms in accordance with the implementation of the meaning of these words. Questions and answers affecting each man's destiny are implicit in Makar's words, pregnant with challenge. Personality defines itself, its rarefying forms, in direct relation to a corollary experience of these words. To be sure, Makar's words are the result of a simple spiritual faith imbued with wisdom and reverence. Faith and spiritual simplicity, as he shows, are, after all, one in their ultimateness. Dostoevsky's own contemplation of the Bible and of other sacred writings had left to him a legacy of religious belief. Not all the complications and subtleties of personality, no matter how legitimate and inevitable, could dim the truth of this conclusion as it crystallized for Dostoevsky into religious imagination, of which *A Raw Youth,* in its explorative nuances, is an astonishing, if unappreciated, result.

Leonid Grossman and other commentators have noted that in *A Raw Youth* we have the highly distinctive and complex style of the late Dostoevsky, a style that in its innovative structural difficulties and obscurities anticipated trends in much of modern art.[4] "Let the readers do a little work themselves," Dostoevsky averred.[5] But unlike his successors among novelists, he did not allow his stylistic experiments to disintegrate into an artistic vacuum. That is, both as a novel and as a segment of his burden of vision, *A Raw Youth* is another creation of a spiritual artist writing out of his moral sense.

This novel is equally responsive to spiritual values in crisis; it testifies to Dostoevsky's abiding religious sense of the importance of the human act. The subjective world of personality, which *A Raw Youth* records, is never without its awareness of the spiritual world in which the visible and the invisible essences of personality conjoin. Here, then, the spiritual law that Makar invokes is ever-present, no matter how pervasive appears the rebellion of personality (and particularly as Dostoevsky renders the form of this rebellion, this chaos). There are human beings with souls to lose or to save. Dostoevsky's preoccupation with personality is, consequently, not completely pure. The graduated formation and experience of personality must ultimately find their completion, their *telos,* in the life of the soul, with its requisite religious consideration of moral action and judgment. The form of aesthetic experimentation could not, in *A Raw Youth,* triumph over Dostoevsky's moral, and religious, conscience. The religious artist in him was far too vigilant for any final aesthetic diversion from the spiritual plane.

Aesthetic and sacramental impulses, even as they collide and possibly unbalance *A Raw Youth,* set up the artistic and spiritual tensions that continuously excited Dostoevsky's genius. But in his "quest for form," in the scheme of his artistic experiments, there was always an un-Flaubertian self-regulating priority that determined the pathways of the metaphysics of his art-form. His literary creation once more ends in religious quest, for, as Father Florovsky insists, the quest for religion in nineteenth-century Russian literature was incontestable: "Dostoevsky was undoubtedly correct when he identified the major theme of his time as religious. It was the problem of faith and unbelief, in their confrontation and conflict."[6]

Confrontation and conflict in *A Raw Youth* not only influence personality but also, more importantly, reveal it. And the revelation itself bodies forth its own force and truth of example, indeed of the fate of personality, in the light of its full response to the challenge of Makar's words. It is a pedagogical novel; it is also an opportunistic one. Dostoevsky's educational purposes blend with his spiritual purposes, insofar as *A Raw Youth* is not only about the search for personality by a young man, Arkady Makarovitch Dolgoruky (the legal son of Makar and the natural son of Andrey Petrovitch Versilov), but also about the infinite process of personality in its inwardness. It would not be far-fetched to say that one is saved or damned by one's thoughts, a fact indicated especially as these are expressed in the mind of Arkady Makarovitch, who slowly discovers his spiritual identity in the actions that surround him. As he awakens to the consciousness of his relation to his father, to his pilgrim-father, and to the other members of his family, above all to his mother, Sofia Andreyevna, his personality expands. A positive and spiritual expansion of his personality is involved; human relations, their achievement as well as their paradox, evolve here in a much softer pattern. In depicting this process the narrative tone is certainly less acerbic than in Dostoevsky's preceding novels. *A Raw Youth* seeks to educate the reader in a much more humane, certainly less demonic way than the other novels would lead one to expect. Out of all the chaos that, socially and intellectually, constitutes the immediate setting, with the stark and cruel city of Saint Petersburg always in the background as the image of despair and dissolution—and it is exactly this chaos that Dostoevsky seeks to convey, there emerges a sense of man increasingly aware of his limits, his "burden of himself."

What *A Raw Youth* does is to meliorate the burden of selfhood and to put personality in contact with the springs of inherited traditional wisdom, with enduring spiritual criteria. In *A Raw Youth* Dostoevsky does not promote or glorify personality. Rather he endeavors to depict personality in its regenerative potentiality, slowly stripped of a self-absorbed personal view of life that is without recourse or loyalty to any spiritual standard. Personality in *A Raw Youth* must be viewed, hence, in its spiritual gradation, as it is purified and refined and as it is liberated from its own demon. The relativistic view of personality, which prevails with such arrogant force in the whole of modern literature (and society), is not for Dostoevsky an unchallengeable element. Personality must invariably testify to the demands of moral conflict and resistance. The spiritualization of personality: Dostoevsky's didactic aim remains steadfast and helps to control the fecundity of ideas in *A Raw Youth*. There is an incessant situational flux that Dostoevsky seeks to emphasize, analogously, in structural ways. This is his method of delineating the deep pressures and paradoxes with which the personality must contend in postulating its own significance, its identity in society, its quintessential wholeness, its innerness.

The dynamics of personality are operative everywhere in *A Raw Youth*. Each of the central characters struggles to particularize his personality; it is the element of struggle that underlines the intrinsic value and validity of personality and that separates it from thingness and pluralistic reductivism. The greater the struggle, the more vivid the personality. Regeneration, as Dostoevsky showed, always has the element of chaos in it. The careful definition of spiritual essence is never easy. Not the possibility of life as a natural phenomenon but of life as a spiritual manifestation is one of Dostoevsky's cardinal points. Infinite possibility of spirit in personality epitomizes the fundamental purpose and significance of *A Raw Youth*. In this possibility he discloses the approximation of grace.

The redemptive quality of his novel is based on hope. But the tyranny of the objective world in spite of its finiteness, or even because of it, has overwhelming force. When this force consumes personality, it destroys spiritual possibility. Personality always finds itself in a state of warfare as the outer world works to legislate its conditions of material existence. Under these conditions personality is enslaved, extinguished; materialization defeats spiritual essence. *The Devils* illustrates this irreversible demonic process, but *A Raw Youth* moves in another way by focusing on the qualitative side of personality. But pain and suffering, as the implicit conditions of such a state, are inevitable, even absolute in their experiential meaning. It is simpler to renounce these conditions, to surrender to the technic spirit and all that it ordains. "The struggle to realize the personality is an heroic one," to quote Berdyaev once more. "Heroism is above all a personal act. The personality is not only related to freedom, but cannot exist without it. To realize the personality is therefore to achieve inner freedom, to liberate man from all external determination."[7]

Berdyaev's words help to explain the indecisiveness and paradoxes of *A Raw Youth*. After exploring the evils of the world in *The Idiot* and satanic energy in *The Devils,* Dostoevsky had no small task in rendering the spiritual uniqueness of personality in an age of "incendiarism" and negation. "From the right of force it is not far to the right of tigers and crocodiles," he had asserted in *The Idiot*. How could personality fight against all the might of a world in which even the value of Value was being abrogated? The nineteenth century, Dostoevsky was all too aware, was imperiously proclaiming the ruin of the religious spirit. "The foundations of society are cracking under the pressure of the revolution brought about by the reforms," Dostoevsky writes in his notebooks. "The sea has become troubled. The borderlines of good and evil have disappeared and *become obliterated*."[8]

Personality, like religious belief, was becoming just another relic of a rejected past. In *A Raw Youth* Dostoevsky's description of the disorder of the times discloses all those adverse secular pressures under which personality must labor. The uneven, tenuous, contradictory, and uncertain directions that any expression of personality takes are coextensive with the spirit of the age. Dostoevsky's image of the whirlpool has its recurring significance here; and the theme of illegitimacy has its corresponding significance. A world without spiritual order is a disinherited world. It has no depth of personal identity and worships idols, especially that of the collectivist mentality. "Work for humanity," one young socialist enthusiast advises in *A Raw Youth*, "and don't trouble about the rest." But the results of such an attitude were, for Dostoevsky, all too apparent, and in *A Raw Youth* its analogues are societal "disorder," "corruption," "meanness," "madness"; "a carnival of mediocrity and ineptitude and nothing else"; "the golden age of mediocrity and callousness, of a passion for ignorance, idleness, inefficiency, a craving for everything ready-made."

Ultimately if personality is to have any validity, it embodies spiritual substance. Its immediate constituents are uniqueness, centrality, certitude, mystery; its process of discovery is discriminating and judgmental. And it must affirm the qualitative courage of its transcendent essences in its encounter with the world. The astonishing number of personal encounters, which erupt in *A Raw Youth* like a series of epiphanies, of visionary moments as it were, dramatizes personality's encounter with the world. At every step dangers and pitfalls dictate the precarious conditions of each encounter. In *The Idiot* Prince Myshkin's encounter with the power of the world revolves around what he represents in his immutability. Two forces, two entities, collide. Probing more ambitiously, and metaphysically, in *A Raw Youth*, Dostoevsky shows how human encounters take on a problematic dimension, for here personality connects with the world. The inner and outer worlds, spirit and fact, transcendence and immanence, meet. This meeting is inevitable inasmuch as personality is always open to experience as it engages in the process of discrimination. Whereas in *The Idiot* encounter has a static pattern of exemplification, for each participating force is rooted in itself and self-contained in the measure of the discrete powers it possesses and conveys, in *A Raw Youth* encounter prescribes a situation in which the flux of change exerts the primary conditions of response. Unlike *The Idiot*, *A Raw Youth* does not present and personify *exempla*. Instead, the conditions of encounter here emphasize the contexts of a special relatedness.

Though necessarily exposed to the requirements of the world, personality must simultaneously fight to defend its own peculiar, and higher, functions, its discrimination, its identity, against the empirical process of secular society.

How is personality not merely to survive as, innately, an agent of discrimination, but also to defend its mission in a world in which all doors to transcendence are locked? How is personality to be saved from the disintegrative process of depersonalization embodied in modern materialism and positivism? How is personality to retain the consciousness of itself? *A Raw Youth* describes the difficulty of answering these questions, and in this difficulty lies much of the anguish that the novel communicates. What happens to personality in a disintegrating world— "in the whirl of the world" (*V mirovorote*)—is Dostoevsky's preoccupying concern. "Disintegration," he writes in his notebooks, "is the principal visible idea" of *A Raw Youth*. "The disintegration is present everywhere, for everything is falling *apart*, and there are no remaining ties not only in the Russian family, but even simply between people. Even children are apart."[9]

*A Raw Youth* must be read with *The Devils* in the immediate background, in which the demoniac conditions of general, social disintegration have already been firmly established. It is the finite situation of precisely such a dissolution that personality has to confront. In *A Raw Youth* Dostoevsky takes personality beyond the historical process; he sees it as much more complex and much higher than mere historical destiny. Personality comprehends in depth the historical meaning of social experience. But this comprehension in its totality attains transcendence in transfiguration, which is the personality's ultimate effort and its greatest destiny.

For Dostoevsky the transfiguration of personality connoted a divine progression. In such a progression the personality moves closer to its origin and experiences the full potential of its creativeness. Yet his view of personality was not sentimental, for he saw that personality, when unhinged by those divisive emotions that nearly destroy Raskolnikov, can be brutally separated from its spiritual inheritance and fate. In this sense Dostoevsky viewed personality as an absolute entity, any compromise of which was an overture to the rationalistic and relativistic impulses that the world has increasingly glorified. The crisis of faith that Dostoevsky saw as a mark of society was equally the crisis of personality. Breakdown was, after all, a corrosive and endemic condition, as *A Raw Youth* illustrates. This novel shows the struggle for personality in a broken society: the greater the breaks and cracks the greater the effort needed for personality to subsist. For some persons this effort is too much and leads to confusion and, worse, to destruction. But the split personality that so many commentators choose to focus on in the novels in purely psychological terms is an utterly insufficient understanding of what Dostoevsky was seeking to show: the psychic disorientation of personality is a sign of deeper levels of distress, of spiritual disorder. (It is worth recalling that "Disorder" was his original title for the novel.) Indeed, Dostoevsky writes in his notebooks, "The reason for the underground is the destruction of our belief in certain general rules. *'Nothing is sacred.'*"[10]

Depersonification and desacralization, Dostoevsky insisted, are interdependent. The absence of God proclaims the absence of personality. Makar, in effect, is voicing precisely this warning, in a novel that recurringly responds to the central question of God. *A Raw Youth* presses on with one of Dostoevsky's greatest thematic concerns, even as it heightens, according to Mochulsky, his one theme, "a depiction of the tragic *Russian chaos.*"[11] If God is no longer sacred, then neither is personality. In place of God a collective will is formulated; in place of personality there is the person. Dostoevsky's sociological premises were, in this respect, both spiritual and prophetic. When his characters distance themselves from the standard of Godhood, they in turn depersonify their own essences. Spiritually and intellectually they rob personality of the truth of its transcendent feeling and transform it into perfunctoriness, thingness. The deniers in his novels are all persons without personality. They have "original ideas" but no abiding standards. In *A Raw Youth* formlessness and rootlessness image this process of debasement. What Dostoevsky writes in *The Diary of a Writer* for January 1876, in retrospect concerning *A Raw Youth,* has added meaning here:

> I took an innocent soul, yet one already touched with the terrible possibility of corruption, with an early hatred for his insignificance and "accidentalness," and with that wideness with which a soul still pure consciously entertains vice in his thoughts,

nourishes it in his heart, and is caressed by it in his furtive yet audacious and wild dreams—all this naturally connected with his strength, his reason, and even more truthfully, with God. These are all the abortions of society, the "uprooted" members of "uprooted" families.[12]

The transfiguration of personality, Dostoevsky believed, involves suffering and is an implicit aspect of the tragic view of life. In *A Raw Youth* the authentic spiritual recognition of the personality's meaning is seen as an organic part of the way in which a fundamental purgation occurs. This purgation of personality is a necessary prelude to the discovery of infinity. Purgation acts as a tempering detriment to the always terrible possibility of corruption. It serves as a reverent discipline, and it anticipates unity of essence and destiny. Its result is the purgation of consciousness as opposed to what has been labeled positivistic individualism, which, as in Raskolnikov, is not only corruptive but also disintegrative. The Absolute is the personality's deepest center, and to penetrate and grasp it is man's destiny. *A Raw Youth* portrays the personality in quest of the Absolute, and though the world of sin is equally present here as in the earlier novels, it is a world in which appear a cleansing of pride, a glimmering of humility, and a craving for the good. Personality is thus seen directing its attention beyond its own self, and longs for harmonious connection with what is outside. There is a conscious and an unconscious awareness of a transcendental force and a longing for some transfiguring form of spiritual growth, symbolized especially in the raw youth's search for his father. This supervening idea of reconciliation and atonement, as a result, accounts for this novel's distinguishing "artistic tonality."[13] The possibility of corruption is not without its attendant possibility of good, which is God.

The contention that *A Raw Youth* is Dostoevsky's purgatory is not an oversimplification. As a transitional novel it comes between the experience of damnation in *The Devils* and that of holiness in *The Brothers Karamazov*. It offers for special contemplation the personality's experience of suffering for purgation. That, as Eliot writes of Dante's *Purgatorio,* "damnation and even blessedness are more exciting than purgation,"[14] has its corresponding truth with respect to most critical reactions to *A Raw Youth* and explains to some extent the neglect of this novel. The dramatic horrors of *The Devils* have no counterpart here, even as the metaphysical focus of *A Raw Youth* is much more restricted, defined as it is by a family setting. Within this setting personality itself is on trial, in the sense that Saint Paul delineates when he says: "Every man's work shall be made manifest: for the day shall declare it, because it shall be revealed by fire; and the fire shall try every man's work of what sort it is" (I Corinthians 3:13).

Personality is intrinsically apocalyptic in Dostoevsky's novels. In the rectilinear world it is always unfinished; it moves, as it must move, beyond the present in fervent expectation of that other world, of that eternal *kairos*. The growth of personality, anchored in suffering, is measured by the intensity of a cleansing and refining process that transfigures it. As the personal and the individual are cleansed of their cloying influences, personality attains rebirth. This is one of the main themes of *A Raw Youth*. It is also Dostoevsky's prophetic recognition of purgatory.

The note of atonement in *A Raw Youth* is distinct. Personality itself can be envisioned as a journey of atonement. Personality is eternalized, as Makar, another of Dostoevsky's pilgrims of the apocalypse, teaches with "marvellous simplicity" and "seemliness." Indeed, in Makar personality achieves expiation, for in and through him Arkady and Versilov discover, in various intersecting stages and degrees, personality in its eternal aspects. The eternalizing of personality is, with respect to the totality of Dostoevsky's burden of vision, tantamount to the final restoration. Personality returns to its divine primacy, to the country of its origin.

The metaphysical schema of the five great novels revolves around this transfiguring process of restoration. *A Raw Youth* is both a perception of the process and a symbolization of hope. Lostness, as an ineradicable consequence of chaos, cannot be the death verdict. Arkady, in exploring the infinite dimensions of personality, penetrates eternity in the bondage of sin and guilt. The imaging form of this exploration is, to recall, that of a whirlpool, as Arkady is carried from one predicament to another, from an encounter with holiness to one with sinfulness, especially as the novel moves to its conclusion and torrential emotions converge in the making of personality. Revelation is at hand when, as Dante would have it, one has seen "the temporal fire and the eternal."

Dostoevsky sees personality in the light of religious action that transforms the inner life of the individual. Suffering, that which Kierkegaard calls "soul-suffering," is the primal quality of this experience, and it constitutes a decisive part of the God-relationship. *A Raw Youth,* as an extension of Dostoevsky's eschatological vision, accentuates his religious imagination as it becomes spiritual art. Inherent in this art, and empowering it, is the idea that human destiny is never meaningless, that it is necessarily significant and tragic—and universally revealing. This transcendent idea finally possesses Arkady and necessarily subordinates his grand idea of obtaining money and power. He is, as has been remarked, one of Dostoevsky's most ardent religious seekers.[15] In a world in which the death of love is a bleak daily fact, Arkady searches desperately, if often confusedly, for the father to whom he wants to bring the gift of love. Surely there could be no more ennobling effort than this. For the expression and affirmation of such a feeling, always something of a mystery to Dostoevsky, Arkady is a suffering servant.

# II

Arkady, Versilov, and Makar are Dostoevsky's poetic incarnations of his metaphysics of personality. In each of them the inner life of personality is of commanding importance. In each there is a revelation. In each there exists an element of divine possibility, for each, whether only partly or fully, experiences, to use Thurneysen's words, "that greatest thing that can awaken in a man: *a consciousness of God.*"[16] Corruption touches all three: each man's personality is, in one way or another, stamped by the kingdom of the world. But if each has temporal experience, each has also a spiritual shock to his sensibility. A transcendental consciousness is a redeeming dimension of personality, a perception of something infinite. There is no quest without pain; pain is a purgative element that ultimately disciplines and widens each man's personality. In his own right each of these men is a pilgrim seeking for "that greatest thing." The effort of such a search is always rending, for it demands the discipline of reverence; it entails the recognition of what lies beyond the world and, ultimately, of personality as an endless Becoming. Each must undergo the religious act of the cleansing and stripping of personality, for as Richard of Saint Victor puts it: "The essence of purgation is self-simplification."[17] Self-simplification is the recognition of self-limitation. In Arkady we have Raskolnikov in his post-Siberian purgative period. There has now been a momentous move, containing the seeds of transfiguration. Possession by individualism gives way to the possession of personality. Purgation seeks illumination. A raw youth climbs the steps to find the brothers Karamazov.

Personality in *A Raw Youth* is necessarily tri-centered, as we are reminded of man, "that thing of threes." Human, like religious, bonds are not reducible to any single category or criterion. Of its very nature, personality is interparticipatory and interdependent: it complements the unending connection that exists between the material and the spiritual worlds, what Dostoevsky spoke of as the "complete universality of mankind." Dostoevsky had a unitive world-view. His spiritual art proceeds from and is sustained by this integrality. Through Arkady, then, there begins the penetration of the personality's consciousness, and through him one attains a comprehension of personality as both spiritual substance and revelation. His youth—he is in his twenty-first year—provides a freshness and a radiance of perception, enabling one to enter and see metaphysical depth. Arkady, the child-man, seeks to learn the truth about his father; he seeks to embolden his discriminating judgment—"for I've come to judge this man." Arkady's search signifies the relationship between childhood and maturity. His search reminds us that the courage of truth and of judgment is intrinsic to the spiritual understanding of one's self in relation to others and, finally, to the mystery and values of personality.

To pursue his search and to attain his goal, Arkady must overcome great barriers that the world always places in the way of spiritual quest. In its immediate conditions his quest takes place within the temporal process, and as such it is characterized by tragic ramifications. But Arkady does not stop his search on this side of existence. His search is not only for his natural but also for his supernatural father, Makar. It has ultimate meaning, as is underlined in the concluding chapter when Arkady submits the manuscript of his autobiography for criticism to his former tutor in Moscow, Nikolay

Semyonovitch, who eventually replies in a long letter. A number of extracts are quoted, but perhaps the most important is the paragraph with which the novel ends. Clearly the final-and-absolute meaning of Dostoevsky's spiritual art requires and encompasses the relative-historical lessons of *A Raw Youth*:

> Then such autobiographies as yours—so long as they are sincere—will be of use and provide material in spite of their chaotic and fortuitous character ... they will preserve at any rate some faithful traits by which one may guess what may have lain hidden in the heart of some raw youth of that troubled time—a knowledge not altogether valueless since from raw youths are made up the generations. (III, xiii, 3)

What we see in Arkady is his eventual transcendence over the dialectical tyranny of ideas. Slowly but steadfastly ideology gives way to piety as Arkady's personality comes into more intimate contact with spiritual love, particularly in his relations with Sofia and Makar. "But then shall I know even as also I am known," Saint Paul says (I Corinthians 13:12). The power of beauty and of love, two of Dostoevsky's dominant themes, opens new doors for Arkady and initiates in him the longing for the spirit of grace. Here Simone Weil's definitions of beauty and of love capture the essence of the power that gradually infuses and cleanses Arkady's personality: "Belief in the existence of other human beings as such is love." "The beautiful is the experimental proof that the incarnation is possible."[18] Once again Dostoevsky makes us aware that spiritual experience, if given the opportunity, can be redeeming. In this respect, the seraphic characterization of Arkady looks back to Prince Myshkin and ahead to Alyosha Karamazov. That is, Arkady attains, in spite of great obstacles, the religious perception of life, one that points beyond to a mysterious ground of existence. What some critics take to be incoherence in *A Raw Youth* is, in reality, mystery.[19] "The finiteness of human life, contrasted with the limitless quality of the human spirit, presents us with a profound mystery. We are an enigma to ourselves."[20] Reinhold Niebuhr's words are especially pertinent to Dostoevsky's aims. As a novel about personality, *A Raw Youth* dramatizes this mystery. Personality is the celebration of mystery.

From the beginning Arkady finds himself in a situation of

mystery. He has not seen his father since he was ten. Then Versilov suddenly summons him to Saint Petersburg to rejoin his family, from which he has been long separated: "I was like an outcast, and, almost from my birth, had been with strangers." The summons, like the relationship, is fateful: "From my childhood upward, my dreams were all coloured by him; all hovered about him as the final goal. I don't know whether I hated him or loved him; but his figure dominated the future and all my schemes of life. And this happened of itself. It grew up with me" (I, i, 7). Arkady comes out of a fearful isolation and proceeds to encounter his destiny; the nascent personality emerges from a dream world. The son is to be re-united with a long-lost father!

The atmosphere of Arkady's return is charged with urgency. The real world in which personality must struggle to mould and also to protect its innerness is filled with dangers, traps, seductions, perplexities, paradoxes. It is a world of *angst*. When Arkady rejoins his "accidental family," he comes filled with hurt and humiliation. He is aware of the illegitimacy of his birth: of how his mother, Sofia Andreyevna, a serf-girl of eighteen, had married Makar Ivanovitch Dolgoruky, a man of fifty, also a house-serf, who worked on Versilov's estate in the province of Tula; how something "had *just happened*" between Versilov, at the time a young widower, and Sofia only six months after her marriage to Makar; how she, "once so pure and . . . of a different species, of an utterly different world," "carried away by some violent emotion," became Versilov's life-long mistress and the mother of his son, Arkady. The memory, too, of his experiences at Touchard's boarding school in Moscow still rankles, for here he was constantly, abusively, reminded that he was "of low origin and no better than a lackey." Under these conditions of sin and guilt, he retreats into a private world of theories and ideas, so as "to be left alone" and, through "obstinacy" and "perseverance," "to become a Rothschild." The whole object of his "idea" is isolation and power, or, to be more precise, what Arkady expresses in his own words: "I only want what is obtained by power, and cannot be obtained without it; that is, the calm and solitary consciousness of strength! That is the fullest definition of liberty for which the whole world is struggling!" (I, v, 3).

Arkady is reacting to evil in the wholeness of his personality. This is Dostoevsky's focus. The imaging constituents of active evil are sin and disorder, which Arkady must confront throughout. His situation is often intolerable, but Arkady never surrenders to the negation that drives other characters in Dostoevsky's novels to madness and suicide. "We are perplexed, but not in despair," Saint Paul writes (II Corinthians 4:8). Arkady's relentless search for his father is not only a search for moral certitude in a time of incertitude but also a search for love, which outweighs all else. This search saves Arkady from his ideas and from the devastations of despair; its germinal presence is transcendent and redeeming.

A Raw Youth is Dostoevsky's most overtly didactic novel, for in the son's search for his father, the novelist plants a significance for all fathers and sons. In this respect it prepares the ground for The Brothers Karamazov. Arkady clears the way for Alyosha; the meaning of love is their common denominator. Versilov's confusion of values marks the beginning of the breakdown of the fatherhood that the old Karamazov personifies. Arkady struggles to affirm the meaning of filial reverence, and his struggle is spiritually heroic. Nowhere else in Dostoevsky's novels is this particular meaning more dramatically re-created than in the incantatory scene depicting Versilov's visit to Arkady, who now lives apart from his family in a "tiny cupboard of a room."

The visit occurs during a period of "shame and disgrace" in Arkady's life. The new freedom and his bursting passions are pushing him more deeply into "the whirl of the world" now that he has been reunited with his family. His personality is in pursuit of self-knowledge. But the meeting does not reveal much of the "secret" of Versilov's life. "This was not at all what I wanted. I was expecting something different, something important, though I quite understood that this was how it must be" (II, i, 2). It is another, a deeper secret that is discovered. When their meeting is concluded, Arkady, candle in hand to light the way, leads his father down the stairs. The affection that he shows for his father, the underlying sense of paternal need and direction that he seems now, more than ever, to be asking of Versilov, the love that connects them, despite the son's desperate gropings and the father's own moral confusion: these aspects of the relationship between Arkady and Versilov attain symbolic realization in the scene. The element of hope that is inherent in this novel is illuminated by the indwelling reverence of this epiphanal scene, pregnant with the image of good. The possibility of the personality's inner change is equally present. Divine Presence informs the very meaning of the encounter; Arkady wants that which Martin Buber describes as the "great relation [that] exists only between real persons" and that "throws a bridge from self-being to self-being across the abyss of dread."[21]

> "These staircases . . ." Versilov mumbled, dwelling on the syllables evidently in order to say something, and evidently afraid I might say something. "I'm no longer used to such stairs, and you're on the third storey, but now I can find the way. . . . Don't trouble, my dear, you'll catch cold, too."
>
> But I did not leave him. We were going down the second flight. . . .
>
> "I've been expecting you for the last three days," broke from me suddenly, as it were of itself; I was breathless.
>
> "Thank you, my dear."
>
> "I knew you'd be sure to come."
>
> "And I knew that you knew I should be sure to come. Thank you, my dear."
>
> He was silent. We had reached the outer door, and I still followed him. He opened the door; the wind rushing in blew out my candle. Then I clutched his hand. It was pitch dark. He started but said nothing. I stooped over his hand and kissed it greedily several times, many times.
>
> "My darling boy, why do you love me so much?" he said, but in quite a different voice. His voice quivered, there was a ring of something quite new in it as though it were not he who spoke.
>
> I tried to answer, but couldn't, and ran upstairs. He stood waiting where he was, and it was only when I was back in the flat that I heard the front door open and shut with a slam. I slipped by the landlord, who turned up again, and went into my room, fastened the latch, and without lighting the candle threw myself on my bed, buried my face in the pillow and cried and cried. It was the first time I had cried since I was at Touchard's. My sobs were so violent, and I was so happy . . . but why describe it? (II, i, 2)

The need for roots and the need for harmony embody Arkady's most fervent needs. They define the way in which he travels in search of values. The absence of these values, which is tied to the long absence of his father, remains for Arkady, and for the other raw youths in the novel, a nagging problem. The characterization of Lambert, Arkady's schoolfellow who

becomes an "expert blackmailer," contains another of Dostoevsky's warnings of what happens in a society in which
people have lost the way on which they can meet with God.
Arkady's "notes" on Lambert are revealing:

> We were going out into the country to shoot, and on the way we
> met a bird-catcher with cages of birds. Lambert bought a canary
> from him. In a wood he let the canary go, as it couldn't fly far after
> being in the cage, and began shooting at it, but did not hit it. . . .
> He was almost choking with excitement. . . . He tied the canary by
> a thread to a branch, and an inch away fired off both barrels, and
> the bird was blown into a hundred feathers. Then we returned,
> drove to an hotel, took a room, and began eating, and drinking
> champagne; a lady came in. . . . Afterwards, when we had begun
> drinking, he began taunting and abusing her; she was sitting
> with nothing on, he took away her clothes and when she began
> scolding and asking for her clothes to dress again, he began with
> all his might beating her with the riding-whip on her bare
> shoulders. I got up, seized him by the hair, and so neatly that I
> threw him on the ground at once. He snatched up a fork and stuck
> it in my leg. (I, ii, 3)

> . . . Lambert told me at sixteen that when he came into his fortune
> it would be his greatest satisfaction to feed on meat and bread
> while the children of the poor were dying of hunger; and when
> they had no fuel for their fires he would buy up a whole wood-
> stack, build it up in a field and set fire to it there, and not give any
> of it to the poor. (I, iii, 5)

> . . . Lambert was young, insolent, and filled with impatient greed
> for gain; he knew little of human nature, and confidently as-
> sumed that all were scoundrels. (III, iv, 1)

Lambert portends the last consequence of a lost father and
an absent God. In him we have Dostoevsky's metastatic representative of the rejection of all forms of moral and spiritual life.
He lacks any standard of order that includes the "consciousness of what hinders life and what facilitates it."[22] He can even
be called Versilov's other son—and Arkady's potential Cain.
The young nihilists of the 1870's who make up the Dergatchev
circle, with whom Arkady gets into a discussion, are much less
brutish than Lambert. But they, too, are impervious to standards of order. Filled with vague and confused ideas about
equality and brotherhood—"One must live in harmony with
the laws of nature and truth," Mme. Dergatchev observes at

one point—these young people exemplify moral and social decay. All the young people in the novel are victims of this decay and vary only in the degree of their disorientation. All of them can be described as sons and daughters of Versilov, who has relinquished all moral and social standards. These young people epitomize not only a fatherless generation but also the disoriented personality. Their capitulation to Satan (whose name in Hebrew means "hinderer") is as pathetic as it is catastrophic.

Will Arkady go the way of his contemporaries? It is this ever-present danger that preoccupies Dostoevsky. Dissolution, disorientation, debasement everywhere impede Arkady's search for values (even as they are portents of the explosion that is to come to Russia in 1917). So widespread and oppressive is the breakdown that everyone and everything in the novel are in a state of disequilibrium. A prophetic disquiet heightens the feeling of apprehension that culminates in the electrifying events "of those three momentous days with which my story concludes," as Arkady puts it. Disappointments lead to disasters, passions become chaos, dreams turn into nightmares. Arkady fights for his soul in the midst of a world in which there is general paralysis of soul. He battles to save the meaning of personality, but he needs help—he needs Versilov, he needs his father: ". . . but what I wanted most of all was *him*. With him I could have decided everything—I felt that; we should have understood each other in two words! I should have gripped his hands, pressed them; I should have found burning words in my heart—this was the dream that haunted me. . . . But where was he? Where was he?" (III, ix, 3)

Arkady's question, in a time of sickness, is as frantic as is the structure of the novel. The question resounds from beginning to end, for it is a prophetic and ultimate question. Versilov's failure to answer discloses the much greater failure of society in the death of God, in the death of personality. In failing to answer his son, Versilov capitulates to the evil that afflicts all generations. "If a man lets it have the mastery," Buber reminds us, "the continually growing world of *It* overruns him and robs him of the reality of his own *I*, till the incubus over him and the ghost within him whisper to one another the confession of their nonsalvation."[23]

Continuously Arkady's rage for order is at war with the

rage of time: with those intrusive forces that defy all laws of constraint, when, as he declares, "things have never been worse than they are now. Nothing is clear in our society. You deny God, you see, deny heroism" (I, iii, 5). Arkady seeks for a spiritual hero, for a spiritual standard, to purge him of those theories that are equally destructive and self-destructive. Thus he reveals a consciousness of personality, as well as of its implicit reconstruction. By the conclusion of the novel Arkady gains a larger insight. He grows within the process of what Kierkegaard speaks of as "existence-spheres," or "stages on life's way." Arkady's personality, to follow through with Kierkegaard's triad, experiences, interrelatedly, aesthetic existence that is essentially enjoyment, ethical existence that is essentially struggle and victory, and religious existence that is essentially suffering.[24]

The upshot of this synthesizing process is the personality's achievement of infinite significance, its contravention of what Arkady terms "the soul of the spider." Purgation is the internal and concrete condition of this experience, which is a determining factor in the personality's spiritual eternalization; it is, hence, a precedent condition to transfiguration. There is a special appropriateness in the contention that before man can be rooted in Christ, he must first be unrooted and uprooted. Personality is to be viewed, then, in its ultimate relationship with God. Here, once more, Dostoevsky renders in his art what Kierkegaard diagnostically posits in his *Thoughts on Crucial Situations in Human Life:* "No man can see God without becoming a sinner."[25]

Versilov occupies a place between Arkady and Makar. Without him Arkady would be meaningless and his personality barren. "This father, who teaches and learns, and this son, who gives and receives are one," writes one critic.[26] The major characters attain their significance either in direct or in indirect relation to Versilov. He personifies that enigma of which Niebuhr speaks, and contains the condition of man. Promise and disappointment remain the polar opposites of his character; the great promise and the great refusal underline his fatefulness. Those ultimate questions that Arkady asks get no definitive answers from Versilov. He is and he is not, he knows and he does not know, he believes and he does not believe, he can and he cannot. These are only a few of the antitheses of

Versilov's personality that are at the heart of Dostoevsky's most probable first reference to him in the notebooks: "A Christian Hamlet."[27]

Versilov's problem vividly silhouettes Arkady's problem. High-born, he has been banished from society because of his scandalous behavior while abroad; once wealthy and powerful, he now lives in poverty, having squandered three fortunes; noble and compassionate, he is the victim of dark forces. "There's no crushing me, no destroying me, no surprising me," he exclaims to Arkady.

> "I've as many lives as a cat. I can with perfect convenience experience two opposite feelings at one and the same time, and not, of course, through my own will. I know, nevertheless, that it's dishonourable just because it's so sensible. I've lived almost to fifty, and to this day I don't know whether it's a good thing I've gone on living or not. I like life, but that follows as a matter of course. But for a man like me to love life is contemptible." (II, i, 3)

In conversations Arkady repeatedly besieges him with questions relating to life-issues: "What's to be done?" "Tell me how, at the present moment, I can be most of use." Versilov's replies are inevitably colored by equivocations, cynicism, paradox, apathy, doubt, irony, indecision. Values and standards have, for him, no substance, no informing role. He fails to communicate any synthesizing principles; in him antitheses and antinomies become obstacles to any attempt to grasp, in the highest spiritual sense, the wholeness of life. He is floundering, and there is something sad about it. He lacks, in the end, spiritual courage to leap above himself. His whole attitude, though it is not the outgrowth of wickedness, issues from abandonment to the forces of chaos. His evil, as it manifests itself, is a lack of direction that belongs to the profane. Versilov's attitude, as Arkady intuits it, has no centrality, no spiritual hallowedness. His inner division is overpowering, opposed to order. Versilov is a father who lacks the essence of fatherhood:

> On one occasion, however, he spoke out, but so strangely that he surprised me more than ever, especially after the stories of Catholicism and penitential chains that I had heard about him.
> "Dear boy," he said one day, not in my room, but in the street, when I was seeing him home after a long conversation, "to love people as they are is impossible. And yet we must. And therefore

do them good, overcoming your feelings, holding your nose and shutting your eyes (the latter's essential). Endure evil from them as far as may be without anger, 'mindful that you too are a man.' Of course you'll be disposed to be severe with them if it has been vouchsafed to you to be ever so little more intelligent than the average. Men are naturally base and like to love from fear. Don't give in to such love, and never cease to despise it. Somewhere in the Koran Allah bids the prophet look upon the 'froward' as upon mice, do them good, and pass them by—a little haughty, but right. Know how to despise them even when they are good, for most often it is in that they are base. Oh, my dear, it's judging by myself I say that. Anyone who's not quite stupid can't live without despising himself, whether he's honest or dishonest—it makes no difference. To love one's neighbour and not despise him—is impossible. I believe that man has been created physically incapable of loving his neighbour. There has been some mistake in language here from the very first, and 'love for humanity' must be understood as love for that humanity which you have yourself created in your soul (in other words, you have created yourself and your love is for yourself)—and which, therefore, never will be in reality."

"Never will be?"

"My dear boy, I agree that if this were true, it would be stupid, but that's not my fault, and I was not consulted at the creation. I reserve the right to have my own opinion about it."

"How is it they call you a Christian, then?" I cried. "A monk in chains, a preacher? I don't understand it!" (II, i, 4)

Dostoevsky hardly sanctions Versilov's kind of evil, though he shows a marked sympathy for his falling soul. The human elements are pitilessly mixed in him. After his seduction of Sofia ("one of those 'defenceless' people whom one does not fall in love with . . . but whom one suddenly pities for their gentleness"), Versilov sobs on the shoulder of Makar and pays him a sum of money for her. He readily recognizes her virtues, "meekness, submissiveness, self-abasement, and at the same time firmness, strength, real strength." "Take note," he tells Arkady, "that she's the best of all the women I've met" (I, vii, 2). If she were to die, he claims, he would kill himself to atone for the wrong he did her. In his feelings toward Makar he admits to having deep shame. At times, too, he is capable of "good works" and of "noble actions" that, concurrently, mean sacrifices on his part, whether of personal reputation or of pecuniary advantage. His love for Arkady comes out, on occasion, instinctively and spontaneously:

> We came out on the canal bank and said good-bye.
> "Will you never give me a real warm kiss, as a child kisses its father?" he said, with a strange quiver in his voice. I kissed him fervently.
> "Dear boy . . . may you be always as pure in heart as you are now."
> I had never kissed him before in my life, I never could have conceived that he would like me to. (II, v, 3)

Tenderness, warmth of heart, magnanimity, and honesty are qualities that Versilov does not fail to affirm.

Above all, the peculiar circumstances of his relationship to Sofia excite and penetrate his conscience, "that court within the soul which concerns itself with the distinction between the right and the wrong in that which has been done and is to be done," as Buber puts it.[28]

> "It was only in Germany that I understood that I loved her. It began with her hollow cheeks, of which I could never think, and sometimes not even see, without a pain in my heart, real physical pain. There are memories that hurt, my dear, that cause actual pain. Almost everyone has some such memories, only people forget them, but it does happen that they suddenly recall them, or perhaps only some feature of them, and then they cannot shake them off. I began to recall a thousand details of my life with Sofia. In the end they recalled themselves, and came crowding on my mind, and almost tortured me while I was waiting for her coming. What distressed me most of all was the memory of her everlasting submissiveness to me, and the way she continually thought herself inferior to me, in every respect, even—imagine it—physically; she was ashamed and flushed crimson when I looked at her hands and fingers, which were by no means aristocratic, and not her fingers only—she was ashamed of everything in herself, in spite of my loving her beauty. She was always shrinkingly modest with me, but what was wrong was that in it there was always a sort of fear, in short she thought herself something insignificant beside me, something almost unseemly in fact. I used really sometimes to think at first that she still looked upon me as her master, and was afraid of me, but it was not that at all. Yet, I assure you, no one was more capable of understanding my failings, and I have never met a woman with so much insight and delicacy of heart." (III, viii, 1)

At the end Versilov has gained the "gift of tears." There is an element of tragic expiation, an epiphanal sense of the opposition of grace and evil. The picture of Versilov and Sofia is one of alleviating wholeness, when the "evil urge" and the "good urge" are united:

> But I know that even now mother often sits beside him, and in a low voice, with a gentle smile, begins to talk to him of the most abstract subjects: now she has somehow grown *daring* with him, but how this has come to pass I don't know. She sits beside him and speaks to him usually in a whisper. He listens with a smile, strokes her hair, kisses her hand, and there is the light of perfect happiness in his face. He sometimes has attacks that are almost like hysterics. Then he takes her photograph, the one he kissed that evening, gazes at it with tears, kisses it, recalls the past, gathers us all round him, but at such moments he says little. . . .
> (III, xiii, 1)

In some resemblances, Versilov belongs to the genus of Stavrogin. But, with a far more compassionate understanding of their basic difference, Dostoevsky is careful to show that Versilov is not a fallen man but a man always in the process of falling. The difference is redeeming, though by no means does Dostoevsky sanction Versilov's conduct. Within the confines of this difference Dostoevsky explores Arkady's developing consciousness, his personality. Versilov's life, as Arkady comes to see, provides parabolic answers to the questions that the son is asking. The answers, even when not supplied directly, are implicit in Versilov's plight and call for dramatic exploitation, as well as for the dramatization of insight. Versilov, insofar as he relates to Arkady's personality, presents a creative peril, a metaphysical element that sharply differentiates him from Stavrogin's death-in-life. Through Versilov, Arkady is tangled in the web of good and evil. The complexity of *A Raw Youth* is, in this connection, typically and necessarily enigmatic. Versilov is another of those crucibles of evil and suffering which Dostoevsky sees as inevitable in the quest for meaning and out of which issue the revelation that Shakespeare recognizes in "There is some soul of goodness in things evil/ Would men observingly distil it out."[29] It is in the full potentiality of this refining process that Versilov is Arkady's revelational experience of personality. In and through Versilov, expiation and resurrection attain a proximate grace, which, in the last sequence, becomes a note of hope. Versilov's hell-torments and soul-state do not, like Stavrogin's, come to a moral impasse when his successors, in the grip of Satan, personify an irrevocable negation.

Disorder-symbols saturate Versilov's pathways, nowhere more apparent than in the scene involving the plain antique ikon bequeathed to him by Makar. The scene occurs in the late afternoon on the day of Makar's funeral, with the members of his family present. Versilov, who had not gone to the funeral, now arrives and begins a strange, almost incoherent speech in which he claims that he is split in two mentally. In his speech and gestures he communicates disorder, culminating in his snatching the ikon: " . . . and with a ferocious swing [he] smashed it with all his might against the corner of the tiled stove. The ikon was broken into two pieces" (III, x, 2). His "second self" is ascendant here, or as Versilov explains:

> "It's just as though one's second self were standing beside one; one is sensible and rational oneself, but the other self is impelled to do something perfectly senseless, and sometimes very funny; and suddenly you notice that you are longing to do that amusing thing, goodness knows why; that is you want to, as it were, against your will; though you fight against it with all your might, you want to." (III, x, 2)

Versilov's act is one of desecration; it is typical of acts throughout the novel. Arkady's cry, "What I want to know is what kind of man *he* is . . . ," is given an answer here. Versilov has inverted value for the "raw youth." Reverence and irreverence, grace and evil, are forever at war in Versilov; he wrestles with his devils.

Disorder-thoughts plague him during his early solitary wanderings, which periodically separate him from his family. "I went away meaning to remain in Europe and never to return home, my dear. I emigrated," he says to Arkady. One afternoon, in a tiny hotel room in a German town, he dreams of Claude Lorrain's "Acis and Galatea," which he calls "The Golden Age." It is the setting sun of the first day of European civilization which Versilov sees in his dream. Versilov's recollection of his wandering abroad, "in melancholy and happiness, and . . . in the strictest monastic solitude," impresses Arkady. He sees in his father's love for humanity an honest feeling, of which his vision of felicity is a telling commentary:

> "I dreamed of this picture, but not as a picture, but, as it were, a

reality. I don't know exactly what I did dream though: it was just as in the picture, a corner of the Grecian Archipelago, and time seemed to have gone back three thousand years; blue smiling waves, isles and rocks, a flowery shore, a view like fairyland in the distance, a setting sun that seemed calling to me—there's no putting it into words. It seemed a memory of the cradle of Europe, and that thought seemed to fill my soul, too, with a love as of kinship. Here was the earthly paradise of man: the gods came down from the skies, and were of one kin with men. . . . Oh, here lived a splendid race! they rose up and lay down to sleep happy and innocent; the woods and meadows were filled with their songs and merry voices. Their wealth of untouched strength was spent on simple-hearted joy and love. The sun bathed them in warmth and light, rejoicing in her splendid children. . . . Marvellous dream, lofty error of mankind! The Golden Age is the most unlikely of all the dreams that have been, but for it men have given up their life and all their strength, for the sake of it prophets have died and been slain, without it the peoples will not live and cannot die, and the feeling of all this I lived through, as it were, in that dream; rocks and sea, and the slanting rays of the setting sun—all this I seemed still to see when I woke up and opened my eyes, literally wet with tears. I remembered that I was glad, a sensation of happiness I had never known before thrilled my heart till it ached; it was the love of all humanity." (III, vii, 2)

But inherent in Versilov's vision of a "humanistic utopia" is a profound sorrow. Hope as a memory of the future disappears, for beyond an existential present there is nothing: God is dead here, banished and forgotten. "The great idea of old" has left men; "the great source of strength that till then had nourished them was vanishing like the majestic sun setting in Claude Lorrain's picture." Man's aloneness is the outcome, this "European civilizer" and "philosophical Deist" proclaims.

It is the humanist ideologue who is speaking here of his Idea, of the thought without which he could not have lived, as he confesses. Dostoevsky's insight into the illusion of humanism is piercing and prophetic. Can there be love without God? Relentlessly Dostoevsky repeats one of his agonizing questions. Versilov wants desperately to answer it in the affirmative; he wants to, but ultimately he cannot, and he knows he cannot. His internal division is proof of this inability; the disorder-pattern of his life and thought revolves around this division. His humanist creed, like his vision, is rent by its inadequacy and incertitude, by its own futile exaggeration of the human prospect. It is a "fantasy," he admits, and the humanist dilemma is immediately, and for all time, crystallized in his admission. For Arkady the parabolic lessons of Versilov's vision are unalterable, and unforgettable, as Nikolay Semyonovitch recognizes in this comment in his long letter: "He [Versilov] is a nobleman of ancient lineage, and at the same time a Parisian communard. He is a true poet and loves Russia, . . . yet almost ready to die for something indefinite, to which he cannot give a name, but in which he fervently believes . . . " (III, xiii, 3). At the very heart of Versilov's vision of felicity one finds the spiritual emptiness that no humanist ideologue can ever permanently dispel; Versilov's greatest virtue is an uncorrupted sincerity, the secularist's limitive counterpart of grace:

> "I picture to myself, my boy," he said with a dreamy smile, "that war is at an end and strife has ceased. After curses, pelting with mud, and hisses, has come a lull, and men are left alone, according to their desire. . . . I have never, my dear boy, been able to picture men ungrateful and grown stupid. Men left forlorn would begin to draw together more closely and more lovingly; they would clutch one another's hands, realizing that they were all that was left for one another! The great idea of immortality would have vanished, and they would have to fill its place; and all the wealth of love lavished of old upon Him, who was immortal, would be turned upon the whole of nature, on the world, on men, on every blade of grass. They would inevitably grow to love the earth and life as they gradually became aware of their own transitory and finite nature, and with a special love, not as of old, they would begin to observe and would discover in nature phenomena and secrets which they had not suspected before, for they would look on nature with new eyes, as a lover looking for his beloved. On awakening they would hasten to kiss one another, eager to love, knowing that the days are short, and that is all that is left them. They would work for one another, and each would give up all that he had to all, and by that only would be happy. Every child would know and feel that everyone on earth was for him like a father or mother. 'To-morrow may be my last day,' each one would think, looking at the setting sun; 'but no matter, I shall die, but all they will remain and after them their children,' and that thought that they will remain, always as loving and as anxious over each other, would replace the thought of meeting beyond the tomb. Oh, they would be in haste to love, to stifle the great sorrow in their hearts. They would be proud and brave for

themselves, but would grow timid for one another; everyone would tremble for the life and happiness of each; they would grow tender to one another, and would not be ashamed of it as now, and would be caressing as children. Meeting, they would look at one another with deep and thoughtful eyes, and in their eyes would be love and sorrow. . . ." (III, vii, 3)

The most shattering extent of Versilov's pattern of disorder appears in his passion for Katerina Nikolaevna, the young widow of General Ahmakov, and the daughter of Prince Nikolay Ivanovitch Sokolsky. The details of this relationship are important only insofar as they shed light on Versilov. He had first met the Ahmakovs while at Ems. By his first wife General Ahmakov had a consumptive daughter, now seventeen years of age, "extremely beautiful, but at the same time very fantastical." Lidya Ahmakov became attached to Versilov and, to the horror of her family, agreed to marry him. However, nothing came of it, for, while in an obviously deranged state, she poisoned herself; shortly afterwards her father, who had led an irregular life and was sickly, also died.

Before these deaths the Ahmakovs had come to dislike and to fear Versilov, particularly the general, whom Versilov, it was said, had, "by hints, inferences, and all sorts of roundabout ways," poisoned with the suspicion that Katerina Nikolaevna was responsive to the young Prince Sergay Petrovich Sokolsky (no relation to the old prince). Versilov had earlier exerted "an extraordinary influence" on Katerina Nikolaevna, but she, too, came to detest him, and it was she who had most fiercely opposed her stepdaughter's marriage. It was conjectured that this opposition came from her own unrequited love of Versilov. In any event, this was what the latter had managed to suggest both to Lidya and to her father. The result was inescapable: "The house, of course, began to be a perfect hell." (Another version was that Versilov had, before his relation with the stepdaughter, made love to Katerina Nikolaevna, who had "met Versilov's declaration with deep resentment and had ridiculed him vindictively.") After the funeral, it should be noted, the young Prince Sokolsky, having returned to Ems from Paris, gave Versilov— "that petticoat prophet"—a slap in the face in a public garden, but the latter did not reply with a challenge. (Indeed, Lidya Ahmakov, before she met Versilov, had been fascinated by the young prince, by whom, after a brief liaison, she had had a baby girl. Out of either friendship or pity, Versilov offered to marry her and later looked after her child.) Finally, Katerina Nikolaevna was also convinced that Versilov possessed a letter that she had written in which she inquired of the now deceased lawyer Andronikov whether it would be possible to put her ailing and feeble father under guardianship or to declare him incompetent during a period in his life when he was wasting his money. Versilov's possession of this compromising letter, she felt, held her fate and could wipe out whatever legacy she would receive from the old prince if he learned of it.

This document, as it happens, is now sewn up in Arkady's coat pocket. Through his possession of the letter Arkady found a great source of power, especially in the earlier stage of his "idea," that he could wield not only over his father but also over Katerina Nikolaevna. ("Yes, the secret consciousness of power is more insupportably delightful than open domination.") As it happens—the various surface coincidences become acute perplexities for most critics—Arkady also falls in love with Katerina Nikolaevna, one of Dostoevsky's "virginal aristocrats,"[30] of no significant beauty, with a face that, as Arkady observes, "is quite countrified," "bashful and chaste." The complications that develop from such a medley of relations are many (and sometimes difficult to follow). But Dostoevsky's paramount purpose, his *préoccupation morale,* is always clear: Disorder multiplies when all central authority, traditional wisdom, and standards are shoved aside.

The novel's structural complications, indeed perplexities, are analogues of this breakdown, as well as of the sporadic, obscure, and impure humanism that Versilov epitomizes. His emotional paroxysms, as the quintessence of the disorder of his self-directing personality, come out at their shrillest in his relations with Katerina Nikolaevna. For Versilov, consequently, everything goes out of control, the loss of which his vicious letter to Katerina Nikolaevna, with special reference to Arkady and to the document she learns he now has, is symptomatic:

> Depraved as you are in your nature and your arts, I should have yet expected you to restrain your passions and not to try your wiles on children. But you are not even ashamed to do that. I beg to inform you that the letter you know of was certainly not burnt

in a candle and never was in Kraft's possession, so you won't score anything there. So don't seduce a boy for nothing. Spare him, he is hardly grown up, almost a child, undeveloped mentally and physically—what use can you have for him? (II, viii, 3)

Arkady's reactions to this letter, which he is given to read by that "old-maidish *babouchka*," Tatyana Pavlovna,[31] are revealing. Earlier, and with complete naïveté, he had told his father of the events leading to his first meeting with Katerina: "I told him honestly that I was ready to kiss the spot on the floor where her foot had rested." But he had not told his father the truth about the letter, which he had decided to destroy. Versilov's letter to Katerina Nikolaevna has cumulative effects on Arkady. He becomes more and more aware of the differences between good and evil, of the nuances of disorder, of that distilling process that T. S. Eliot speaks of when he writes that "unless there is moral resistance and conflict there is no meaning." Arkady's instinctively moral reactions to Versilov's immoral charges are evident. What we have here is a seminal recognition of sin:

I turned white as I read, then suddenly I flushed crimson and my lips quivered with indignation.

"He writes that about me! About what I told him the day before yesterday!" I cried in a fury.

"So you did tell him!" cried Tatyana Pavlovna, snatching the letter from me.

"But ... I didn't say that, I did not say that at all! Good God, what can she think of me now! But it's madness, you know. He's mad ... I saw him yesterday. When was the letter sent?"

"It was sent yesterday, early in the day; it reached her in the evening, and this morning she gave it me herself."

"But I saw him yesterday myself, he's mad! Versilov was incapable of writing that, it was written by a madman. Who could write like that to a woman?"

"That's just what such madmen do write in a fury when they are blind and deaf from jealousy and spite, and their blood is turned to venom. ... You did not know what he is like! ... What possessed you to tell him! What induced you to tease him! Did you want to boast?"

"But what hatred! What hatred!" I cried, clapping my hand on my head. "And what for, what for? Of a woman! What has she done to him? What can there have been between them that he can write a letter like that?"

"Ha—atred!" Tatyana Pavlovna mimicked me with furious sarcasm. (II, viii, 3)

Not long after this event Arkady becomes seriously ill. By chance, he is found by Lambert, who learns much from Arkady's ravings: " . . . the expert blackmailer had anyway dropped on a trustworthy scent." In a fateful action Lambert manages to steal the letter from an unconscious Arkady and to replace it with a piece of notepaper of the same size. Earlier Arkady had resolved to return the letter to Katerina Nikolaevna, whom, like his father, he both hates and loves. (He dreams of her at one point: "I clutched her hands; the touch of her hands sent an agonizing thrill through me, and I put my lips to her insolent crimson lips, that invited me, quivering with laughter.") Versilov's cunning and bold daughter of his legal marriage, Anna Andreyevna, also has designs on Arkady's letter, inasmuch as she feels that it would quickly insure her pending marriage to the old prince.

The plot is all too thick with complications and coincidences; nonetheless these serve Dostoevsky's purpose of heightening the pattern of disorder that culminates in Versilov's actions. Disorder is not only the absence of standards of behavior or the dispersion of all meaning and authority. It represents the incredible, the contradictory, the scandalous, the discordant, the bizarre symptoms of the fragmentation of Value. Versilov's ambivalent relation to Katerina Nikolaevna essentializes disorder of passion, for Dostoevsky once again, as always, the most brutalizing, all-embracing symbol. In this relationship the theoretical aspects of disorder that appear throughout *A Raw Youth* achieve a concrete sensualization.

Whenever Versilov and Katerina Nikolaevna meet, disorder appears as "a vision of unhappiness and pain," to apply Berdyaev's phraseology. At the approaching climax of the novel, the confrontation between them dramatizes the intensity of passion in disaggregation. (Arkady chances to overhear their entire conversation.) They have not seen each other for two years, and this meeting adds a tone of finality to their relationship. A moment of tension now emerges as Versilov asks the painful question: "Tell me the truth for once, and answer me one question. . . . Did you ever love me, or was I . . . mistaken?" The question is contrapuntal when one recalls

Arkady's desperate questioning of his father. It is equally desperate. Katerina Ivanovna replies that she did love him once, but only for a short time. Her replies are invariably transparent in their honesty: " . . . I look on you as a man of great intellect. . . . I always felt there was something ridiculous about you."

Versilov's anguish, in the face of these remarks, is always in evidence. Like Arkady he yearns to assuage the desperation of his disordered state of mind and soul; his words are symbolic of disorder: "I picture you in my mind whenever I'm alone. I do nothing but talk to you. I go into some squalid, dirty hole, and as a contrast you appear to me at once. But you always laugh at me as you do now. . . ." And to her protestation—"I came here to tell you that I almost love you"—he responds: "All I know is that in your presence I am done for, in your absence, too. It's just the same whether you are there or not, wherever you may be you are always before me. I know, too, that I can hate you intensely, more than I can love you." Katerina meets his anguish with gentleness: "Let us part as friends, and you will be for me the most earnest and dearest thought in my whole life." The scene is filled with pathos; the eavesdropping Arkady finds the depths of spiritual degradation insufferable to watch, as Versilov begs of her for one charity more: " . . . don't love me, don't live with me, let us never meet; . . . *only don't marry anyone!"* (III, x, 4)

This confrontation, with its stress and excitement, is a prelude to the final storm scene. It is a microcosm of the novel. The pain of separation; the frenzy of disappointed love; the frantic questions and trembling answers; revenge, venom, jealousy, threats, deceptions, cynicism, hatred: evil as misdirection now gallops on towards catastrophe. "There was no time to reflect," Arkady recalls. Inevitably disorder ensues. Versilov, *"cet homme noir,"* and Lambert join forces, as confusion and villainy merge, to trap and destroy *"Mme. la générale."* The blackmailer knows how to use the power of the document to exploit Katerina Nikolaevna, even as Arkady now discovers, to his horror, that Lambert has stolen the letter.

The final scene, once again with a spying Arkady present, occurs in Tatyana Pavlovna's flat. Versilov and Lambert arrive. Lambert, with letter in hand, enters the room while Versilov waits outside. Standing before Katerina Nikolaevna, who is sitting on the sofa, Lambert shouts at her. He wants thirty thousand roubles for a letter that he claims is worth one hundred thousand. His threats are interlaced with insults: "Don't be obstinate, madam, be thankful that I'm not asking much, any other man would ask for something else besides . . . you know what . . . which many a pretty woman would not refuse in such trying circumstances, that's what I mean. . .; ha-ha-ha! *Vous êtes belle, vous!*" (III, xii, 5). Impetuously, indignantly, Katerina Nikolaevna rises and spits in his face. Furious, he pulls out a revolver, "clutching her by the shoulder, and showing her the revolver—simply, of course, to frighten her." Versilov and Arkady run in at the same instant, with Versilov snatching the revolver from Lambert and hitting him on the head with it. Arkady's recollection of the actions following attests to Versilov's loss of control and sums up his father's tense history:

> She saw Versilov, turned suddenly as white as a sheet, gazed at him for some moments immovable with indescribable horror, and fell into a swoon. He rushed to her. . . . He caught her as she fell unconscious, and with amazing ease lifted her up in his hands, as though she were a feather, and began aimlessly carrying her about the room like a baby. It was a tiny room, but he paced to and fro from corner to corner, evidently with no idea why he was doing so. In one instant he had lost his reason. He kept gazing at her, at her face. . . . He went up and laid her down on it [the bed], stood over her, and gazed at her face. . . . He would have shot her and then himself, but since we would not let him get at her, he pressed the revolver against his heart; I succeeded, however, in pushing his arm upwards, and the bullet struck him in the shoulder. At that instant Tatyana Pavlovna burst into the room shrieking; but he was already lying senseless on the carpet beside Lambert. (III, xii, 5)

The scene is one of utter disarray. Versilov, powerless in an overwhelming whirl, is a weak, indecisive, travailing, confused man, and hence a natural victim of disorder. A purgative element seems to color the entire happening, and we see the resultants of human imperfection. The informing note here, as throughout, is one of compassion, of suffering together, which for Dostoevsky is "the chief law of human existence." Thus, a certain reticence, or withholding, of judgment is in attendance; good and evil, no less than judgment and mercy, constitute the opposing but fluctuating forces of tension and contention. Murder has been thwarted. (This is Dostoevsky's only novel in which murder is absent.) Extremes, as tragical things, are mitigated. The novel's metaphysics, we are reminded, is continually purgatorial. As one who witnesses his father's defeat, Arkady gains insight, as his father speaks to him symbolically, parabolically. He penetrates the depths, so to speak. The action, really the action that cannot bring itself to be, is allayed by a meditational note hesitantly intermixing judgment and mercy. Father and son continue to learn from each other; their relationship is both a mutual development and a mutual self-recognition, which evolve with difficulty and pain. But nothing is conclusively simple and direct, as Versilov illustrates.

# III

At the end Versilov lies in purged quietude. He has nothing more to give to his son. But Arkady is not father-forsaken. He carries with him the lasting memory of his "other father," the pilgrim Makar. This memory, containing the hope of calm after storm, connects past and future. Essentially Makar is an hagiographic figure, but he is always something more: the embodiment of supernal fatherhood. Unexpectedly seeing Makar for the first time, Arkady cannot escape contemplating some special power, or light. His is a mystic's impression of that combination of "unspeakable power" and "deep humility," for what Arkady experiences is a consciousness of "otherness":

> What I saw there completely astounded me; I had never expected anything of the kind, and I stood in the doorway petrified. There was sitting there a very grey-headed old man, with a big and very white beard. . . . He was, it could be discerned, tall, broadshouldered, and of a hale appearance, in spite of his invalid state, though he was somewhat thin and looked ill. He had a rather long face and thick but not very long hair; he looked about seventy. (III, i, 2)

In him the "raw youth" perceives the possibility of completion; Makar is a means of Arkady's re-education. Catharsis is the essence of this re-education, even as it is the passage to il-lumination and to a full working consciousness. Versilov is self-centered personality, Makar is God-centered. Arkady owes his education to both fathers: to the one he owes his birth, to the other his re-birth.

Makar is the epitome of that Russian wanderer who, as Dostoevsky later says in his famous address on Pushkin, needs the happiness of all men wherein to find his peace.[32] Makar's spirit, in life as in death, radiates throughout the novel. Even when Versilov would prefer to deny such a presence and even when, on occasion, he derides it, he can hardly escape it. Thus, during their travels Versilov and Sofia always receive two letters a year from Makar containing "ceremonious hopes, greetings and blessings." Besides, every three years or so Makar visits Versilov, staying for five days or a week at most with Sofia, who always has her own lodgings apart from Versilov: " . . . Makar Ivanovitch did not loll on the sofa in the drawing-room, but always sat discreetly somewhere in the background." Compassion, not judgment, inheres in his pres-ence. The image of the raging whirlpool subsides in his pres-ence, which embodies the everlasting need for spiritual respite. When Versilov confesses his sin to him, Makar remains silent, silence as a "living stillness" being one of his virtues. Rever-ence is another of his virtues, which he communicates with mysterious power. After their meeting, Arkady is not quite the same, for Makar has helped ignite a change in him as his waking dream shows: "I lay with my face to the wall, and suddenly I saw in the corner the patch of glowing light which I had been looking forward to with such curses, and now I remember my whole soul seemed to be leaping for joy, and a new light seemed penetrating to my heart" (III, 1, 3). The relationship between pilgrim and raw youth here is in a pur-gatorial stage; in *The Brothers Karamazov* it attains complete spiritual and poetic fruition in the relationship between Father Zossima and Alyosha.

Not only moral virtues but also theophanic powers are associated with Makar. When Arkady finds that the pain of disorder is beginning to overcome him, he flees to Makar's room, "as though there were in it a talisman to repel all enticements, a means of salvation, and an anchor to which I could cling." He stands for spiritual order, for wholeness. The recurring shocks of disorder that intersperse *A Raw Youth,* like those goblin-footfalls that E. M. Forster has made famous in the English novel, seem to retreat whenever Makar appears. His words, on those occasions, provide spiritual wisdom. Makar has a profound spiritual beauty. He is a work of spiritual art which can be approached only from a distance; he is the soul of the beautiful.[33] Contact with him is access to a sacrament. Makar is the only hope of salvation from despair's damnation, something that Arkady is doubtlessly aware of: "What attracted one first of all . . . was his extraordinary pureheartedness and his freedom from *amour-propre;* one felt instinctively that he had an almost sinless heart" (III, iii, 2). Makar is not only the limitless illumination of love but also the limitless power of grace.

During his serious illness, to recall, Arkady remains unconscious for nine days. He is given Versilov's room, where he is faithfully nursed by his mother. On the afternoon of the fourth day, after he recovers consciousness, he suddenly hears "in the midst of the profound stillness" some words "pronounced in a half-whisper . . . followed by a deep-drawn sigh." These words come from his mother's room, in which he first sees Makar. The words are the Jesus Prayer, the voice is Makar's: "Lord Jesus Christ, have mercy upon us." Arkady will never forget what he hears and then sees. In Makar he comprehends "the sense of God," the "spirit stretching towards God." For Arkady, the old pilgrim is, as Simone Weil would say, "the mirror of grace"—"the gateway to God."

There is a sacred character to the forms of Arkady's education that keep in check the secular influences. From Makar he learns the meaning of "Blessedness," even as the pilgrim's name indicates. From his mother, Sofia Andreyevna, he learns the meaning of "Divine Wisdom." She is a continuing extension of Dostoevsky's "sophiological" interest, in concert with one of the basic concerns of his spiritual art. Makar and Sophia must be viewed together from beginning to end, for together they project Dostoevsky's idea of spiritual synthesis, which is to be seen in startling contrast to the disorder that inheres in the secular humanism of Versilov. "All her life," writes Dostoevsky of Sofia, "in fear and trembling and reverence, she had honoured her legal husband, the monk, Makar Ivanovitch, who with large-hearted generosity had forgiven her once and for ever" (III, i, 3). Sofia Andreyevna must bear the onus of a profane world, the power of which has victimized her by destroying her innocence. In the face of unremitting suffering she must endure. (Characteristically, she advises her daughter [and Arkady's sister], Liza, who is with child by Prince Sergay: "Bear it.")

Throughout Sofia remains a sacramental symbol of sanctity, the memory of which Arkady cannot forget as he recalls his earliest childhood memory of his mother taking him to a village church: " . . . I remember clearly only at one moment when I was taken to the church there, and you held me up to receive the sacrament and to kiss the chalice; it was in the summer, and a dove flew through the cupola, in at one window and out at another . . . " (I, vi, 3). Later Arkady also recalls how once when she visited him at Touchard's, he felt ashamed of her: "I only looked sideways at her dark-colored old dress, at her rather coarse, almost working-class hands, at her quite coarse shoes, and her terribly thin face; there were already furrows on her forehead . . . " (II, ix, 2). During this visit even the mean Touchard and his wife, who scorn her when she first arrives, are made momentarily helpless by her humility. It is Divine Wisdom as the Mirror of the Being of God that Sofia manifests here, as throughout: "Mother turned towards the church ['St. Nikolay's, the red-colored church opposite Touchard's'], and crossed herself three times; her lips were trembling, the deep bell chimed musically and regularly from the belfry. She turned to me and could not restrain herself, she laid both hands on my head and began crying over it" (II, ix, 2).

The memory of Sofia's power of sanctity is shared by Versilov, who cannot think of "her hollow cheeks . . . without a pain in my heart, real physical pain." It is the pain of purgation that Versilov refers to, for in Sofia one is plunged in "the divine furnace of purifying love."[34] His desire for Katerina Nikolaevna opens him up to the most irrational disorders, which periodically reduce him to nothingness. In contact with Sofia he comprehends and sees the deeper things. He comes closer to an insight that cleanses the self. His encounters with Katerina Nikolaevna, it will be remembered, are mercilessly restrictive and oppressive; he becomes a prisoner of the darkness. Sofia, on the other hand, helps him to escape his prison; helps him to apprehend feeling-states that "earthly man" too often ignores or rejects. His memories of his life with Sofia well up spontaneously; he cannot shut them off, such is their power, which is "torturous" and "distressing," to use Versilov's own words. In Sofia, Versilov perceives spiritual qualities peculiar to Divine Transcendence: littleness, unworthiness, awe, self-abasement. In contact with her Versilov comes into contact with the God he denies. Through her he attains purgation on the edge of redemption.

*A Raw Youth* contains what can be called Dostoevsky's merciful provision. That is to say, the complexity of the novel's concept and the lack of a pronouncement of judgment, so baffling to critics, have an intrinsically biblical context that helps to clarify, if not to strengthen, the light that this novel brings. "The son shall not bear the iniquity of the father," Ezekiel declares, "neither shall the father bear the iniquity of the son: the righteousness of the righteous shall be upon him, and the wickedness of the wicked shall be upon him" (18:20). No less urgently than the great exilic Hebrew priest and prophet, Dostoevsky portrays in this novel the absence of God from life and, more specifically, the resultant disorder when people become, in Ezekiel's words, a "rebellious house." And no less than Ezekiel, Dostoevsky speaks of doom but also of hope: for, even as in the restored land, so too in the restored personality, "God is there." How we make each other's destiny is one of the dramatized lessons of this novel. In his experience and in his recognition of this process, Arkady slowly realizes a spiritual transformation, a remaking of the self: "But that new life, that new way which is opening before me is my 'idea,' the same as before, though in such a different form, that it could hardly be recognised.... My old life has passed away completely, and the new is just beginning" (III, xiii, 2). It is altogether appropriate that *A Raw Youth* has the form of autobiography: confession is preparation for communion. The "new life" that Arkady now seeks is encounter with the regenerative values of spirit that Ezekiel connects with the moral struggle to make "a new heart and a new spirit."

# Chapter Five

# SAINTLINESS
## The Brothers Karamazov

> *Then flew one of the seraphims unto me,*
> *having a live coal in his hand, which he*
> *had taken with the tongs off the altar:*
> *And he laid it upon my mouth, and said,*
> *Lo, this hath touched thy lips; and thine*
> *iniquity is taken away, and thy sin*
> *purged.*
>
> Isaiah 6:6-7

> *For not one sparrow can suffer & the*
> *whole Universe not suffer also*
> *In all its Regions, & its Father & Sav-*
> *iour not pity and weep.*
>
> —William Blake, *Jerusalem*

# I

*The Brothers Karamazov* (1879-1880), Dostoevsky's last novel, shows how affirmation comes out of denial, and, above all, how saintliness overcomes satanism. Maxim Gorky goes so far as to call *The Brothers Karamazov* "a fifth Gospel" in which Dostoevsky's "preoccupation with supra-moral goodness, Christ-like-ness,"[1] attains its greatest intensity, its *paradiso*. In this novel he is doing some extraordinary things as a great visionary artist and prophetic novelist—as a "realist of distances" who sees "near things with their extensions of meaning and thus...[sees] far things close up."[2] That is to say, Dostoevsky undertakes to defy categorically the threats and the arrogance of "rational assertions" in the course of his envisioning and then affirming the ultimate reality of the sacred, the spiritual, the numinous, the theonomous.

Essentially this affirmation is derived from a vision that "is genuinely and radically dialectical," or as one writer would have it: " ... it is by means of the very power of the demonic—of the profane—that an epiphany of the sacred occurs."[3] The passage from an immersion in the profane, "the non-religious mood of everyday experience," to a yielding to and a reconciliation with the ultimate, "the depth of one's experience, the awareness of the holy," in Tillich's phraseology, constitutes the evolving and the major pattern of experience in *The Brothers Karamazov.* For in this novel, which must signify for Dostoevsky as well as for his readers the highest state of spiritual progression, he comes as close as one can to touching the *mysterium tremendum,* and hence to intuiting what is hidden and esoteric, what is beyond conception or understanding, what is nonrational or suprarational: to a growing and profound "consciousness of a 'wholly other,'" or a divine otherness. This experience, "thrillingly vibrant and resonant"[4] while it lasts, must be seen as being a struggle to approach the holy and to glimpse the nature and modes of its manifestations, its numina. On the outcome of this encounter depends the ultimate, the eschatological, experience which Dostoevsky views as crystallizing in the miracle of redemption.

"Miracle is the dearest child of Faith," declares Schiller. In his notebooks relating to *The Brothers Karamazov* Dostoevsky writes that "much is inexplicable in this world without miracles."[5] (It was with good reason that Thomas Mann coupled Dostoevsky and Schiller as "children of spirit," as "saintlike.") He renders precisely the miraculous in the person of Father Zossima. And it is through the old monk that he strives to achieve a dual interacting process belonging to the highest function of a religious poetry that breaks for us the shackles of habit. Artistically, this break-through is communicated as an epiphany of the sacred. Religiously, or spiritually, it is transposed into the experience of the holy, which in the end, according to Otto, must be "recognized as that which commands our respect, as that whose real value is to be acknowledged *inwardly.*"[6] Father Zossima, embodying both the experiential and the epiphanous facets of an artistic process that the German poet Richard Dehmel identified with "embrac[ing] the world in love and lift[ing] it up to God," contains Dostoevsky's consummate view of the whole of "human existence as a tension between earthly suffering and a striving for a lofty ideal."[7]

Father Zossima dramatizes Dostoevsky's continual efforts to make the Word become flesh. In him we recognize the furthest advancement of Dostoevsky's concept of the sacred and the mysterious as ever-present numinal energies in the universe. "I am a frightful hunter after mysteries,"[8] Dostoevsky writes of himself. Father Zossima is Dostoevsky's ecstatic conception of the world, the image in which—and the point at which—mystery and miracle, holiness and redemption cohere in presaging the "subsurface unexpressed future Word." In him the aesthetic, or the secular, element is converted by the spiritual, or the religious element when, Dostoevsky states, "the Holy Spirit is the direct understanding of beauty, the prophetic cognition of harmony and, therefore, a constant striving for it."[9] Father Zossima epiphanizes the most mystical dimension of Dostoevsky's spiritual art. Aesthetically and ideologically he becomes the medium of and for the experience of the holy, when the artistic proximity to the divine wondrously approximates the religious experience of the divine. Once again Otto helps us to gauge the intensity and value of the experience, the transfiguration, when he writes:

> The point is that the "holy man" or the "prophet" is from the outset, as regards the experience of the circle of his devotees, something more than a "mere man".... He is the being of wonder and mystery, who somehow or other is felt to belong to the higher order of things, to the side of the numen itself. It is not that he himself teaches that he is such, but that he is experienced as such.[10]

"That he is experienced as such": these words indicate the very nature and significance of Father Zossima, a type "of the universally human," Zweig declares, "soaring upward towards God."[11] As a form of the beautiful containing measure and harmony, he represents an essential facet of Dostoevsky's belief (as well as of his aesthetics) that "the world will become the beauty of Christ."[12] Through Father Zossima, Dostoevsky reveals an intuitive, and symbolic, apprehension of paradisiacal heights, just as in the figure of Stavrogin in *The Devils* he reveals a knowledge of "satanic depths." The "religious" experience that Dostoevsky seeks to portray in Father Zossima instances at the same time a meditation on the "double eternity," Death and Resurrection. Father Zossima is a fictionalized meditation as well as a meditative *homo fictus* lifted up to a metaphysical plane. Both as an image of reconciliation and as an image of redemption he personifies the miracle of how "the eternal penetrates . . . life in time,"[13] to use Guardini's words.

Undoubtedly Father Zossima constitutes an integral part of a novel in which the applied Christian content of Dostoevsky's aesthetic theory is readily observed. He stands for something real and yet ideal, transcendental and timeless. To Dostoevsky he exemplifies the Christian aesthetic which lies beyond the pale of Russian Orthodoxy *per se*. That is, Father Zossima is Dostoevsky's vision of a Christianity refined and purified to its highest point; a universalized vision, in which Dostoevsky has overcome his own prejudices and limitations, his own religious idiosyncrasies necessarily occasioned by such excrescences as Slavophilism and some of the rigid traditions of the Eastern Church. With Father Zossima, Dostoevsky soars, even if precariously, into a realm of pristine Christianity, but only after purging himself of religionist elements that are mere secularizations—personality, dogma, legalism, and ritual, for example, those inevitable entrapments of temporalized *ecclesia,* Eastern as well as Western. Father Zossima, in short, is Dostoevsky's vision of prophetic Christianity, and of Christianity beyond historicism. Indeed, in Father Zossima he meditates on the whole religious process of this de-creation, on the promise of redemption, from a fallen and philistine Christianity. The purity of this vision, this pan-Christian vision, it needs constant stressing, is arrived at through the artistic process, and arrived at in a novel in which, as Blackmur remarks, "it is the novelistic force which gives poetic justice to the religious."[14]

With Bishop Tihon in *The Devils* and with the old pilgrim Makar Ivanovitch Dolgoruky in *A Raw Youth,* Father Zossima comprises "the most wise teachers of life." Actually, the figure of Father Zossima enlarges upon the earlier figure of Makar, intensifying and heightening the kerygmatic qualities of the "beautiful serenity" and the "positively beautiful" which comprise that "old monk" ("a very greyheaded old man, with a big and very white beard") in his life and travels. That Makar is a precursor of Father Zossima is not difficult to see. Like Zossima he has a "benign serenity, an evenness of temper, and what was more surprising than anything, something almost like gaiety" (I, vii, 2).[15] And like Father Zossima "he retains a pure position," "a sinless heart,"[16] in the face of inextinguishable pain and suffering in life. In his love of man and of the whole of nature, which he sees garbed in a boundless and radiant mystery—

> What is the mystery? [Makar asks, and then goes on to reply:] Everything is mystery, dear; in all is God's mystery. In every tree, in every blade of grass that same mystery lies hid. Whether the tiny bird of the air is singing, or the stars in all their multitudes shine at night in heaven, the mystery is one, ever the same. And the greatest mystery of all is what awaiteth the soul of man in the world beyond. (III, i, 3)

—he anticipates both physically and pneumatically the holiness consummated in the figure of Father Zossima.

More, Makar anticipates a monastic ideal foreign to Byzantine Christian austerity and asceticism. His "gaiety of heart, and therefore 'seemliness,'" looks directly ahead to Father Zossima's sanctification of the "gladness" of life when, as the *staretz* affirms, "every day that is left me I feel how my earthly life is in touch with a new infinite, unknown, but approaching life" (VI, 1).[17] From Makar to Father Zossima we view an organic pattern of development, a steadily evolving spiritual vision and merging Christian ethos, rooted in the sacred mystery of the created world. It is a vision and a world that are detheologized, freed from the restrictions of creed and the particularizations of dogma, and that embrace "living life" in communion with the Divine.

Makar and Father Zossima are images of a divine *sophia,* earthly and yet metaphysical. Dramatically they reflect Dostoevsky's own contemplation of the theme of mystical naturalism that is intrinsic in a spiritual vision which never loses sight of a supernal power, but that concurrently bathes in the majesty of the immediate physical world in which God's immanence remains as an irrevocable, interpenetrating hint of a higher dimension—and as gleams of an ultimate experience that must have their beginning in sensuous ways. The recognition of this fact is tantamount to an "experiential transformation," as Guardini expresses it. Similarly, Mochulsky conceives of it in these words: "To the pure heart paradise opens itself on that ground." Which is to say, "on that ground" of theophanic experience which Makar describes ecstatically with reference to his pilgrimage to the monastery of Our Lady for the holy festival:

> We spent the night, brother, in the open country, and I waked up early in the morning when all was still sleeping and the dear sun had not yet peeped out from behind the forest. I lifted up my head, dear, I gazed about me and sighed. Everywhere beauty passing all utterance! All was still, the air was light; the grass grows— Grow, grass of God, the bird sings—Sing, bird of God, the babe cries in the woman's arms—God be with you, little man; grow and be happy, little babe! (III, i, 3)

An "inspirer of Dostoevsky" was the great Russian Saint Tikhon of Zadonsk (1724-83). The first drafts of both *The Life of a Great Sinner* and *The Brothers Karamazov* contain the name "Tikhon," which was subsequently changed to "the Hermit" and then to the "Elder Zossima." Dostoevsky was well acquainted with the life of Saint Tikhon and it is probable that during his years in Siberia he had heard of or read the saint's writings (e.g., *Of True Christianity, The Spiritual Treasury, Letters from a Cell*), the style of which definitely colored the writing of Book VI, "The Russian Monk," in *The Brothers Karamazov*. Dostoevsky "found in the simple Russian saint his initial idea of perfection"[18] and, as he noted in *The Diary of a Writer,* a great "historical ideal" from which the Russian people "would be learning beautiful things."[19] In a letter to A. N. Maikov, dated March 25, 1870, he clearly shows just how much Saint Tikhon meant to him, to the extent that this saint had furnished him with a prototypal image and ideal aesthetically and spiritually realized in *The Brothers Karamazov:*

> The whole of the second story [in *The Life of a Great Sinner*] will take place in a monastery. I have fostered all my hopes upon this second story.... I wish, in this second story, to portray as its main figure Tikhon Zadonsky, naturally under a different name, but he will also be a bishop and will live in retirement in a monastery.... I know the monastic world, I have known the Russian monastery since childhood.... If only I could depict a *positive* holy figure.... It is true that I am not going to create but only portray a real

Tikhon whom, long ago, with deep delight, I received into my heart. If I succeed I shall account it a great achievement.[20]

Nor is it difficult to see the high qualities of Saint Tikhon's life and writings which Dostoevsky found attractive and which influenced the creation of the figure of Father Zossima. G. P. Fedotov rightly speaks of this attraction in terms of Saint Tikhon's "charitable and kenotic personality." Saint Tikhon, it should be pointed out, lived during the time of spiritual and monastic revival in Russia, following a period of religious lassitude and doctrinaire religionism, all too often apparent only as external signs of piety and morality, which gripped Russian Orthodox society throughout the seventeenth century. In many ways his solitary life of prayer and his acts of charity to the poor, his guidance of and exhortations to the many visitors and pilgrims who came to see him at the monastery of the Blessed Virgin at Zadonsk, his preaching of and attempts to effect a national regeneration, epitomized the direction of this spiritual revival. Indeed, Saint Tikhon, stressing the radiance of Christlike life and divine love, was "a living reply"[21] to those who embraced atheism and antireligionism. As James H. Billington asserts, "at Zadonsk, Tikhon took the role of the spiritual elder out of the narrow confines of the monastery into the world of affairs, becoming the friend and counselor of lay people as well as monastic apprentices."[22]

Billington's words accentuate the broader basis of interrelationship between the historical role of Saint Tikhon ("a Westernizing kenotic") and the fictional image of Father Zossima. Of course, it cannot be denied that any comparison of these two figures shows, as has been remarked, "a disparity which is greater than the likeness": viz., Father Zossima contains "a Christian humanism, a serene freedom and cosmic mysticism of Mother Earth, which were entirely foreign to the melancholy recluse of Zadonsk."[23] But the point that needs to be understood is that Father Zossima served for Dostoevsky as an artistic transfiguration. Thus he went far beyond mere historical reality or fact, originally acting as a spermatic inspiration. "In the ecstatic Pater Seraphicus," Nadejda Gorodetsky reminds us, "the novelist revealed something at which St. Tikhon, out of the depths of his hidden spiritual life, only hinted."[24] Father Zossima, then, renders a metamorphosed Saint Tikhon without doctrinal curtailment or presuppositions. He is a "hint" of a new spiritual conscience, and he lives in the light of the coming resurrection.[25] He is a culminating, seraphic vision of peace and reconciliation, the point at which, it can be said with Saint Paul, "The night is far spent, the day is at hand."[26]

If it is Saint Tikhon who inspired some of the deeper religious ramifications of Father Zossima's significance, it is Father Ambrose (1812-92), elder of the famous monastery of Optina Pustyn ("the desert of Optina"), who actually provided some of Father Zossima's exterior qualities. Dostoevsky visited this monastery for a few days in June 1878, not long after his little son Alyosha had died and just as he had started writing *The Brothers Karamazov*. Accompanied by his young friend Vladimir Soloviev, at the time a promising philosopher, he went to the Optina for consolation. During his stay he was particularly impressed by the *staretz* Ambrose,[27] with whom he had three meetings. The visual and atmospheric aspects of the hermitage, located near the small town of Kozelsk, in the province of Kaluga, are amply reproduced in Dostoevsky's own description of the physical properties of the hermitage and of the particular cell in which Father Zossima lived.

Dostoevsky and Soloviev were not the only ones making a pilgrimage to the Optina. The Slavophile publicist Ivan Kireevsky, the novelist N. V. Gogol, the critic N. N. Strakhov, and the "aesthetic monoman" (as he called himself) Konstantin Leontiev had also, at one time or another, visited the hermitage in order to seek spiritual comfort. And during his lifetime Count Leo Tolstoy repeatedly visited the monastery, located some hundred miles from Yasnaya Polyana. His discussions with Father Ambrose prompted him on one occasion to praise the elder as a "holy man." "I talked with him and my soul felt light and joyous. When one speaks with such a man one really feels the nearness of God."[28] At the end of October in the fateful year 1910, when he left his family for good, Tolstoy again set out for the Optina. (His sister Marya was a nun at the convent of Sharmandino, approximately eight miles from the monastery.) "Apart from everything else," he now wrote to his wife, "I can no longer live in these conditions of luxury ... and I am doing what old men of my age commonly do: leaving the worldly life to spend the last days of my life in peace and solitude."[29] Tolstoy died on November 7, 1910, at the railroad station of Astapovo, still in the neighborhood of Optina Pustyn and still possessed by that inner turmoil, that "infinite, irresistible despair and loneliness," which tortured him to the very end.

Both the figure of Father Ambrose, bearded, tall, thin, and stooping, and the surroundings of Optina Pustyn, simple and poor, made a profound impression on Dostoevsky's religious consciousness and his aesthetic sensibility. Father Zossima bodies forth the strength of this impression. In his preachings and in his religious position, he is a composite of Saint Tikhon and Father Ambrose, who in turn belong to a special tradition of Russian Orthodox monasticism. This tradition goes back to Saint Nil Sorsky (1433-1508), who advocated a monastic life based on spiritual freedom, on tolerance of heretics, on compassionate love, and on moderation.[30] "There is a time for silence," Saint Nil taught his followers, whom he treated as friends, "and a time for quiet conversation, a time for prayer and a time for sincere obedience."[31] Some of his other teachings were these: "With regard to eating and drinking, let the practice of each monk be adjusted to his physical and spiritual capacity, avoiding satiety and greediness."[32] "It is a mistake to seek a more advanced state than our progress justifies; we should pursue the middle way and await the right moment."[33] "Therefore neither should we have gold and silver and other unnecessary ornaments in our possession, but only what is necessary to the church."[34] These teachings and the spiritual principles inherent in them are echoed by Father Zossima's "exhortations": "Equality is to be found only in the spiritual dignity of man, and that will only be understood among us" (VI, 3). "Remember particularly that you cannot be a judge of any one. For no one can judge a criminal, until he recognises that he is just such a criminal as the man standing before him, and that he perhaps is more than all men to blame for that crime" (VI, 3). "Seek no reward, for great is your reward on this earth: the spiritual joy which is only vouchsafed to the righteous man. Fear not the great nor the mighty, but be wise and ever serene" (VI, 3). "Always decide to use humble love. If you resolve on that once for all, you may subdue the whole world" (VI, 3).

By his opposition to ritualistic formalism and to monastic authoritarianism and discipline, as well as by his repudiation of living authorities (for he considered the "Holy Writings" as the only true authority), Saint Nil went counter to the Byzantine-Muscovite religious thinking which had prevailed in Russia for hundreds of years. (It is not difficult to see why the Russian liberal intelligentsia admired him.) In this connection he was vigorously opposed by Saint Joseph of Volokolamsk (1439-1515) and his followers, the so-called "Josephites," who stressed order, discipline, obedience, and autocracy. Saint Nil and his "friends," it should be noted, formed what is called a "skete" (or "skit"), a monastic way of life "neither eremitical nor cenobitical, but a middle way which avoided the disadvantages of both."[35] Their retreat was located in a wild and solitary spot in the forest bordering the Sora River, in northern Russia. Saint Nil remained here till the end of his life. In 1503 he attended an ecclesiastical council held in Moscow. Saint Joseph was also among those present. At this gathering Saint Nil advocated various controversial monastic reforms, including the dispossession of lands by the monasteries. His radical proposals were defeated by Saint Joseph and his administration-minded sympathizers, who were also responsible for the subsequent persecutions of Saint Nil and his followers.

The ideology of the Josephites remained firm until the eighteenth century, when the inherently liberal religious thinking of Saint Nil reappeared in the persons of Saint Tikhon and Father Païsius Velichkovsky (1722-94), the latter a great Optina elder whose Slavonic translation of a Greek ascetic-mystical anthology entitled the *Philokalia* played an important part in the Russian monastic revival at the end of the eighteenth and the beginning of the nineteenth centuries. The form of this contemplative monastic life and Orthodox culture flourished throughout this period in Optina Pustyn, which held "itself to be the heir and depository in a special sense of Païsius' tradition."[36] In the person of Father Zossima, Dostoevsky dramatized some aspects of this revived spiritual tradition, with its stress on prayer and love and on the interior life, which embraced not only Saint Nil, but also Isaac the Syrian, Saint Sergius of Radonezh, Saint Tikhon of Zadonsk, and Father Ambrose. "By the power of his artistic insight," Father Florovsky writes in his *Puti russkogo bogoslovia*, "Dostoevsky discovered and understood this seraphic current in Russian piety and prophetically continued it."[37]

# II

Dostoevsky himself considered Book V, "Pro and Contra," which contains the celebrated Legend of the Grand Inquisitor, and Book VI, "The Russian Monk," as the quintessential parts of *The Brothers Karamazov*. Both parts comprise antithetical energies, or rhythms: the first is one of negation and destruction, whereas the second is one of affirmation and creation—an "opposed heartbeat" to Ivan's prose poem. To his influential friend C. P. Pobedonostev, whom he called "a healing spirit" and who, it is sometimes claimed, though somewhat tenuously, not only influenced the composition of the novel but also "suggested" the creation of the figure of Father Zossima, Dostoevsky wrote concerning Book VI, "I have written this book for the few and consider it to be the culminating point of my work."[38] The fact remains that on "The Russian Monk" Dostoevsky "expended more effort" than on any other book in the novel. The reasons for his extra effort are not hard to understand. In a letter dated September 13, 1879, he comments on the extraordinary nature and aims in writing Book VI. "My main worry and care just now is with regard to the necessity of refuting the atheistic thesis. I intend to give the answer to the whole negative side in *The Russian Monk*. I tremble for it and wonder whether it will be a *sufficient* answer...."[39] And later, on May 10, 1879, he writes concerning the role of Father Zossima: "Pater Seraphicus. The death of the Elder. I consider this the climax of the novel."[40]

Dostoevsky fully knew, as only a prophet can, the irrevocable reality of the facts of the history of his time; he knew, that is, that what he was trying to do in "The Russian Monk" ran counter to the tendencies and actualities of an age seeking after new gods. That he had his doubts as to what he was doing in his presentation of Father Zossima is clearly indicated. "I think I have not sinned against reality," he wrote to Liubimov. "I only wonder if I have succeeded."[41] For Dostoevsky, Father Zossima was a figure who embodied something larger than life, who transcended everyday experience in communion with a greater power and a greater world. In Father Zossima he envisioned the organic metamorphosis of the human condition—a redeeming moment of encounter with the manifestly divine. No wonder that words failed to disclose the significance of his purpose. "I myself think that I have not expressed even a tenth part of what I wanted."

It would not be excessive to suggest that, in Father Zossima, Dostoevsky was searching for those converging aesthetic and religious levels of meaning that in visual art appear in the Pancreator of the Byzantine mosaic at Ravenna; or in El Greco's painting of Christ dead in the arms of the eternal Father; or in William Blake's "Promise of Redemption." A comparable stillness of contemplation seems to surround Dostoevsky's "Pater Seraphicus," who speaks to all time and all men. Hence, Father Zossima is not merely a dramatic figure, an artistic portrayal, but a visionary, universal power, both permanent and immanent, that speaks from "out of the whirlwind." Hence, also, he must be defiant of the transient demands of particular dramatic usage and idiom, because he says what he says from the center of a universal experience and a meaning for all time and all men. And for these reasons, too, Dostoevsky can hardly violate on aesthetic levels the supernatural experience of sanctity that Father Zossima captures, precisely because it is an experience of "the alpha and the omega" that in its depth arises from the beginning of time and will continue to the end of time. Such an experience cannot, must not, be personalized, subjected to a Heracleitian flux, for it challenges art. Rather, it must be rendered in its immemorial wisdom and purity, in its spiritual depth and permanence. Dostoevsky in his letter to Liubimov seems to be underlining precisely those elements when he writes: "Although I myself hold the same opinions which he [Father Zossima] expresses, yet if I expressed them personally *from* myself, I should express them in a different form and in a different style. But he could not speak in a different style, nor *express himself in a different spirit* than the one which I have given him."

Essentially, Father Zossima must be viewed as experience beyond art, vision beyond reality, spirit beyond flesh, life beyond death. Not only the skills of the craft of fiction but the eternals of spiritual art go into the portrayal of the old monk. If he signals for Dostoevsky the metamorphosis of the human condition, he also signals the metamorphosis of art—when art itself becomes a contemplation of the divine. As a prophetic figure Father Zossima contains those intuitive powers of discernment and truth that make him "the great healer," "the saint and custodian of God's truth," to quote Dostoevsky. Gide has observed that there is not a single great man in all of Dostoevsky's novels, with the exception of Father Zossima, "the noblest figure the Russian novelist had drawn."[42] But his greatness, Gide insists, is not as the world generally reckons it. Rather, it is the greatness that we must associate with saintliness, with holiness. Father Zossima, in a word, represents spiritual greatness and is the product of spiritual art. In this respect he signifies for Dostoevsky a spiritual force, invisible and unregarded, that, as rendered in art, lives and breathes in the very destiny of man. As such the figure of Father Zossima is also the moment of confrontation, or as Dostoevsky wrote to Liubimov: "If I succeed, I shall achieve a good work: *I will compel people to admit* that a pure, ideal Christian is not an abstraction, but a vivid reality, possible, clearly near at hand...."[43]

Understandably, Dostoevsky was concerned with the response that the figure of Father Zossima would generate. He was writing, after all, in an age in which moral crisis was in the air, and precisely that social, intellectual, and religious crisis in Western society that exploded with the Great War in 1914. How authentic, how effective, how convincing would Father Zossima be? Would he be able to withstand the kind of gospel that the archintellectual Ivan Karamazov espoused, or the brutally compromised religious philosophy that the Grand Inquisitor promulgated? Would his doctrine of love and compassion, of "lovingkindness," be able to militate against the increasing emphasis on the dynamics of power increasingly pervading European civilization? Father Zossima, Dostoevsky well realized, was an abstract image of a believing faith in an age on the threshold of the "crisis of faith," the age that Raskolnikov envisioned with prophetic terror in his dream, as found in the Epilogue to *Crime and Punishment,* and that Dostoevsky had first reflected on in his *Winter Notes on Summer Impressions.* Hard questions and hard facts seemed to constitute the real meaning of existence as the nineteenth century was coming to its ominous end. And Father Zossima, speaking for the joys of a life of faith and prayer, was ostensibly an anachronism with which a "modern age" would have little patience.

Since the publication of *The Brothers Karamazov,* Father

Zossima has aroused precisely the impatience that modern man has continually disclosed in response to metaphysics as a whole and to figures like Father Zossima who are rooted in metaphysics. Thus he has gone the way of metaphysics in modern times, into the realm of the obscure, the unreal, the intangible, the senseless. Most modern critics have seen to it! Interestingly, his dismissal can be traced back as early as 1882, when Konstantin Leontiev's *Nashi Vovye Khristiane* appeared. Leontiev (1831-91), a Russian writer and thinker, a military surgeon in the Crimean War, a consular official in the Near East, underwent a spiritual crisis in 1871 and lived for a time at Mount Athos. Prior to his death he took monastic orders at the Optina Monastery. Espousing formal aesthetic criticism and admiring the pagan art of Hellas and Constantinople and the spirit of the Renaissance, Leontiev considered Tolstoy's *Anna Karenina* the most artistically perfect work of art; and for a model of aesthetic simplicity, he believed that one had to go to George Sand's *Lucrèce Floriani*.

In Leontiev, Berdyaev concludes, we sense "a pointless aristocratic squeamishness and superficial aestheticism."[44] These elements are clearly communicated in Leontiev's judgment of Dostoevsky's "monstrous" novels, which can "only excite a few psychopaths, living in badly furnished rooms."[45] He claimed that they were "non-beautiful," inelegant, joyless, oppressive; that they re-created in tone, atmosphere, and characterization what was dissolute and debased; and that they continued some of the vulgar techniques and elements of the Gogolian school of writing. He felt that *The Brothers Karamazov* failed to pass the tests of "true Orthodoxy" or to perpetuate the Christianity of the Holy Fathers and of the Elders of Mount Athos and the Optina. (John Middleton Murry, advancing a similar thesis, later suggested that Father Zossima—and Dostoevsky with him—was "a Christian after the order of Ernest Renan."[46]) Father Zossima, Leontiev charged, was neither Father Ambrose nor an authentic Orthodox "type," but an offshoot of the overall "superficial and sentimental make-believe" of the novel: an aspect, in a word, of Dostoevsky's "rosy Christianity."

Most of the modern criticism of the figure of Father Zossima and of the artistry of Book VI in the novel stands in direct succession to Leontiev's. The most common criticism is that Father Zossima lacks convincing reality and offers unrealistic solutions to spiritual problems. The part of the novel in which he appears is said to be disordered, strange, prolix, digressive, "an endless dissertation, introduced apparently *à propos de bottes,* on the duties of a Russian monk."[47] Dostoevsky, it is charged, "is carried away by the moral-religious didactic element in Zossima."[48] Even a sympathetic and penetrating critic like Ernest J. Simmons describes Father Zossima's religious philosophy as stagnant and humiliating: "It is a negation of the whole ideal of progress."[49] Another critic calls the section on the Russian monk "unfortunate." The life and maxims of Father Zossima, he goes on to assert, are presented in "the naïve meandering style of a sermon," which lacks depth and focus and which runs toward "spiritual diffusion and boring prolixity." "The style excludes dimensions of personality, moreover, which are vital to substantive argument."[50] Still another critic, in a shriller vein, summarizing the typical, if arrogant, impatience of many modern critics and readers in the West, avers that "there are times when Father Zosima is dangerously near to becoming an intolerable old bore and his 'Conversations and Exhortations' are an inartistic excrescence"![51] In fact, the entire novel is, according to Joseph Conrad, "an impossible lump of valuable matter. It's terrifically bad and impressive and exasperating. . . . It sounds to me like some fierce mouthings from prehistoric ages."[52]

Such evaluations of Father Zossima inevitably disclose sharp misconceptions and misunderstandings and are a part of the debased values and loyalties in modern society. They are symptomatic of the crisis of faith that has gripped Western civilization since the middle of the nineteenth century. In this connection they are the distillation of a skeptical, often cynical, and prejudiced spirit as opposed to the prophetic spirit and that "new and dangerous faith" which, Hesse believed, Father Zossima announced. But the "modernism" of the assessments of Father Zossima is strangely paradoxical. Dismissing the old monk as an image that is dead and no longer relevant, this criticism fails to see that Father Zossima is indicative of Dostoevsky's struggle to abolish time itself and that he personifies "that inner man who has emerged from a rebirth."[53] (The significance of the biblical epigraph to the novel— "Verily, verily, I say unto you, except a corn of wheat fall into the ground and die, it abideth alone: but if it die, it bringeth forth much fruit" [John 12:24]—assumes its proper relevance here.) Indeed, Father Zossima can be described in terms of a "new revelation," a "new Christianity," as well as a reborn Orthodoxy, and a new freedom. In him Dostoevsky not only anticipated the demands of the modern spirit for something that is religiously existential, as both the history and the ambitions of religious thought in the twentieth century have revealed, but also went beyond modernism, to defy, it can be said, a static modernism (and a static criticism, as well).

# III

Dostoevsky invests Father Zossima with the burden of vision. His presence in the novel is prophetic. It must stir up something new and reverberate against a spirit of religious decay and sterility; it must energize, like some "Holy Event," a change in man; it must act like a prophetic "announcement" and contain, concurrently, what is peculiar to prophecy—a mission and a function, a declaration and a meditation. And we must bear in mind that as a prophetic figure Father Zossima is also the bearer of the "charismatic" power, the power of grace, the "splendor" of which is transmitted after his death to another man[54]—to Alyosha—"in whom there is spirit." To miss the point of this prophetic power in Father Zossima, and in Alyosha, is to miss the continuing dramatic movement of the novel itself, from beginning to end, and which gives it its justification and meaning.

From a surface look Father Zossima appears to lack vitality and to suffer from inanition. He is imaged as a "dying saint." Death hovers in his presence, and he is pictured as "dying of weakness and disease." Even his cell has "a faded look." Death and life, life and death—these are the great tensions that he embodies. He is of this world, but at the same time he belongs to the other, the next world. His knowledge of life is temporal and supratemporal. Infinite understanding and compassion radiate from him; blessed tranquillity, profound patience, abiding and pure love, and reverence are not only the qualities of his being but also the conditions of the realm that he personifies and inspires. To the old Karamazov he is "the most honest monk among them." To the youngest Karamazov, Alyosha, he is that "some one or something holy to fall down before and worship." The immediate physical projection of the elder, as rendered by Dostoevsky, consists of traits that underline suffering, venerability, wisdom. The details of his physical appearance inevitably bring to mind portraits of famous saints found in Byzantine iconography, with which Dostoevsky was undoubtedly familiar:

> He was a short, bent, little man, with very weak legs, and though he was only sixty-five, he looked at least ten years older. His face was very thin and covered with a network of fine wrinkles, particularly numerous about his eyes, which were small, light-coloured, quick, and shining like two bright points. He had a sprinkling of grey hair about his temples. His pointed beard was small and scanty, and his lips, which smiled frequently, were as thin as two threads. His nose was not long, but sharp, like a bird's beak. (II, 2)

There is nothing, however, in Father Zossima that communicates sadness, pessimism, or ethereal detachment. A rigoristic Byzantine asceticism does not inform his life or message; he is "not at all stern" but "always gay," "joyful," "smiling." "His mind was quite clear; his face looked very tired, yet bright and almost joyful" (IV, 1). Though sick and weary, he remains active in his ministry, exhorting, imposing penance, absolving, reconciling, blessing. A divine *sophia* inheres in him as he teaches the importance of "infinite, universal, inexhaustible love." The tone of his teachings is distinctly human and humble, bringing to mind affinities with Saint Nil Sorsky. Indeed, Father Zossima is not averse to jesting as he talks with his fellow monks and with visitors. "I've been teaching you so many years," he says, "and therefore I've been talking aloud so many years, that I've got into the habit of talking, and so much so that it's almost more difficult for me to hold my tongue than to talk, even now, in spite of my weakness, dear fathers and brothers" (IV, 1).

Whatever he says is part of a constant attempt not so much to instruct others as "to share with all men and all creation his joy and ecstasy, and once more in his life to open his whole heart" (IV, 1). His view of those who follow the monastic life is balanced and existential: "For monks are not a special sort of men, but only what all men ought to be" (IV, 1). Both his person and his teachings are the antithesis of the religious extremism of Father Ferapont—"kneeling all day long at prayer without looking round," living on bread and water, and wearing irons weighing thirty pounds under his coat. It is not necessarily the life of devoutness or of fasting and observing silence, Father Zossima insists, in word and practice, which gives meaning to religion; for such a life can all too often ignore the most intrinsic relation, the finest harmony, that exists among all men. "For know, dear ones, that every one of us is undoubtedly responsible for all men and everything on earth, not merely through the general sinfulness of creation, but each one personally for all mankind and every individual man" (IV, 1). The knowledge of this responsibility, he stresses, "is the crown of life for the monk and for every man" (IV, 1).

When we consider the structure of *The Brothers Karamazov,* and chiefly the fact that "The Russian Monk" constitutes exactly the middle part of a novel containing twelve books and an epilogue, we must be impressed by the centralizing importance of Father Zossima's role. For he is, in essence, the one who seeks to reconcile the factious elements of a family that in itself dramatizes a schism of soul. He understands completely the nature of human suffering: "Alyosha noticed that many, almost all, went in to the elder for the first time with apprehension and uneasiness, but came out with bright and happy faces" (I, 5). Instinctively aware of the nature of sin, he "was more drawn to those who were more sinful, and the greater the sinner the more he loved him" (I, 5). His compassion, his patience, his understanding and wisdom are infinite, as well as steadfast in the face of the mockery, the cynicism, the boisterous indifference, and the sarcasm of some of those whom inevitably he meets. Yet "he blessed them all and bowed low to them" (II, 3). Significantly, he tells his young disciple Alyosha "to care for most people exactly as one would for children, and for them as one would exactly for the sick in hospitals" (V, 1). (Indeed, are not the Karamazovs "children of darkness," childlike and sickly in their illusions, their rebellion, their urges? Do they not need to be cared for?)

If Father Zossima is a healing spirit, if he represents an enduring sacredness in the midst of the profane, he is also that marvelous sanctifying force in the novel that absorbs the recurring blows of life. Disbelief, disharmony, and cruelty rage all around him; he is at the very center of turmoil and hatred. Yet, he endures all and signifies hope and connection. Quietly but perseveringly, even heroically, he withstands the cynical and ruthless subversions of his meaning and message, the pitiless defiance of his gospel of love and belief and hope by the "Euclidean earthly mind," with its abrasive rational assertions, its terrifying end-of-the-world conceptualizings—the cold, cruel, grim, hopeless negativisms which Ivan Karamazov voices with an indignation and authority that seem to defy rebuttal, so forceful are his "conclusions" and his view of life and man. "To my thinking, Christ-like love for men is a miracle impossible on earth. He was God. But we are not gods" (V, 4). "It's not that I don't accept God . . . it's the world created by Him. I don't and cannot accept [it]" (V, 3). "If all must suffer to pray for the eternal harmony, what have children to do with it, tell me, please?"

Far from being a dull or pedestrian sermon, "The Russian Monk" constitutes the most visionary part of the novel. Its quietness, perhaps even its passivity, is the true source of its strength, for it reminds us of the need for meditation if life itself is to be saved from nothingness. Father Zossima serves as the antithesis to the obsession with flesh that we observe in the old Karamazov and to the riot of mind that possesses Ivan. In a way he stands at midpoint between the sensual and the rational, and he dramatizes what is immutable. He provides in his own life-experience and in his teachings the occasion to reflect on the meaning of existence. His presence in the novel is a sustaining counterpoint to shrill extremes. Father Zossima stands for contemplation, when man seeks to attain himself beyond flesh and beyond mind, as well as for conscience, when man must summon himself to himself. Too, he reminds us that the drama of life includes meaning that lies outside the domain of the purely functional demands of existence. Life is something more than flesh and mentality, something more than the excitation of sense. And he reminds us that contemplation of life verges on contemplation of the mystery of death. In short,

Father Zossima reminds us that Dostoevsky "is the prophet of the *other life*."[55]

Dostoevsky, it has been remarked, "stands deep within the uncertainties of his work, not somewhere above them or beside them."[56] The Karamazovs depict the secular dimensions of uncertainties connected primarily with the problems of flesh and mind. They embody earthly entities and preoccupations which consume various stages of the seen life. It is their thingness that we feel throughout the novel. With them we experience the multifaceted, the relentless immediacies of life. They are our elemental, our urgent encounters with the elements—with the world, and in it. They are our longings and disappointments, our struggles, our sinnings, our hopes, our naked selves and requirements. With the world, and in it, the Karamazovs are this world, the world reacting to and against itself in the most elemental ways. As a family and as individuals, the Karamazovs are witnesses to and participants in the spectacle of life. In the depth and breadth of their experiences, small and great, they portray for us the human condition in all its fleeting variability—economic, social, emotional, religious. In the Karamazovs we know ourselves as we are and as we live, creatures of a day. Their passions are our passions; their joys are our joys; their nights are our nights. Unwavering necessities of existence, in the face of the uncertainties of existence, color and distort their responses to the world. The limits of time itself make them captives. The Karamazovs are prisoners of life in time.

# IV

Father Zossima is more than just an elder; he is also a great teacher. His teachings are passed on and propagated by his followers, especially Alyosha. It is the life of the spirit that he teaches. So uplifting are his teachings that Alyosha and the other monks "had unquestioning faith in . . . [his] miraculous power." The story of Father Zossima's life, which Alyosha recorded on the basis of the old monk's last conversation with his friends and which appears under the heading "Biographical Notes," constitutes a kind of holy book on which one is asked to meditate. What is emphasized is the way in which Father Zossima, who came of a family of landowners, had been in the army in his youth, and served as an officer in the Caucasus, recalls some "precious memories" of his home and of his study of the Bible and of books of Scriptural history. Throughout the novel these memories achieve an epiphanous role and serve to underscore revelations that take on deeply spiritual connotations and lead to the affirmation of spiritual values. They record miraculous moments, prophetic encounters, sacred signs and numina that crystallize spiritual change and conversion and lead to an awareness of the divine and to an experience of otherness. Awe, wonder, and gladness accompany these memories, which assume the form of a human link.

Buber has remarked that the spark which leaps from him who teaches to him who listens and learns "rekindles a spark of that fire which lifted the mountain of revelation 'to the very heart of heaven.'"[57] Such a transmission evidences the relationship between Father Zossima and Alyosha (and later between Alyosha and the schoolboys). Together they represent the continuity of the values of spirit, as well as the encounter of generations. Time and again, to recall Buber, an older generation "comes to a younger with the desire to teach, waken, and shape it; then the holy spark leaps across the gap."[58] In this respect Father Zossima must be viewed as a *didaskalos* whose teachings, touched by eternity, return us to the *Logos*. In himself he is the great reminder, the great memory, the great teaching. In "The Russian Monk" Dostoevsky seeks to evoke precisely the wisdom and the strength of this teaching. But Alyosha is not the only pupil whom Father Zossima is "forming" and "making."[59] All men are the object of his concern; his world-view is both prophetic and universal. Indeed, Father Zossima's teaching has as its purpose that of affording one rebirth into a better life. "Spirit begets and gives birth; spirit is begotten and born; spirit becomes body."[60]

"The Russian Monk" follows Book V, "Pro and Contra." It follows, that is, the exposition of Ivan Karamazov's rebellion and his famous "poem in prose," "The Grand Inquisitor." In this light the meaning of rebirth is enhanced. Nor is it insignificant that at the end of Ivan's "poem" Jesus approached the Inquisitor "in silence and softly kissed him on his bloodless aged lips. That was all his answer." Father Zossima represents an added aspect of this "answer." He is the rendering of religious life, and religious "answer," the holding fast to the God that Ivan repudiates, the essence of the humility which refuses to exist outside God. He is faith emerging in the midst of unfaith, an answer to the possibility of nothingness. In his life and work Father Zossima shows the importance of making a choice in the world and of accepting the reality of the world, of living at harmony with the powers of the world but not of becoming absorbed by them as Ivan did. Alienation from the world leads to the rejection of the world. Thus, Father Zossima declares, Alyosha will go forth from the walls of the monastery and "live like a monk in the world." "You will have many enemies, but even your foes will love you," he tells his young disciple. "Life will bring you many misfortunes, but you will find your happiness in them, and will bless life and will make others bless it—which is what matters most" (VI, 1). And here we are reminded of Karl Jaspers' contention that remoteness from the world gives an inward distinction, whereas immersion in it awakens what is human in selfhood. "The former demands self-discipline; but the latter is love."[61]

For Father Zossima the word "love" connotes *kerygma* and *pistis*: it is the only answer, the only struggle, the only mystery, the only redemption. "Brothers, love is a teacher; but one must know how to acquire it, for it is hard to acquire, it is dearly bought, it is won slowly by long labour. For we must love not only occasionally, for a moment, but for ever. Everyone can love occasionally, even the wicked can" (VI, 3). Love conquers pride (of the kind that we find in Father Ferapont, for instance) and overcomes despair. It serves as the beginning of life, in "kindness and mercy."[62] It reveals God to man; it relates man to God. It frees men and announces a new "way"—"the way of hallowing." "Love a man even in his sin," Father Zossima exhorts, "for that is the semblance of Divine Love and is the highest love on earth. Love all God's creation, the whole and every grain of sand in it. Love every leaf, every ray of God's light. Love the animals, love the plants, love everything. If you love everything, you will perceive the divine mystery in things" (VI, 3). For Father Zossima love assumes the highest spiritual value, and it arouses an experiential transformation, the "experience of paradise," of divine immanence. The failure of love is tantamount to damnation, to hell. "Fathers and teachers, I ponder 'What is hell?' I maintain that it is the suffering of being unable to love" (VI, 3). Father Zossima's words here crystallize the innermost conflict and crisis of the novel. They also give a clue to a knowledge that comes from a higher dimension and that is transposed into spiritual art.

And yet in *The Brothers Karamazov* love also presents the overwhelming paradox. The struggle for and the absence of love: these comprise the terrible conditions of life; these are the very problems of human nature that make of life the dichotomy that it is and that practically devour poor Ivan. Father Zossima affords the knowledge of this desperation. Through him we are able to share in a vision that in itself objectifies the burden of mortality. Father Zossima asks to help and to sustain us under the crushing weight of this burden. Pater Seraphicus! Truly he is such, as Ivan claims, for Alyosha—and for us. Father Zossima's preoccupation with love adumbrates its difficulties, its elusiveness. Ivan's contention that "for any one to love a man, he must be hidden, for as soon as he shows his face, love is gone" (V, 4) is not without relevance here. Throughout the novel love is there and is not there, as Dmitri Karamazov discovers to his grief. Its presence is as painful as its absence. It requires so much of one, Father Zossima indicates, that it becomes a trial to which not only Dmitri but all men are summoned. (We can well recall Miguel De Unamuno's sage words: "Love is the child of illusion and the parent of disillusion; love is consolation in desolation; it is the sole medicine against death, for it is death's brother."[63]) When the prosecutor in the course of the trial speaks of "the broad Karamazov character" as "capable of combining the most incongruous contradictions, and capable of the greatest heights and of the greatest depths," he is at the same time describing the paradox of love. Of all the characters in the novel only Father Zossima is fully aware of this truth. Seeking to alleviate the human condition, he is also striving to renew it, to save it from itself.

The story of Father Zossima's life serves to emphasize the place of spiritual illumination as it alters one's vision of life. In particular, Father Zossima notes the great importance of certain "precious memories" in his life, such as his fond recollections of his study of the Bible (for instance, the parts relating to Abraham and Sarah, to Job, to the parables of Jesus Christ, and to the conversion of Saint Paul) and of his study of a book of Scriptural history, *A Hundred and Four Stories From the Old and New Testament.* Through these recollections he strives to show how his own life can take a new direction. He recounts how as a youth he spent eight years in a military cadet school at Saint Petersburg and how he later became an officer. "Drunkenness, debauchery and devilry were what we almost prided ourselves on," he confesses. He tells of falling in love with a girl who later marries another man, while Zossima is away on military duty. Eventually, he insults his rival, an action that brings on a duel. Just before the duel, in a bad temper, he cruelly beats Afanasay, his orderly. Guilt-stricken, he thinks: "This is what a man has been brought to, and that was a man beating a fellow creature! What a crime! It was as though a sharp dagger had pierced me right through" (VI, 2). And then he thinks, too, of his brother, seventeen-year-old Markel, who had died when Zossima was still a child. He remembers what Markel said on his deathbed to his servants: "My dear ones, why do you wait on me, why do you love me, am I worth your waiting on me?" (VI, 2)

From Afanasay, Zossima now begs forgiveness and drops at his servant's feet and bows his head to the ground. Other crucial words uttered by Markel have further impact on Zossima: " . . . in truth we are responsible to all for all, it's only that men don't know this. If they knew it, the world would be a paradise at once" (VI, 2). When the duel takes place, his rival "had the first shot," which just grazes Zossima's cheek and ear. Zossima thereupon takes his own pistol and flings it far away into the woods. A new form of courage emanates from Zossima as a result of these experiences. For in making the decision to bow to his orderly and not to shoot at his rival, Zossima has overcome his own proud will. More importantly, he has come to grips with a difficult question, that of human dignity—the question that is so central to the novel. In the story of Father Zossima's early years, especially up to the age of twenty-five when he became a monk, human dignity is finally affirmed. This affirmation, Dostoevsky shows, can be the process of a good, precious memory, which in itself is touched by God.

At the end of the novel, during Ilusha's funeral, Alyosha similarly returns to the meaning of a good memory in life, especially a memory of childhood and of home. A sacred memory preserved from childhood, Alyosha says to the boys who gather around him at Ilusha's stone, can be the best education for one. "If a man carries many such memories with him into life," Alyosha declares, "he is safe to the end of his days, and if one has only one good memory left in one's heart, even that may sometime be the means of saving us" (Epilogue, 3). In *The Brothers Karamazov* memory is seen to assume mystical and spiritual significances. As a vehicle of grace in an Augustinian sense, it connects not only life and life but also life and eternity. It fuses the conscious and the unconscious. It exempts us from oblivion and reaffirms divine immanence. It generates hierophantic powers, when, as Eliade points out, "*something sacred shows itself to us*,"[64] evoking and revealing the power of the *Logos* in life. The hierophantic, in this respect, is a major esoteric element of spiritual art. "Poets are the hierophants of an unapprehended inspiration," Shelley declares. His words summarize a special function of Dostoevsky's work.

With the approach of Father Zossima's death, Alyosha and the other monks "anticipated miracles and great glory to the monastery in the immediate future from his relics" (I, 5). When he does die, however, "a smell of decomposition began to come from the coffin." This incident shatters the hopes of his followers. To Alyosha it is "one of the bitterest and most fatal days of his life," for Father Zossima, he felt, "instead of receiving the glory that was his due, was suddenly degraded and dishonoured." It was as if Providence had suddenly hidden its face "at the most critical moment." If "the breath of corruption" proves to be such a terribly disappointing episode for Father Zossima's supporters, it serves to sharpen the "frantic outcries of bigots" like Father Ferapont. "The unbelievers rejoiced, and as for the believers some of them rejoiced even more than the unbelievers, for 'men love the downfall and disgrace of the righteous,' as the deceased elder had said in one of his exhortations" (VII, 1). For Alyosha the "unseemly" incident is "a crisis and turning-point in his spiritual development." His immediate reaction is one of abject disillusionment, and at one point he even repeats Ivan's words to the effect that he rebels not against God but simply against His world. ("He is rebelling against his God and ready to eat sausages," quips the wily Rakitin.)

Returning again to the elder's cell where the coffin is standing, Alyosha falls on his knees and prays. In the meantime Father Païssy reads from the biblical story of the marriage at Cana in Galilee when Jesus works the first miracle of turning water into wine. As Father Païssy reads, Alyosha starts to listen, but, exhausted, he begins to doze. The pages of this chapter recounting this episode exemplify what has already been called the hierophantic power and function of spiritual art. They also illustrate Dostoevsky's use of biblical language and meaning under the guise of fiction. The entire episode synthesizes vision and miracle, life and eternity. At the same time the role of Father Zossima in the novel and story is further heightened. For Alyosha suddenly has a vision of "the little, thin old man, with tiny wrinkles on his face" coming up to him. The elder appears joyful and laughs softly: " ... he, too, had been called to the feast. He, too, at the marriage of Cana in Galilee ... " (VII, 4). He speaks to Alyosha and raises him by the hand. From every aspect the incident breathes mystical joy and ecstasy; there is a pervasive, even overpowering, spiritual mood created in these pages. The emphasis is on rebirth, on a renewed faith, dramatically rendered in a thoroughly hierophantic scene.

Father Zossima, as he appears to Alyosha, personifies miracle. These moments, as they are described, are moments of holiness, of revelation, when art converts and is converted. ("Artistic and religious vision," Robert Louis Jackson tells us in his study *Dostoevsky's Quest for Form,* "are ultimately one vision, reveal the same absolute reality.") Father Zossima constitutes the miracle of vision at a point of infinite significance in Alyosha's life. "We are drinking the new wine, the wine of new, great gladness ... " (VII, 4). The hierophantic power of Dostoevsky's art here is crystallized as divinity itself is glimpsed, as in a dream, or in a memory that flashes in the mind and communicates to us some meaningful experience. For in a very deep sense Father Zossima is now part of the Spirit when something happens to man—to Alyosha. He pleads with his young disciple to make the beginning, to see Him, to believe in Him, to be reborn in Him. "Do not fear Him," he counsels Alyosha. "He is terrible in His greatness, awful in His sublimity, but infinitely merciful. He has made Himself like unto us from love and rejoices with us. He is changing the water into wine that the gladness of the guests may not be cut short. He is expecting new guests, He is calling new ones unceasingly for ever and ever.... There they are bringing new wine" (VII, 4).

"Changing," "expecting," "calling," "bringing": these words are essentially hierophantic words which attempt to capture the charged significance of the entire episode that is Alyosha's vision. And likewise they inform the nature of his response. Something "glows" in his heart and "fills" it with rapture. "He stretched out his hands, uttered a cry and waked up" (VII, 4). Suddenly, "as though thrown forward," he goes right up to the coffin. "Something strange was happening to the boy." The momentousness of the happening, dramatized with artistic skill, is consummated in a majestic passage that directly follows Alyosha's gazing "for half a minute at the coffin, at the covered, motionless dead man that lay in the coffin, with the ikon on his breast and the peaked cap with the octangular cross on his head":

> He did not stop on the steps either, but went quickly down: his soul, overflowing with rapture, yearned for freedom, space, openness. The vault of heaven, full of soft, shining stars, stretched vast and fathomless above him. The Milky Way ran in two pale streams from the zenith to the horizon. The fresh, motionless, still night enfolded the earth. The white towers and golden domes of the cathedral gleamed out against the sapphire sky. The gorgeous autumn flowers, in the beds round the house, were slumbering till morning. The silence of earth seemed to melt into the silence of the heavens. The mystery of earth was one with the mystery of the stars.... (VII, 4)

As mystical as this part of *The Brothers Karamazov* is—possibly the most mystical of anything Dostoevsky wrote—it does not end on a passive note. We see Alyosha suddenly throwing himself down on the earth, embracing it, kissing it, "sobbing and watering it with his tears." Father Zossima's words, "Water the earth with the tears of your joy and love those tears," return to him and echo "in his soul."

For Alyosha this mystical experience has as its media vision and voice, supersensual auditory and visual intuitions which bring man's finite being, his "seeing self," into contact with the Infinite Being, the Absolute. What Dostoevsky seeks to dramatize here is what is paramount to such an experience

in the mystic life; visionaries from Saint Teresa to Blake and ·
down to John Masefield believed that the messengers of the
invisible world knock persistently at the doors of the senses,
with visions and voices, symptoms of transcendental activity.[65] Alyosha apprehends "that other world," "in a flash,"
as it were. "And never, never, all his life long," writes Dostoevsky, "could Alyosha forget that minute. 'Some one visited
my soul in that hour,' he used to say afterwards, with implicit
faith in his words" (VII, 4). That "some one," of course, is
Father Zossima, who, as Mochulsky declares, "teaches about
the soul's ascent to God."[66] For Alyosha this ascent is now
marked by the discovery of a great new strength, all the more
required to steel him against the subsequent happenings in the
tragic history of the Karamazov family. His visionary experience is energizing in its ultimate contexts:

> ... something firm and unshakeable as that vault of heaven had
> entered into his soul. It was as though some idea had seized the
> sovereignty of his mind—and it was for all his life and for ever
> and ever. He had fallen on the earth a weak boy, but he rose up a
> resolute champion, and he knew and felt it suddenly at the very
> moment of his ecstasy. (VII, 4)

As a result of what is termed "the organic growth of his
transcendental consciousness,"[67] Alyosha now "longed to forgive every one and for everything, and to beg forgiveness. Oh,
not for himself, but for all men, for all and for everything" (VII,
4). His vision cannot be viewed as exclusively God-conscious. It
is that, and something more, in the sense that Alyosha's very
purpose and task, from this point on in the story, will revolve
around what Father Zossima had earlier told him: " ... to care
for most people exactly as one would for children, and for some
of them as one would for the sick in hospitals" (V, 1). Alyosha's
visionary experience has enabled him to make his ascent and
to experience the mystic states of ecstasy ("a synonym for
joyous exaltation, for the inebriation of the Infinite") and
rapture ("a violent and uncontrollable expression of genius for
the Absolute"; "the violent uprush of subliminal intuitions").
But the end of this vision for Alyosha is not the attainment *per
se* of what mystics term the "Unitive Life," or that "final
triumph of the spirit, the flower of mysticism, humanity's top
note: the consummation towards which the contemplative life,
with its long slow growth and costly training, has moved from

the first."[68] The highest and most perfect in its forms, "standing at the highest point of the mystic ladder," the Unitive Life, "though so often lived in the world, is never of it. It belongs to another plane of being, moves securely upon levels unrelated to our speech; and hence eludes the measuring powers of humanity."

For if we are to judge by what befalls Alyosha after his mystic experience, not the contemplative (and ultimately the unitive) life but rather the familiar, concrete, everyday life is to be his fate. His *askesis,* the "dark night of the soul" when the "mysterious death of selfhood" occurs and the soul is "initiated into the atmosphere of Eternity, united with the Absolute," is merely antecedent to his own interior and exterior exposure, in the fullest sense, to "the primitive force of the Karamazovs," "a crude, unbridled, earthly force." For good reason does Dostoevsky stress in his Author's Note that Alyosha "carries within himself the very heart of the universal." His vision has enabled him to touch the divine and, in effect, to gain another "breath of life" by which he is renewed and strengthened to face, to withstand, the travails he is to undergo: the murder of his father, the prosecution of his brother Dmitri, the brain sickness of Ivan—in short, the whole gamut of affliction and catastrophe endemic to the human condition: doubt and death, hatred and cruelty, despair and destruction, temptation and sin. Alyosha's destiny, as Father Zossima prophesies in the early pages of the novel, will not be easy. "I bless you for great service in the world," the elder tells him. "Yours will be a long pilgrimage. And you will have to take a wife, too. You will have to bear *all* before you come back. There will be much to do. . . . You will see great sorrow, and in that sorrow you will be happy" (II, 7). And indeed, to contend with this sorrow, to care for man "as one would for the sick in hospitals," Alyosha's Divine Encounter serves quintessentially as a strengthening, as a preparation for his "sojourn in the world."

His mystic vision, thus, does not fall into quietism, so dynamic is it in its roots and its potentiality, so extraordinary is its meaning as seen in the light of the movement of the novel and Alyosha's role in it—a role so dynamic that one is surprised that it is little remarked on by critics who are satisfied merely to complain that Alyosha and Father Zossima do not provide a "clear moral guide."[69] Evelyn Underhill in her book

*Mysticism* gives the best explanation of the kind of visionary experience that Alyosha has and, at the same time, clarifies the thrust of its direction and the nature of its meaning:

> Whereas vision of the passive kind is the expression of thought, perception, or desire on the part of the deeper self: active vision is the expression of a change in that self, and generally accompanies some psychological crisis. In this vision, which always has a dramatic character, the self seems to itself to act, not merely to look on.[70]

In the persons of Father Zossima and Alyosha we have a single positive spiritual-earthly force. Alyosha is an extension of Father Zossima in a secular way. To view and to estimate Alyosha's actions in the novel is really to comprehend a transfiguration of Father Zossima himself. That is, Alyosha continues his elder's work as "the great healer," continues it in another arena, one certainly more problematic and dangerous than that of the monastery. Whereas Father Zossima bows down at Dmitri's feet—a prophetic symbol of this unhappy man's future suffering—Alyosha is an active witness to his brother's search for salvation and actually helps to give him "new life," as seen in this dialogue:

> Once more they kissed hurriedly, and Alyosha was just going out, when Mitya suddenly called him back.
>
> "Stand facing me! That's right!" And again he seized Alyosha, putting both hands on his shoulders. His face became suddenly quite pale, so that it was dreadfully apparent, even through the gathering darkness. His lips twitched, his eyes fastened upon Alyosha.
>
> "Alyosha, tell me the whole truth as you would before God. Do you believe I did it [the murder of the father]? Do you, do you in yourself, believe it? The whole truth, don't lie!" he cried desperately.
>
> Everything seemed heaving before Alyosha, and he felt something like a stab at his heart.
>
> "Hush! What do you mean?" he faltered helplessly.
>
> "The whole truth, the whole, don't lie!" repeated Mitya.
>
> "I've never for one instant believed that you were the murderer!" broke in a shaking voice from Alyosha's breast, and he raised his right hand in the air, as though calling God to witness his words.
>
> Mitya's whole face was lighted up with bliss.

"Thank you!" he articulated slowly, as though letting a sigh escape him after fainting. "Now you have given me new life. Would you believe it, till this moment I've been afraid to ask you, you, even you. Well, go! You've given me strength for to-morrow. God bless you! Come, go along! Love Ivan!" was Mitya's last word. (XI, 5)

# V

The center of Father Zossima's *raison d'être,* giving him flesh and purpose, is his hope for "that grand and simple-hearted unity." His spiritual ideal, however, is all along rejected primarily by Ivan Karamazov's blasphemy in the denial of the meaning of God's creation. Ivan, to quote Albert Camus, "incarnates the refusal of salvation."[71] Another critic goes so far as to say that though unable "to receive Alyosha," because of "Dostoevsky's unclarity or our blindness," modern man can receive Ivan with "a terrible kind of delight." For Ivan, he contends, "is a true gift to us all, perhaps Dostoevsky's supreme gift."[72] In him one finds his self-portrait, inasmuch as "the God that is dead for him is dead for us; and his Karamazov-God of tension and terror is often the only one we are able to find."[73] These arguments, which for Dostoevsky would have been symptomatic of the logic emerging from the Crystal Palace, his image of a debased materialistic culture, particularly as it is found in his *Winter Notes on Summer Impressions,* instance the kind of reaction both Father Zossima and Alyosha draw forth. Too often there has been precisely this refusal to accept the role and significance of the elder, as well as that of his follower, within the economy of *The Brothers Karamazov.* Implicit in this refusal is an insistence on the abstract quality of the saintly figure.

Undoubtedly one reason for the denigration of Father Zossima is that his pastoral work, on which basis he can be judged, is not only inconclusive but even negative, insofar as it does not provide clearly defined and estimable advantages or remedies. The message of suffering, of love, humility, and patience hardly (ever) qualifies alone for actualized success. Even Father Zossima's own example of life, as well as his message, contributes to turmoil, as seen in the hostility of some other monks, like Father Ferapont, who felt that the elder failed in monastic asceticism characterized and ultimately judged by the presence or the absence of "invisible warfare." "He did not keep the fasts according to the rule. . . ," Father Ferapont screams. "He was seduced by sweetmeats ladies brought . . . to him in their pockets, he sipped tea, he worshipped his belly, filling it with sweet things and his mind with haughty thought . . . " (VII, 1).

If Father Zossima was too radical in his behavior, he was also too radical in his doctrines. In his notebooks Dostoevsky planned for Father Zossima to say: "Love men in their sin, love even their sins."[74] Although the second part of this injunction was later eliminated from the text, its appearance in the notebooks further predicates Dostoevsky's radical intention to give Father Zossima a revolutionary religious significance—that "new saintliness" the modern world has yet to comprehend. No words can better summarize the daring of what Dostoevsky had in mind, what he sought to personify in the figure and purposefulness of Father Zossima, than these of a later religious thinker and prophetic genius, Simone Weil (1909-43): "We live in an age which is quite without precedent: to-day there is nothing in being a saint. We need a saintliness proper to the present moment, a new saintliness, which is also without precedent."[75]

Obviously, this "new saintliness," of which Father Zossima is very much a prototype in modern literature, was alien to Father Ferapont, who represents a moribund ecclesiasticism. Dostoevsky dramatizes in Father Zossima the problematic aspects of faith even as he renders in the entire novel the crisis of faith. The old monk, Thurneysen notes, embodies "the eschatological tension that gives life its meaning"; indeed, this "eschatological tension develops into eschatology itself."[76] And for Dostoevsky the religious situation, with all its paradoxes and uncertainties, as rendered in Father Zossima and subsequently in Alyosha, comprises the focal point of this tension. To a great extent Father Zossima is Dostoevsky's answer to Ivan; he provides the occasion for reflection on the "eternal questions," particularly on the opposition of good and evil. Father Zossima embodies the metaphysical view of and concern with human life. He symbolizes proximity to God, just as Ivan symbolizes distance from God. In a deeply dramatic sense Dostoevsky uses Father Zossima, whether as an active presence or as a name on the lips of some other characters, as a means of keeping one's attention fixed upon divine truth. He constitutes for Dostoevsky, in the metaphysics of his art, a sacred force comprising love and attention in the midst of immense evil. As we come to see in the various confrontations in *The Brothers Karamazov,* Father Zossima is not only a sacred force but also a contact with purity, effecting a transformation in evil. "But if through attention and love," Simone Weil tells us, "we project a part of our evil upon something perfectly pure, it cannot be defiled by it; it remains pure and does not reflect the evil back on us; and so we are delivered from the evil."[77]

It is Simone Weil who helps us most to discover the various and subtle levels of meaning in Father Zossima. When Berdyaev divided people into two classes, the "dostoievskites" and the "non-dostoievskites," he pronounced a truth which the modern world has witnessed with ever-increasing urgency. In Simone Weil, whom Camus saluted as "the only great spirit of our time," we have a paragon "dostoievskite" whose own writings are in themselves astonishing commentaries on the Russian novelist's metaphysics. Perhaps it would be best to conclude this interpretation of Father Zossima, and of *The Brothers Karamazov,* in the light of some of her writings, particularly her essay "The Love of God and Affliction." Affliction (*malheur*), she says, though inseparable from physical suffering, "is something apart, specific and irreducible," an uprooting of life, a destroyer of personality. It takes possession of the soul, destroys it, and then marks it for slavery. "Affliction is above all anonymous; it deprives its victims of their personality and turns them into things. It is indifferent, and it is the chill of this indifference—a metallic chill—which freezes all those it touches, down to the depth of their soul."[78] Primarily, it contains the truth of the human condition; that is, it epitomizes man's infinite fragility and his constant exposure to "the mechanism of necessity." It is not a psychological state, but rather "a pulverization of the soul by the mechanical brutality of circumstances." The possibility of affliction, writes Simone Weil in words which deserve to be quoted, is always present:

All the three sides of our being are always exposed to it. Our flesh is fragile; it can be pierced or torn or crushed, or one of its internal mechanisms can be permanently deranged, by any piece of matter in motion. Our soul is vulnerable, being subject to fits of depression without cause and pitifully dependent upon all sorts of objects, inanimate and animate, which are themselves fragile and capricious. Our social personality, upon which our sense of existence almost depends, is always and entirely exposed to every hazard. These three parts of us are linked with the very centre of our being in such a way that it bleeds for any wound of the slightest consequence which they suffer. Above all, anything which diminishes or destroys our social prestige, our right to consideration, seems to impair or abolish our very essence—so much is our whole substance an affair of illusion.[79]

It is true that the themes of purgation, resurrection, holiness, repentance, and theodicy run throughout and interpenetrate in *The Brothers Karamazov*. But these themes are mainly the manifestations and constituents of what must remain basic in the structure and in the intended purpose of the novel—to dramatize a condition of affliction in life. No character in this novel of affliction is spared affliction—physically, socially, or spiritually. Each endures in the most painful, unexpected, and inexplicable ways a sense of deracination, depersonalization, weakness, disintegration. The fragility of each character, even of the saintly ones, appears in numerous and sometimes enigmatic ways. The supreme victimizer, as well as the ultimate human process, affliction has "the power to seize the very souls of the innocent and to possess them as sovereign master. At the very best, he who is branded by affliction will only keep half his soul." Father Zossima (and eventually Alyosha) is the only one of the major figures in the novel who comprehends this condition. The power of his vision, and hence of his prophetic faith, is rooted in his own experiences of suffering and joy and in his recognition of the fact, to quote Simone Weil, "that the substance of the universe is necessity and that the substance of necessity is obedience to a perfectly wise Love."[80]

The so-called passivity attributed to Father Zossima is not that at all. In contrast to the rebelliousness, even the madness, that grips the other characters in *The Brothers Karamazov*, it is his acceptance of the universe and his obedience to God that give Father Zossima quietude and confidence. He sees the universe as no other person sees it: he accepts the fact that man by himself has not created the world nor can he control it. Again, Simone Weil's remarks are invaluable here in illuminating Father Zossima's power—the mysterious, hierophantic power that Dostoevsky endows him with in the novel: "It is affliction that reveals, suddenly and to our very great surprise, that we are totally mistaken" ["that the world is created and controlled by ourselves"]. . . . "To be a created thing is not necessarily to be afflicted, but it is necessarily to be exposed to affliction. Only the uncreated is indestructible."[81] Man is vulnerable, and thus afflictive, Father Zossima teaches; hence, he must also accept this condition. "Affliction, when it is consented to and accepted and loved, is truly a baptism."[82] The two poles, the two essential truths of Christianity, are the Trinity ("perfect joy") and the Cross ("perfect affliction"), Simone Weil emphasizes. "It is necessary to know both the one and the other and their mysterious unity, but the human condition in this world places us infinitely far from the Trinity, at the very foot of the Cross. Our country is the Cross."[83]

She also notes that "affliction without the Cross is hell," that the one thing enabling man to accept affliction "is the contemplation of Christ's Cross."[84] Father Zossima's knowledge of this truth, it can be said, opens the door to the wholly "other reality," whereas Ivan's rejection of any "mysterious unity," or "higher harmony" as he puts it, ends in the *cul de sac* of rebellion. "What good can hell do," Ivan cries to Alyosha as he expounds his theory of the "unatoned" suffering of children, "since those children have already been tortured? And what becomes of harmony if there is hell? I want to forgive. I want to embrace. I don't want more suffering. And if the sufferings of children go to swell the sum of sufferings which was necessary to pay for truth, then I protest that the truth is not worth such a price" (V, 4). Ivan, surely the most afflicted of Dostoevsky's characters, here protests against the hell of affliction. For him there can be neither contemplation nor consolation, inasmuch as he believes that God is absent. Even if Ivan can agree with Father Zossima that man is the slave of necessity, he disagrees, violently, that man is also the son of her Master. Unlike Father Zossima, he cannot be obedient to God.

In *The Brothers Karamazov* Dostoevsky's vision of evil in

the world, in the forms of affliction and crime, achieves its consummate prophetic validity. In the person of Father Zossima, in the essence of his utter goodness and compassion, Dostoevsky strives to show how immensely difficult and painful it is for us to accept his spiritual insights or sympathize with his spiritual values. Our distance from Father Zossima reflects the distance between us and God. This, in effect, is what accounts for Father Zossima's so-called "unreality," "unclarity," "immobility."[85] Father Zossima's constant awareness of the inseparability of, even the dialogue between, Creation and Passion is that which gives him meaning and prophecy in the novel. His message of love attests to the Creation; his own death attests to the Passion. "The tremendous greatness of Christianity comes from the fact that it does not seek a supernatural remedy against suffering, but a supernatural use of suffering."[86] Thus Simone Weil wrote in her notebooks. Her words underline Father Zossima's unique place in *The Brothers Karamazov* as well as Dostoevsky's own religious orientation, which, as it emerges in this novel, transcends any religious system.

Man must not, Father Zossima shows, struggle against the Absolute. Nor must afflicted man wait for God in silence. "He who is capable not only of listening," Simone Weil declares, "but also of loving hears this silence as the word of God. The speech of created beings is with sounds. The word of God is silence. God's secret word of love can be nothing else but silence. Christ is the silence of God."[87] Father Zossima personifies this silence in the midst of affliction: " ... the Lord *is* in his holy temple: let all the earth keep silence before him,"[88] a Hebrew prophet admonishes. The numinous value of this silence is suggested by Father Zossima's attitude and by the manner in which he communicates with and counsels others.[89] His silence of waiting is what enables him to break through the horror and ugliness of the affliction around him. He sees and understands this affliction without ceasing to love. This is a secret of his power. This is why he remains in constant touch with God. This contact, in turn, gives him a profounder knowledge of man's suffering. Thus, Father Zossima also knows the last secret of this suffering. He knows, in Simone Weil's words, that if man "remains constant, what he will discover buried deep under the sound of his own lamentations is the pearl of the silence of God."[90]

The pain of affliction and the cry of terror prevail in Dostoevsky's last novel. Again and again he seems to be saying that the possibility of escaping or defeating this human condition is remote, if at all existent. Even if man can follow after God, he cannot be God. For one seeking to defy such a truth will meet with Ivan's fate. This fate—the common fate of all men—is reflected in the crushed, twisted, terrified, broken world in view in *The Brothers Karamazov*. The frenzied movement, the lacerations, the grim dialogue, the questionings of Dostoevsky's people—young and old, sons and fathers, men and women—testify repeatedly to the extent of man's affliction and to the forms of his protest against it. But all human actions and reactions must ultimately be viewed in the framework of chronology. "Time's violence rends the soul: by the rent eternity enters," it is said. Father Zossima represents Eternity insofar as his teachings transcend *chronos*. We can understand, therefore, why he is always characterized by pure and absolute goodness, by quietness, by patience—virtues which he gladly shares with others even as he shares the burden of their sin and affliction. Father Zossima, writes Dostoevsky, "had acquired the keenest intuition and could tell from an unknown face what a new comer wanted, and what was the suffering on his conscience. He sometimes astounded and almost alarmed his visitors by his knowledge of their secrets before they had spoken a word" (I, 5).

Father Zossima embodies Dostoevsky's concept of a new kind of sanctity. He has emptied himself of any false divinity and social idolatry. For him there is no such thing as an easy or safe Christianity reached by institutionalized conventions or means. "It is necessary to uproot oneself. To cut down the tree and make of it a cross, and then to carry it every day."[91] It is this process of de-creation that Father Zossima undergoes and that gives him a clear understanding of human destiny and of the "greater reality." To be sure, Christianity is for him the changeless Word of peace, but it is first of all the Word of suffering, of affliction. He stands at the point where Christianity meets the world of the Karamazovs, the real world. And it is at this point of confrontation that divine truth and the absurdity of the human condition itself must reach each other across the abyss. Father Zossima is terribly aware of this chasm in time and space, just as he is aware of the supreme fact that, as Simone Weil phrases it, "Sin is nothing else but the failure to recognize human wretchedness."[92] (The whole of Dostoevsky's art and thought are, in fact, encompassed by these words.) Father Zossima is thus also aware of the impossibility and the contradiction made implicit in life by the mystery of suffering. His function is to connect the divine and the created worlds, to act as intermediary whose very essence and meaning must be experienced as a regeneration of religious consciousness. In him the sacred and the profane conjoin.

Far from being ineffectual, Father Zossima's Christianity is radical and existential. It could be said that his Christianity is Dostoevsky's answer to the inert Christianity that Ivan Karamazov castigates and refuses. That *this* Christianity can enter profane life and alter it: such is Father Zossima's message and at the same time the poetic, the creative, significance assigned to him in the novel. As a prophet Dostoevsky felt the poetic need, which he related to what is spiritual, to create in *The Brothers Karamazov* a religious figure pertinent to a world in which increasingly both philosopher and theologian were surrendering to the dialectics of a modern cosmology. "When the philosophers abandon the metaphysical threshold," St.-John Perse has said, "it falls to the poet to take upon himself the role of metaphysician: at such times it is poetry, not philosophy, that is revealed as the true 'Daughter of Wonder.' . . ."[93] This is the role which Dostoevsky assumes in this novel more than in any other in his pentalogy; and Father Zossima is, more than any other of his people, the poetic revelation of the novelist's metaphysics of a "new saintliness."

# A CRITICAL NOTE

*The Burden of Vision* is the result of twenty years of studying, teaching, and writing about Dostoevsky's *oeuvre*, particularly the five great novels. For me the critical pursuit has constituted a long meditation. In general this volume belongs to criticism dealing with the relationship between literature and religion; in particular it illustrates the critical process as meditative criticism. Let me assert, immediately and unequivocally, that the word *meditation* has for me a sharply etched internal critical context that is religious in origin and principle; it is cogently defined in *The Oxford English Dictionary*: "That kind of private devotional exercise which consists in the continuous application of the mind to the contemplation of some religious truth, mystery, or object of reverence, in order that the soul may increase in love of God and holiness of life."

Criticism always requires of the practitioner courage of judgment and commitment. If his work is to reflect any value of integrity at all, the critic must take a stand, especially when his discriminations run counter to the times. Today the meditative critic's task is difficult, for he lives in a hostile period. The forces of modern empiricism and liberalism, once "the wave of the future," are now in control, as any glance at the cultural map will readily confirm. For a critic to use words like "reverence" and "meditation," or to invoke as his larger critical contexts and moral direction the religious essences in a definition in *The Oxford English Dictionary,* is to invite opposition. Not only must he confront the power of the doctrinaire empiricists and liberals, but he must also contend with their most proliferating legatees: the relativists, whose insidious attitudes resist any standards that make for moral centrality and spiritual tradition.

One cannot expect this critical situation to change. American secularization and, to a worse extent, Russian paganization are now ascendant, daily facts of life which constitute in their respective ways a "common faith" from which to deviate leads to painful consequences. What F. R. Leavis has to say about current social-intellectual conditions stresses the point: "The fact is that in the world of triumphant modernity, the world of power-centres from which the quantity-addicted machinery is controlled, directed and exploited, literature in the old sense has ceased to matter." Spiritual truths, moral attitudes and judgments, metaphysical premises, religious beliefs: these elements of life and art have become casualties of that modern world that Dr. Leavis indicts. And the consequences are telling. The whole tone of life bears the resonance of a materialistic and technological ethos. What started out historically as experimental and progressivist has been transformed, as Dostoevsky himself showed, into chaos and nihilism. Nothing matters; nothing has value. This spirit of negation prevails, as is dramatized in the mammoth problems besetting education. At the center of these problems there is constant evidence of moral desuetude. A critic who refuses to see or to interpret the conditions of this menace does a disservice to the critical function.

In its own special way the critic's burden of judgment is as sacred as the artist's burden of vision. This burden is moral in essence and function. It cannot be otherwise if criticism is to have any integrating value. Today moral values are much scorned, confined to quotation marks—or to excisable parentheses. The moral real, if it is not treated as a luxury, is viewed as a relic of a discarded past. Its absence must be assessed in the framework of the modern religious situation that Dostoevsky's friend and admirer, the philosopher Vladimir Soloviev, discerned in his book *The Justification of the Good* (1897). Morality, he says, is a common denominator of all religions, grows from a religious soil, and sustains a religious sensibility. Too often critics of literature forget this basic truth of human existence. Such slighting of truth is both a symptom and a concomitant of the relativist mind in the modern age. In dismissing the implications and significance of moral sensibility, a critic contributes to the fragmentation of human experience. That is to say, he disregards the moral meaning that the written and spoken arts give to human action. Such a critic practices what can be called a criticism of denial. It is a denial of what is of ultimate value to art and specifically to what, in relation to Dostoevsky's novels, I term spiritual art. "For a writer, what men think and do is quite as important as what they are. A novelist creates a world of action and therefore he has to deal with motive, with morality. All novels are concerned from first to last with morality." These words of Joyce Cary, found in his remarkable little book *Art and Reality* (1958), are the words of a novelist testifying to the novelist's, and the critic's, moral responsibility.

The moral dimension is one that the critic must sustain as a part of his function, as an intrinsic aspect of his convictions, and as a characteristic of his own quest for meaning and order. "It is scarcely possible for literary criticism," observes Austin Warren, "to eschew participation in the deep need and search of our time, for general principles of order." This search for direction reveals a criterion of criticism. It also reveals the critic's attempt to communicate standards of discrimination that he discovers, defines, and applies as "general principles of order." Within this framework the critic must recognize the existence of basic spiritual needs, without which the human picture is incomplete. Here it is not at all improper to say that spiritual art like Dostoevsky's necessitates spiritual criticism. Along with analysis, comparison, evaluation, it calls for a critical act of reverence and meditation. Nor is it improper to claim that only the critic's own possession of a religious awareness enables him to elucidate an artist's religious consciousness.

In an age when empirical criteria regulate the theory and practice of criticism, the maintenance of a religious awareness in criticism is tenuous. The current state of criticism is one in which obsession with the value of change has reached the point of rejecting religious and even humanistic standards. The critic has become a slave to the habit of generalizing, measuring, aggregating, and averaging human experience. He is more apt to speak of the "socio-economic capabilities of change" than of moral and religious significances. The critic is thus caught in our modern impasse.

Current social and intellectual attitudes, especially since the end of World War II, have accelerated the tendency to discount and just as often to scorn not only a religious metaphysics but also a critical metaphysics. One can see in the whole of education and of general thought and critical intelligence a hardening empirical national spirit that threatens to destroy the critic's pursuit and responsibility. Indeed we have moved from beyond a crisis of criticism to a betrayal of criticism, the betrayal often coming from critical theorists and practitioners themselves. Examples of betrayal are there for all to see in the curriculum, in the classroom, in journalistic criticism, and in the associational process. There is a quick willingness on the part of literary scholars to accept the conclusions that, in our "post-culture," as George Steiner phrases it, literary criticism is dying and moral criticism is dead. We live in and must accept a world of hard facts in which "empirical research," according to John M. Ellis's *The Theory of Literary Criticism* (1974), can now provide the best solutions to critical questions about the nature and function of literature. Hope must lie in the work of the social scientists and "empirical sociologists." "It is a question of research into the structure of society and into the relation of that social structure to the structure of literary texts," Professor Ellis continues, "in which the usual empirical methods of investigation and relevant abstraction must be used; purely conceptual analysis can go no further." That such a claim for "logical analysis" is so boldly ' made and can count on support from within the academy says something about our moral climate and our cultural crudity. From every indication we are establishing an empirical fascism.

Dostoevsky's five great novels are a prophetic picture of the inner life, with all of its spiritual and religious wants, struggling against precisely that cold spirit of fact that the empiricists acclaim. His fiction serves to remind the critic of the need to discern the qualitative states of human consciousness that the empiricists would consign to the logicians. Between the critical spirit and positivist empiricism, then, there is a clash of first principles. The critical spirit requires meditation—and moral discrimination—if only to resist the quantifying imperiousness of material efficiency and utilitarian expediency. Today such resistance is more urgent than ever, for the critic, if he is to remain critical in his task, must refuse to surrender to that preoccupation with immediacy and social relevance to which respectability is given. The pressures of modern economic life on "man in society" have hastened empirical demands and influences. But there are wider and deeper contexts of life, as Dostoevsky believed, which are constituently spiritual and religious. By discouraging these contexts, Americanization and Russianization, in spite of their ideological antagonisms, are united in contributing to a situation in which the full and vigorous interplay of critical awarenesses has been, at the very least, considerably diminished. Any careful reading of Dostoevsky's novels as spiritual art should alert one to the dangers of the empirical *Putsch*. In the absence of spiritual and religious dimensions of life and art, the American can look forward to the perversity of Professor Ellis's volume and the Russian to the terrorism that Alexander Solzhenitsyn decries. One dares not forget that it is the killing of spirit that must engage the artist's vision and must trouble the critic's conscience.

Standards are indispensable to the critic, and he bears a responsibility to his beliefs if he is to avoid working in a vacuum. Standards of themselves, without the reconciling influence of belief, of breadth of concern, become purely functional and formalistic. A critic has especial need to keep alive the older religious tradition and metaphysics, which are being blotted out by the empirical ethos. The need for one to contemplate the broader world and to meditate on its meaning becomes urgent as the pressures of social adaptability predominate and administer one's view of things. We can never discount social beliefs in relation to life and art; neither can we discount our religious needs. We need to be made aware of more than just our own time; we need, more than ever, to perceive a hidden realm of language and beliefs, that realm into which Dostoevsky's novels draw us with incomparable power. The point here is that, though we are informed again and again by some of our more enlightened critical theorists that we have to view literature as, say, an entity of interrelationships, insofar as "man's cultural life is one," the religious dimension is invariably singled out as being always important *but* always suspect. Religious interpretations of art, we are told, are legitimate only by a writ of strict critical qualifications, the specifics of which Rene Wellek throws out in a discussion of the history of Dostoevsky criticism when he focuses on "the émigré writers—who correctly perceive the religious and mystical inspiration of Dostoevsky's work—[but who] also misunderstand its nature if they extract a message from it, a system of doctrines and precepts." Perhaps Professor Wellek wants to remind us that we live in the world of Darwin and not in that of Plato. But unwittingly perhaps he also reminds us of the particular appropriateness and wisdom of Wallace Stevens's words that

> . . . The epic of disbelief
> Blares oftener and soon, will soon be constant.

The critic who seeks to show the connection between literature and religion and specifically, as in *The Burden of Vision,* between the novelist and his metaphysics, seeks to go back to origins. To be afraid of or apologetic about such a task is to yield to the literary empiricists, to the values of the marketplace. We have come to see in the whole of modern society the exaltation of material over spiritual values, the undermining not only of the religious tradition but also, as Irving Babbitt complained, of the humanistic tradition. The mounting difficulties of conserving traditional attitudes and standards threaten the critic's most important goals and even his identity. He is heir, that is to say, to precisely those conditions of spiritual anarchy that lacerate Dostoevsky's fictional world.

Spiritual art can serve as spiritual discipline, and it should be one of the critic's major aims to evaluate the moral facets of the interaction. To evade the task by asserting that it is an arbitrary imposition of a critic's own religious and philosophical views on a writer contributes to spiritual anarchy. What we continually observe in so much of literary criticism is not an attempt to find some principle of unity and order but a readiness to surrender to the laws of natural flux. One need only consider the reviewing media, as well as the literary reputations that are made by them, to realize the extent of what I have called the empirical *Putsch.* Standards of virtue and wisdom are now scorned by many critics (and by most educators, it seems), who have joined forces, in Edmund Burke's phrase, with "sophisters, economists, and calculators." The great advances being made by these forces imperil the very survival of the critical spirit that is in any way allegiant to a vision of order that has moral, metaphysical, and religious roots.

The critic cannot seek comparative safety in formalistic methodology or, as is happening particularly at present, in social parochialism. For the critic who affirms the need for the conservation of order in a time of violent disorder, the task is, qualitatively and selectively, moral. A primary function of the critic is to make distinctions and to face the fact of evil. Far from being examples of a "decadent romanticism" or of a "lack of composition," as some interpreters insist, Dostoevsky's major fiction demands precisely this discriminating moral responsibility. A failure to satisfy the demand is due to indolence or cynicism; it is a failure, really, to implement critical standards and discipline, words that the empiricists have corrupted. A cheap, pluralistic contemporaneity obviously precludes a concern with cohering moral values. Many critics, following the lead of the philosophers, deride a metaphysical approach to literature. Yet it is very much a misrepresented approach, the criteria of which are not in the least unclear or irrelevant. William Troy identifies them in "Time and Space Conceptions in Modern Literature," which is to be found in his *Selected Essays* (1967): "When we speak of a metaphysical approach to literature, therefore, we do not mean that critical exercise which consists of summarizing a set of ideas and then showing how they have been applied or demonstrated in particular works. It is rather that approach which consists in showing the similarity of the problems consciously dealt with by metaphysics to those consciously or unconsciously expressed in literature." These words best describe my own critical orientation, especially as it is crystallized in *The Burden of Vision*. To attempt to isolate Dostoevsky's art and thought from his religious metaphysics is to ignore the basic processes of his vision.

Moderation and boldness must inform the critic's final attitude towards literature. Without moderation he is prone to the sin of *hubris,* and his critical prejudices move in extremes. Without boldness he cannot have a clear perspective or express a steadfast conviction. Moderation provides balance; boldness assures commitment. Their reconciliation creates a critical synthesis of values and standards, creates what I call a reverent discipline. How to penetrate and arrest the artist's vision remains for the critic the highest challenge. And, beyond this, how to distinguish permanent truths from temporary truths must finally test the critic's strength of judgment. This challenge and this judgment comprise the burden of criticism.

But no burden can ever be borne, whether by the artist or by the critic, without the support of faith. Whatever charges are made to the contrary, as seen throughout history, the essential nature of this faith is religious. Its power can be gauged by the unending war waged against it. Modern literature provides for us an abundant, a rich, and a lasting record of the critical claims that I am making here. No less than the modern artist, the modern critic can never completely hide from that truth which D. H. Lawrence recognizes as a force for life when he writes in one of his letters: "I do think that man is related to the universe in some 'religious' way, even prior to his relation to his fellow men. . . . There is a *principle* in the universe, toward which man turns religiously—a life of the universe itself." In Dostoevsky's five great novels, as I try to show in *The Burden of Vision,* the religious way and the religious principle to which Lawrence alludes are the substance of spiritual art.

Dostoevsky's achievement confirms me in my judgment that for too long the critic has been retreating before the adversary's most assailing question: "Where are your proofs?" Surely the time has come for the critic to ask the question of all questions: "Where is your faith?"

\* \* \* \* \*

The chapter on *Crime and Punishment* appeared under the title "In Sight of the Logos: Dostoevsky's *Crime and Punishment* As Spiritual Art" in *St. Vladimir's Theological Quarterly* (Volume 15, Number 3). The chapter on *The Devils* appeared under the title "Dostoevski and Satanism" in *The Journal of Religion* (Volume 45, Number 1). And the chapter on *The Brothers Karamazov* appeared under the title "Pater Seraphicus: Dostoevsky's Metaphysics of a 'New Saintliness'" in the volume containing my collected essays, *The Reverent Discipline: Essays in Literary Criticism and Culture* (Knoxville, Tennessee, 1974). All three have been revised for inclusion in this book.

Here I should explain that, twenty years ago, this was the first book that I ever started to write. In its present form and in its basic areas of critical concern, *The Burden of Vision* represents the most coherent expression of my approach to Dostoevsky's fiction as spiritual art. In defining, amplifying, clarifying, compressing, and unifying this critical approach, I can see in retrospect that the manuscript has necessarily gone

198 / THE BURDEN OF VISION

through various stages of preparation and of presentation. I can see, too, that in order to complete this book in the light of the criteria which I discuss in the preceding Note, which has for me personal, historical significance, this "first book" has had to wait for its appearance. The delay does not surprise me. I have come to know that if the meditative process is to be the highest critical process, it must evolve not as a geometric formulation of parts but as a process in time, a process of which Saint Paul was aware in saying: "Meditate upon these things; give thyself wholly to them; that thy profiting may appear to all" (I Timothy 4:15).

In typing the different versions of the manuscript, my secretary, Miss Mary E. Slayton, has shown patience and generosity; throughout she has encouraged me with her understanding of and sympathy with my aims. In editing the manuscript my friend Miss Martha Seabrook has shown concern and skill with the written word; this final version owes everything to her painstaking search for clarity of thought and language.

# NOTES

*Chapter One:* **SCHISM** Crime and Punishment

1. *Dostoevsky,* trans. Keith R. Crim (Richmond, 1964 [1921]), p. 44.

2. *A History of Russian Literature: From the Earliest Times to the Death of Dostoyevsky (1881)* (New York, 1927), p. 353.

3. All references to *Crime and Punishment* are included within the text, with Roman numerals indicating the parts and Arabic figures the chapters. Throughout, David Magarshack's translation in Penguin Books (1951) is used.

4. See Donald Fanger, *Dostoevsky and Romantic Realism: A Study of Dostoevsky in Relation to Balzac, Dickens, and Gogol* (Cambridge, Mass., 1965), p. 94.

5. See Ralph Harper, *The Seventh Solitude: Man's Isolation in Kierkegaard, Dostoevsky, and Nietzsche* (Baltimore, 1965), p. 1.

6. See *Tolstoy or Dostoevsky: An Essay in Old Criticism* (New York, 1959), pp. 133 ff.

7. Julius Meier-Graefe, *Dostoevsky: The Man and His Work,* trans. Herbert H. Marks (London, 1928), p. 141.

8. Trans. Willard R. Trask (New York, 1961 [1957]), p. 203.

9. See his discussion of *Crime and Punishment* in *Dostoevsky: His Life and Work,* trans. Michael A. Minihan (Princeton, 1967 [1947]), pp. 270-313.

10. Page 117.

11. "On the Meaning of Repentance," a typescript copy of an unpublished essay, p. 5.

12. See Richard B. Sewall, Chapter 4, "The Tragic Form," *The Vision of Tragedy* (New Haven, 1962).

13. See *The Notebooks for Crime and Punishment,* ed. and trans. Edward Wasiolek (Chicago, 1967).

14. See L. A. Zander, *Dostoevsky,* trans. Natalie Duddington (London, 1948), pp. 67 ff.; and Romano Guardini, *Religiöse Gestalten in Dostojewskijs Werk* (Munich, 1951), pp. 65 ff.

15. "Dostoevsky in *Crime and Punishment,*" *Partisan Review* (Summer 1970), pp. 407-409.

16. *Three Masters,* trans. Eden and Cedar Paul (New York, 1930), pp. 209-210.

17. *Eleven Essays in the European Novel* (New York, 1964), p. 136.

18. Trans. Arthur Wills (New York, 1952), p. 120.

19. "The *Iliad,* Poem of Might," *Intimations of Christianity Among the Ancient Greeks,* trans. Elisabeth Chase Geissbuhler (Boston, 1958), p. 31.

20. *Dostoevsky,* trans. Donald Attwater (New York, 1957 [1934]), pp. 100-101.

21. This phrase comes from Sir Maurice Bowra's *The Prophetic Element,* The English Association Presidential Address (Oxford, 1959), p. 11. Cf. Sir Herbert Grierson: "Sin, moral evil, as the source of all we suffer, righteousness and repentance as the promise of better things—these are the recurring themes of prophetic poetry." *Milton and Wordsworth: Poets and Prophets* (London, 1937), p. 17.

22. *Aspects of the Novel* (New York, 1963 [1927]), p. 125.

*Chapter Two:* **TERROR** The Idiot

1. "Thoughts on Dostoevsky's *Idiot,*" trans. Stephen Hudson, *English Review,* XXXV (1922), 194; *Blick ins Chaos* (Bern, 1920), p. 27.

2. *The Idea of the Holy,* trans. John W. Harvey (New York, 1958 [1923]), pp. 12-13.

3. Quoted in Robert Louis Jackson, *Dostoevsky's Quest for Form* (New Haven, 1966), p. 242, n. 65.

4. All references to *The Idiot* are included within the text, with Roman numerals indicating the parts and Arabic figures the chapters. Throughout, David Magarshack's translation in Penguin Books (1955) is used.

5. *The Living Thoughts of Kierkegaard,* presented by W. H. Auden (New York, 1952), p. 30. For a valuable interpretation of Kierkegaard's religious thought see Reidar Thomte's *Kierkegaard's Philosophy of Religion* (Princeton, 1948).

6. "Thoughts on Dostoevsky's *Idiot,*" 195.

7. "The sword without, and terror within, shall destroy both the young man and the virgin, the suckling also with the man of gray hairs" (Deuteronomy 32:25).

8. "Dostoevsky's Idiot: A Symbol of Christ," trans. Francis X. Quinn, *Cross Currents,* VI (Fall 1956), 372.

9. *Fyodor Dostoevsky: A Critical Study* (New York, 1966 [1924]), p. 152.

10. *Neglected Powers: Essays on Nineteenth and Twentieth Century Literature* (London, 1971), p. 192. See also Berdyaev, *Dostoevsky,* p. 44.

11. "Dostoevsky's novels might be defined as psychological dramas pivoting on the problem of personality. This is still one of the central problems of our time." See Frank Friedeberg Seeley, "Dostoevsky's Women," *Slavonic and East European Review,* XXXIX (June 1961), 303-305.

12. Page 353.

13. "The Hovering Fly," *Essays of Four Decades* (Chicago, 1968), p. 118.

14. *The Tragic Vision* (Chicago, 1966), pp. 209 ff.

15. *Dostoevsky,* p. 33.

16. Robert Lord, *Dostoevsky: Essays and Perspectives* (Berkeley, 1970), pp. 81 ff.

17. D. A. Traversi, "Dostoievsky," *Criterion,* XVI (July 1937), 590.

18. Zander, p. 122.

19. *Fear and Trembling,* trans. Walter Lowrie (Princeton, 1941), pp. 61-62.

20. "Wherefore seeing we also are compassed about with so great a cloud of witnesses, let us lay aside every weight, and the sin which doth so easily beset us, and let us run with patience the race that is set before us" (Hebrews 12:1).

21. *Tolstoy or Dostoevsky: An Essay in Old Criticism,* p. 152.

22. Page 153.

23. Vyacheslav Ivanov, *Freedom and the Tragic Life: A Study in Dostoevsky,* trans. Norman Cameron (New York, 1957 [1952]), p. 100.

24. "For from within, out of the heart of men, proceed evil thoughts, adulteries, fornications, murders, thefts, covetousness, wickedness, deceit, lasciviousness, an evil eye, blasphemy, pride, foolishness: All these evil things come from within, and defile the man" (Mark 7:21-23).

25. Richard Curle, *Characters of Dostoevsky* (New York, 1966), p. 72.

26. "The night is far spent, the day is at hand: let us therefore cast off the works of darkness, and let us put on the armour of light" (Romans 13:12).

27. See vol. I (Chicago, 1951), 11-15.

28. N. M. Lary, *Dostoevsky and Dickens: A Study of Literary Influence* (London, 1973), pp. 79 ff.

29. *Systematic Theology,* III (1963), 30.

30. "Three Masters: The Quest for Religion in Nineteenth-Century Russian Literature," *Mansions of the Spirit: Essays in Literature and Religion,* ed. George A. Panichas (New York, 1967), p. 160.

31. *Systematic Theology,* II (1957), 69.

32. *Ibid.,* 68.

33. *Ibid.,* 78.

34. Quoted in *Encyclopedia of Poetry and Poetics,* ed. Alex Preminger (Princeton, 1965), p. 821.

35. "A Conversation with Doctor Abraham Joshua Heschel" (National Broadcasting Company, Inc., 1973), p. 10. This is a mimeographed copy of a special Eternal Light program (NBC Television Network, Sunday, Feb. 4, 1973, 2-3 P.M. EST).

36. *My Belief: Essays on Life and Art* (New York, 1974), p. 134.

37. *Systematic Theology,* III, 398 ff.

38. "Heal the sick, cleanse the lepers, raise the dead, cast out the devils: freely ye have received, freely give" (Matthew 10:8).

39. *Tragic Wisdom and Beyond,* trans. Stephen Jolin and Peter McCormick (Evanston, 1973), p. 145.

40. "And if Christ be in you, the body is dead because of sin; but the Spirit is life because of righteousness" (Romans 8:10).

41. Paul Tillich, *The Shaking of the Foundations* (New York, 1948), p. 57.

42. *Ibid.,* p. 61.

43. *Who is Man?* (Stanford, 1965), p. 79.

44. See V. V. Zenkovsky, "Dostoevsky's Religious and Philosophical Views," *Dostoevsky: A Collection of Critical Essays,* ed. René Wellek (Englewood Cliffs, 1962), pp. 132, 142-145.

45. *Ibid.,* p. 139.

46. *Some Lessons in Metaphysics,* trans. Mildred Adams (New York, 1969), pp. 27 ff.

47. "Dostoevsky's Religious and Philosophical Views," pp. 140, 141.

48. Quoted by Zenkovsky, p. 142.

49. The words quoted are from poem #65, *The Poems of Gerard Manley Hopkins,* ed. W. H. Gardner and N. H. MacKenzie (London, 1967), p. 100.

50. See Gerard Manley Hopkins' sermon "The Paraclete," *A Hopkins Reader,* selected and with an Introd. by John Pick (Oxford, 1953), 279-287.

*Chapter Three*  SATANISM  The Devils

1. *Satan,* ed. Père Bruno de Jesus-Marie, O.C.D. (New York, 1952), p. 455.

2. *The Christian Faith,* ed. H. R. Mackintosh and J. S. Stewart (Edinburgh, 1928), p. 170.

3. Paris, 1926, p. 141.

4. Khot' ubei, sleda ne vidno,
   Sbilis' my, chto delat' nam?
   V pol'e bes nas vodit vidno
   Da kruzhit po storonam.

5. Ernest J. Simmons, *Dostoevsky: The Making of a Novelist* (New York, 1962), p. 247; Michael H. Futrell, "Dostoyevsky and Dickens," *English Miscellany,* VII (Rome, 1956), 78.

6. Edward Hallett Carr, *Dostoevsky, 1821-1881: A New Biography* (London, 1931), p. 227; Traversi, "Dostoievsky," 597-598; Georg Lukács, "Dostoevsky," in *Dostoevsky: A Collection of Critical Essays,* p. 155; Irving Howe, *Politics and the Novel* (New York, 1957), p. 63.

7. Curle, p. 138.

8. Dmitri Merejkowski, *Tolstoi as Man and Artist: With an Essay on Dostoievski* (New York, 1902); Ivanov, *Freedom and the Tragic Life;* Berdyaev, *Dostoevsky;* L. A. Zander, *Dostoevsky.*

9. *Dostoevsky: A Collection of Critical Essays,* p. 6.

10. We are reminded here of T. S. Eliot's comment: "The persons who enjoy these writings *solely* because of their literary merits are essentially parasites; and we know that parasites, when they become too numerous, are pests." *Selected Essays* (New York, 1950), p. 344.

11. *Dostoevski the Adapter* (Chapel Hill, 1954), p. 175.

12. *A History of Russian Philosophy,* I, trans. George L. Kline (London, 1953), 415.

13. *Service Book of the Holy Orthodox-Catholic Apostolic Church,* comp., trans., and arranged from the Old Church-Slavonic Service Books of the Russian Church and collated with the Service Books of the Greek Church by Isabel Florence Hapgood, 3d ed. (Syrian Antiochian Orthodox Archdiocese of New York and All North America, 1956), p. 272.

14. *A Treasury of Russian Spirituality,* ed. G. P. Fedotov (London, 1952), p. 227. The selections from Saint Tikhon were translated by Helen Iswolsky.

15. All quotations from Dostoevsky's novel are taken from Constance Garnett's translation of *The Possessed* (New York, 1936), containing a Foreword by Avrahm Yarmolinsky and his translation of the hitherto-suppressed

chapter "At Tihon's"; and from David Magarshack's translation of *The Devils* (Baltimore, 1953). The references to *The Devils* are included in the text, with Roman numerals indicating the particular part and Arabic figures the chapter and the section.

16. Trans. Constance Garnett, New York, 1950, VI, 3.

17. *Master Builders* (New York, 1939), pp. 209-210.

18. *Writings from the Philokalia on Prayer of the Heart,* trans. E. Kadloubovsky and G. E. H. Palmer (London, 1951), p. 29.

19. *Images of Good and Evil,* trans. Michael Bullock (London, 1952), p. 34.

20. *Cain: A Mystery* in *The Poetical Works of Lord Byron* (London, 1894), p. 459.

21. *The Brothers Karamazov,* III, 3.

22. All references relating to Ivan and the devil are from Book XI, chap. 9 ("The Devil: Ivan's Nightmare"), pp. 771-791 in Mrs. Garnett's translation of *The Brothers Karamazov.*

23. *The Brothers Karamazov,* VI, 3. Cf. Rudolf, Otto: "It might be said that Lucifer is 'fury,' the ὀργή, hypostatized, the *mysterium tremendum* cut loose from the other elements and intensified to *mysterium horrendum.*" *The Idea of the Holy,* n. 2, pp. 106-107.

24. "Immer stärker wird der Eindruck: Das Innere dieses Mannes ist leer." (The impression becomes more and more strong: The man is empty inside.)
"Er besitzt einen scharfsehenden Verstand, eine mächtige Körperkraft, einen ungeheuren Willen aber sein Herz ist öde." (He possesses an acute intellect, powerful physical strength, a phenomenal will power, but his heart is desolate.) *Religiöse Gestalten in Dostojewskijs Werk,* p. 318.

25. *The Destiny of Man,* trans. Natalie Duddington (London, 1937), p. 280.

26. All references to Stavrogin's confession are from Avrahm Yarmolinsky's translation of "At Tihon's," in Mrs. Garnett's translation of *The Possessed,* pp. 689-736.

27. *The Devil's Share,* trans. Haakon Chevalier (Washington, 1944), p. 30.

28. Page 460. See also Paul Ramsey's illuminating study, "God's Grace and Man's Guilt," *Journal of Religion,* XXXI (1951), 30-34.

29. "Er ist der ärmste aller Menschen. Ein grosses Mitleid kommt einem um ihn—aber der Satan ist ja auch wahrhastig keine Majestät! Was neuzeitliche Satanismen und Moralumwertungen von der "Grösse des Bösen" sagen, ist nur Papier. Der Satan ist der Betrogene einfachhin; der von sich selbst Betrogene. Er ist ganz kahl. Er ist in gar nichts grossartig. Er ist der armselige 'simius Dei.'"

30. See Elizabeth Welt Trahan, "The Golden Age—Dream of a Ridiculous Man?" *Slavic and East European Journal,* XVIII (Winter 1959), 354.

31. "We are today lost in a pseudo-intellectualism which, by claiming a final authority and logical clarity that it in no sense possesses, has made chaos in the world of thought." G. Wilson Knight, *The Christian Renaissance* (New York, 1963), p. 4.

32. This phrase is from Albert Camus' Foreword to *The Possessed: A Play in Three Parts,* trans. Justin O'Brien (New York, 1960), p. vi. Thomas Merton, however, contends that Camus does not endorse Stavrogin's brand of evil: "It seems to me that in treating Stavrogin as 'the spiritual adventure and death of a modern hero' Camus is certainly speaking ironically. He certainly takes with

the fullest seriousness the moral nihilism of Stavrogin, and even sees him as a prime example of the kind of evil forces in the world that you and I would characterize as satanic, and which Camus really condemns with all his force as disastrous nihilism. I do not by any means think that Camus considers Stavrogin a sort of sympathetic Promethean character or even a 'hero of the absurd' like his Sisyphus. Stavrogin represents the totalist revolutionary who uses violence to subject everything to pure will, the arbitrary application of the principle that 'if God is dead everything is permitted.'" Letter from Thomas Merton to George A. Panichas, Apr. 3, 1967.

33. Cf. Josiah Royce: "It is not those innocent of evil who are fullest of the life of God, but those who in their own case have experienced the triumph over evil. It is not those naturally ignorant of fear, or those who, like Siegfried, have never shivered, who possess the genuine experience of courage; but the brave are those who have fears, but control their fears. Such know the genuine virtues of the hero." *Studies of Good and Evil: A Series of Essays upon Problems of Philosophy and of Life* (New York, 1898), pp. 1-28.

## Chapter Four: PURGATION  A Raw Youth

1. Trans. George Reavey (New York, 1959), p. 160.

2. *Ibid.*, pp. 162-163.

3. All references to *A Raw Youth* are included within the text, with uppercase Roman numerals indicating the part, lowercase Roman numerals the chapters, and Arabic numbers the sections. Throughout, the Modern Library Edition, trans. Constance Garnett (New York, 1956), is used.

4. Leonid Grossman, *Dostoevsky: His Life and Work,* trans. Mary Mackler (Indianapolis, 1975), p. 527.

5. Quoted in Grossman, p. 527.

6. "Three Masters: The Quest for Religion in Nineteenth-Century Literature," pp. 158-159.

7. *Solitude and Society,* pp. 197-198.

8. Edward Wasiolek, ed., *The Notebooks for A Raw Youth,* trans. Victor Terras (Chicago, 1969), p. 27.

9. *Ibid.*, p. 37.

10. *Ibid.*, p. 426.

11. Page 497.

12. Trans. Boris Brasol (New York, 1954), p. 160.

13. See Mochulsky, p. 505.

14. *Selected Essays,* p. 214.

15. See Zander, p. 11.

16. Page 81.

17. Quoted in Evelyn Underhill, *Mysticism* (New York, 1955 [1911]), p. 204.

18. *Gravity and Grace,* trans. Emma Craufurd (London, 1963 [1947]), pp. 56, 137.

19. For example, see Carr, *Dostoevsky, 1821-1881. A New Biography,* p. 254; Nathan Rosen, "Breaking Out of the Underground: The 'Failure' of *A Raw Youth,*" *Modern Fiction Studies* (Autumn 1958), pp. 225-239; Ronald Hingley,

*The Undiscovered Dostoevsky* (London, 1962), pp. 162-174; Edward Wasiolek, *Dostoevsky: The Major Fiction* (Cambridge, Mass., 1964), pp. 137-144.

20. Reinhold Niebuhr, *Discerning the Signs of the Times: Sermons for Today and Tomorrow* (New York, 1946), p. 161.

21. *Between Man and Man,* trans. Ronald Gregor Smith (New York, 1948), p. 175.

22. Romano Guardini, *The Virtues: On Forms of Moral Life,* trans. Stella Lange (Chicago, 1967 [1963]), p. 2.

23. *I and Thou,* trans. Ronald Gregor Smith (New York, 1952 [1923]), p. 46.

24. *Stages on Life's Way,* trans. Walter Lowrie (Princeton, 1940), p. 430.

25. Trans. David F. Swenson (Minneapolis, 1941), p. 9.

26. Meier-Graefe, p. 256.

27. *The Notebooks for A Raw Youth,* p. 24.

28. *Eclipse of God* (New York, 1952), p. 115.

29. *Henry V,* IV, i, 4.

30. See Nathan Rosen, "Chaos and Dostoyevsky's Women," *Kenyon Review* (Spring 1958), pp. 257-277.

31. Meier-Graefe, p. 240.

32. *The Diary of a Writer,* p. 968.

33. See Simone Weil, *Gravity and Grace,* p. 136.

34. Quoted in Underhill, p. 221.

*Chapter Five:* **SAINTLINESS** The Brothers Karamazov

1. *The Letters of T. E. Lawrence,* ed. David Garnett (New York, 1939), p. 492.

2. *The Added Dimension: The Art and Mind of Flannery O'Connor,* ed. Melvin J. Friedman and Lewis A. Lawson (New York, 1966), p. 237.

3. Thomas J. J. Altizer, *Mircea Eliade and the Dialectic of the Sacred* (Philadelphia, 1963), p. 114.

4. Otto, pp. 13 ff.

5. Quoted in Jackson, *Dostoevsky's Quest for Form,* p. 90.

6. Page 51. (My italics.)

7. Jackson, p. 176.

8. *Ibid.,* p. 82.

9. *Ibid.,* p. 57.

10. Page 158.

11. *Three Masters,* p. 231.

12. Jackson, p. 56.

13. *Religiöse Gestalten in Dostojewskijs Werk,* p. 108.

14. *Eleven Essays in the European Novel,* p. 217.

15. See n. 3, chap. 4.

16. *Religiöse Gestalten in Dostojewskijs Werk,* p. 95.

17. All references to *The Brothers Karamazov* are included within the text,

with Roman numerals indicating the books and Arabic numbers the chapters. Throughout, the Modern Library Edition, trans. Constance Garnett (New York, 1950), is used.

18. Nadejda Gorodetsky, *Saint Tikhon Zadonsky* (London, 1951), p. 180.

19. Page 203.

20. Gorodetsky, p. 183.

21. *Ibid.*, p. 193.

22. *The Icon and the Axe* (New York, 1966), p. 202.

23. *A Treasury of Russian Spirituality,* ed. G. P. Fedotov (London, 1952), p. 185.

24. Page 187.

25. Mochulsky, p. 636.

26. Romans 13:12.

27. Dmitry F. Grigorieff, "Dostoevsky's Elder Zosima and the Real Life Father Amvrosy," *St. Vladimir's Seminary Quarterly,* Vol. 11, No. 1 (1967), 22-34.

28. Aylmer Maude, *The Life of Tolstoy* (London, 1953), p. 75.

29. Countess Alexandra Tolstoy, *The Tragedy of Tolstoy,* trans. Elena Varneck (New Haven, 1933), p. 254.

30. Constantin de Grunwald, *Saints of Russia* (New York, 1960), pp. 87-103.

31. *Ibid.*, p. 97.

32. Fedotov, p. 93.

33. Grunwald, p. 96.

34. Fedotov, p. 93.

35. *Ibid.*, p. 87.

36. *Ibid.*, p. 281.

37. Grigorieff, p. 32.

38. Gorodetsky, p. 185.

39. *Ibid.*, p. 185.

40. *Ibid.*, p. 186.

41. Simmons, p. 358.

42. *Dostoevsky* (New York, 1961), p. 89.

43. Simmons, p. 357.

44. *Konstantin Leontiev* (London, 1940), p. 148.

45. *Ibid.*, p. 148.

46. Page 238.

47. Lytton Strachey, *Spectatorial Essays* (New York, 1964), p. 175.

48. Jackson, p. 121.

49. Page 363.

50. Mark Spilka, "Human Worth in *The Brothers Karamazov,*" *Minnesota Review* (Jan.-Apr. 1965), pp. 42, 43.

51. Gerald Abraham, *Dostoevsky* (London, 1936), pp. 132-133.

52. *Letters from Joseph Conrad, 1895-1924,* ed. Edward Garnett (Indianapolis, 1928), p. 240.

53. *Religiöse Gestalten in Dostojewskijs Werk,* p. 108.

54. *The Writings of Martin Buber,* ed. Will Herberg (New York, 1961), p. 170.

55. Henri de Lubac, *The Drama of Atheist Humanism* (New York, 1963), p. 245.

56. Thurneysen, p. 83.

57. *The Writings of Martin Buber,* p. 324.

58. *Ibid.,* p. 319.

59. *Ibid.,* p. 318.

60. *Ibid.,* p. 318.

61. *Man in the Modern Age,* trans. Eden and Cedar Paul (London, 1951), p. 184.

62. Hosea 2:19.

63. *Tragic Sense of Life* (New York, 1954), p. 132.

64. Page 11.

65. Underhill, pp. 268, 270.

66. Page 636.

67. Underhill, p. 380.

68. *Ibid.,* p. 413.

69. Thomas J. J. Altizer and William Hamilton, *Radical Theology and the Death of God* (Indianapolis, 1966), p. 81.

70. Page 290.

71. *The Rebel,* trans. Anthony Bower (New York, 1954), p. 51.

72. Altizer and Hamilton, p. 84.

73. *Ibid.,* p. 84.

74. Mochulsky, pp. 588-589.

75. *Waiting for God,* trans. Emma Craufurd (New York, 1951), p. 99.

76. Page 44. For a detailed appraisal of some of the philosophical and existential problems found in *The Brothers Karamazov* see Ellis Sandoz, *Political Apocalypse: A Study of Dostoevsky's Grand Inquisitor* (Baton Rouge, 1971).

77. *On Science, Necessity, and the Love of God,* ed. and trans. Richard Rees (London, 1968), p. 149.

78. *Ibid.,* p. 170.

79. *Ibid.,* pp. 184-185.

80. *Ibid.,* p. 187.

81. *Ibid.,* p. 193.

82. *Ibid.,* p. 191.

83. *Ibid.,* p. 187.

84. *Ibid.,* pp. 194, 195.

85. *Ibid.,* p. 154.

86. *The Notebooks of Simone Weil,* II, trans. Arthur Wills (London, 1956), 386-387.

87. *Waiting for God,* p. 197.

88. Habakkuk 2:20.

89. Otto, pp. 68 ff., 210 ff.

90. *On Science, Necessity, and the Love of God,* p. 198.

91. Simone Weil, *Gravity and Grace,* trans. Arthur Wills (New York, 1952), p. 86.

92. *Ibid.,* p. 176.

93. *Two Addresses,* trans. W. H. Auden and Robert Fitzgerald (New York, 1966), p. 11.

# INDEX

Semyonovitch, Nikolay *(A Raw Youth)*, 126-127, 140
Seraphic figures, 55, 56, 127, 159
Sewall, Richard B., 38
Sex, 11, 41, 42, 61, 62, 66, 77, 97, 106
Sh., Prince *(The Idiot)*, 62
Shakespeare, William, 16
—*Hamlet*, 134
—*Macbeth*, 23
—*Tempest, The*, 113
Shame, 25, 97, 107, 129, 135, 136
Shatov *(The Devils)*, 97, 108
Shelley, Mary: *Frankenstein*, 27
Shelley, Percy Bysshe, 90, 176
Siberia, Russia, 23, 44-46, 74, 126, 157
Silence, 27, 39, 70, 71, 148, 169, 178, 187
Simmons, Ernest J., 166
Sin, 12, 14, 15, 27, 28, 52, 63, 88, 91, 96, 111, 124, 128, 129, 133, 143, 148, 152, 156, 169, 171, 173, 180, 183, 188, 189
Slavophilism, 155
Sofya Matveyevna *(The Devils)*, 103
Sokolsky, Prince Nikolay Ivanovitch *(A Raw Youth)*, 141
Sokolsky, Prince Sergay Petrovich *(A Raw Youth)*, 141, 150
Solitude, 26, 52, 91, 138, 158, 160; *via solitaria*, 53
Solon, 32
Soloviev, Vladimir, 159
—*Justification of the Good, The*, 191
Solzhenitsyn, Alexander, 194
Soul, The, 17, 18, 19, 20, 48-49, 51, 56, 57, 62, 69, 71, 78, 84, 87, 89, 95, 96, 100, 102, 104, 105, 106, 110, 112, 116, 117, 125, 132, 133, 135, 136, 137, 138, 145, 149, 169, 178, 179, 180, 185, 188, 190; in torment, 23-46
Spirit of Place, 11, 17, 19; in *Crime and Punishment*, 26, 27, 40; of Saint Petersburg, Russia, 25-41, 49, 55, 118, 128, 175. *See also* Darkness
Spiritual art, 10, 22, 46, 54, 59, 74, 80, 87, 125, 127, 149, 164, 174, 176; definition of, 15, 16; and meditative criticism, 21, 190-198

Standards, 85, 132, 134, 144, 192, 194, 195, 196
Stavrogin, Nikolay Vsyevolodovitch *(The Devils)*, 62, 90-111, 154
Stavrogin, Varvara Petrovna *(The Devils)*, 100, 102, 103
Steiner, George, 26, 62, 193
Stevens, Wallace, 195
Strakhov, N. N., 46, 159
Suffering, 11, 12, 15, 19; and affliction, 185-189; in *Crime and Punishment*, 25, 32, 38, 39; in *The Idiot*, 48, 53, 66, 70, 74, 76, 80, 85, 87; of personality, 119, 123, 124, 125, 133, 137, 144, 147, 150; and Saintliness, 156, 168, 169; and Satanism, 96, 103, 105
Suicide, 18, 23, 38, 41, 43, 104, 129
Superman, 31-46
Supernaturalism, 20, 51, 54, 65, 115, 126
Svidrigaylov *(Crime and Punishment)*, 28-44, 62
Switzerland, 49, 59, 64, 74, 85, 99, 111

Tatyana Pavlovna *(A Raw Youth)*, 143-146
Terentyev, Ippolit *(The Idiot)*, 50, 51, 55, 60, 63, 64
Terror, 25, 27, 115; aesthetics of, 54; of God, 53; "holy terror," 54; in *The Idiot*, 47-88
Theology, 16, 22, 77, 78, 84, 189
Thurneysen, Eduard, 24, 45, 57, 125, 183
Tihon, Bishop *(The Devils)*, 105, 106, 107, 108, 155
Tillich, Paul, 14, 47, 74-78, 80, 82, 153
—*Systematic Theology*, 75
Time, 16, 18, 19, 73, 82, 86, 93, 133, 155, 166, 171, 188, 198; and Eternity, 21, 36, 57, 65, 78, 180; "murder" of, 77
Tolstoy, Count Leo, 33, 95, 159-160
—*Anna Karenina*, 165
Totsky *(The Idiot)*, 66, 70
Touchard *(A Raw Youth)*, 128, 130, 150
Tragedy, 15, 16, 20, 23, 24, 27, 37, 39, 91, 114, 125, 126, 137, 147; tragic vision, 19, 38, 75, 77